# Calcutta Conversations

Cultural Conversations

# Calcutta Conversations

*Edited by*

Lina Fruzzetti and Ákos Östör

*with Notes by*

Tarun Mitra

Chronicle Books
An Imprint of DC Publishers
New Delhi
2003

Chronicle Books is an imprint of DC Publishers.

*Distributed by*
Orient Longman Limited
Bangalore  Bhopal  Bhubaneshwar  Chandigarh
Chennai  Ernakulam  Guwahati  Hyderabad  Jaipur
Kolkata  Lucknow  Mumbai  New Delhi  Patna

ISBN 81-8028-009-8

Typeset in Goudy
by Eleven Arts, New Delhi
Printed in India by Pauls Press, New Delhi
Published by DC Publishers
D-27 NDSE Part II, New Delhi 110 049

## Calcutta's Amazing Astonishing Titillating Games

Strange things happen in Calcutta,
Oh brother, I saw the Howrah bridge,
It left me half dead,
Calcutta is an unbelievable place.

I went along the underground
I saw cars driving over houses.
People from the village say in wonder,
"Why the houses don't fall over!
What a place Calcutta is!"

When I went to Calcutta,
I saw the underground railway,
I, Dukhushyam, was thunderstruck,
I have such a hard time imagining,
Oh, Calcutta is such a strange city

I went to the "babus,"
they called me over
and bought my "pats" cheap to sell abroad.
I ask you, does that make my sorrow any less.
We have no rice to put in our stomachs
Calcutta is an unbelievable place.

Went to a cinema hall
Saw so many men and women
Well, if I was to tell the truth
No one will speak well of me.
Calcutta is a strange place.

I see men with hair like women
and women wearing men's clothes.
Oh babu, this isn't a foreign land after all
so why do they wear such clothes.
Calcutta is a strange place.

I saw on the bus from Moyna
women sitting on the top of the roof
what is left then (to do)?
Now the only thing left
is for the women to take up the plough.
Calcutta is a peculiar place.

I haven't said anything of importance
I have only studied till the first grade
All of you here are educated people
Please forgive me
Calcutta is a strange place.

Well, Dukhushyam Chitrakar is my name
I come from Naya in Pingla Thana.

# Acknowledgments

The Wayland Collegium of Brown University funded an earlier phase of the research including a year long seminar on *Theater as a Social Process*.

We are grateful to our friends in Calcutta who supported our attempts to understand their city. We owe special thanks to Tarun Mitra, Aditi Nath Sarkar and Aditi Sen for their work and encouragement.

We are indebted to Nilanjana Chatterjee for her transcription of the discussions; Katherine Grimaldi for typing the first version and Matilde Andrade for making numerous corrections to subsequent versions of the manuscript.

Our departed friend, Supreo Bonnerjee epitomized the spirit of Calcutta and along with his friends we remember his love for the city.

We wish to thank Dukhushyam Chitrakar, artist, for allowing us to use a translation of his poem "*Ajab Shahar* Kolkata" which is reproduced on pages v-vi. The jacket design is also based on his work.

We are grateful to the interviewees and their successors for granting us permission to reproduce the conversations in our book.

Other Works by Lina Fruzzetti
*The Gift of a Virgin: Women, Marriage, Ritual and Kinship
in Bengali Society* (1983, 1993)
*Women, Orphans, and Poverty Social Movements and Ideologies
of Work in India* (1998)

Other Works by Lina Fruzzetti and Ákos Östör
*Concepts of Person: Kinship, Marriage, and Caste in India*
edited with Steve Barnett (1982, 1992)
*Ritual and Kinship in Bengal* (1984)
*Culture and Change Along the Blue Nile: Courts, Markets
and Strategies for Development* (1989)

Other Works by Ákos Östör
*The Play of the Gods: Locality, Ideology, Time, and Structure
in the Festivals of a Bengali Town* (1980, Forthcoming New Ed., 2004)
*Europeans and Islanders in the Western Pacific* (1981)
*Culture and Power: Legend, Ritual, Bazaar and Rebellion
in a Bengali Society* (1984)
*Vessels of Time: Temporal Change and Social Transformation* (1993)
*Making Forest of Bliss: A Conversation between Robert Gardner
and Ákos Östör* (2001)

Films by Lina Fruzzetti and Ákos Östör
*Seed and Earth* with Alfred Guzzetti and Ned Johnston (1995)
*Khalfan and Zanzibar* with Alfred Guzzetti (2000)
*Fishers of Dar* with Amandina Lihamba and Steven Ross (2001)

Films by Ákos Östör
*Loving Krishna* with Allen Moore (1985)
*Sons of Shiva* with Robert Gardner (1985)
*Serpent Mother* with Allen Moore (1985)
*Forest of Bliss* with Robert Gardner (1986)

# Contents

যথাবিহিত সম্মান পুরঃসর নিবেদন মিতি

# An Invitation to Adda in Calcutta

In the cool of the evenings, on weekends, and holidays, or any other time during the day or night that seems convenient, small groups of people, mostly men, gather in coffee houses, tea shops and other places to talk about the events and issues of the day concerning the neighborhood, the city, or the world. They discuss politics, music, art, literature and just about everything else. They engage in a time-honored tradition, a most engaging feature of Calcutta life: the pursuit of good conversation, *adda*, in one Bengali word.

*Adda* is many things: "shooting the bull" as some Calcuttans would put it, a no-holds-barred encounter, nothing censored, nothing sacred. It is a free and equal encounter since no one is above anybody else, everyone is heard, no one person is deferred to. Here friendship means more than caste, religion, or occupation. Small *adda* groups meet regularly in the local tea or *paan* or other shops, others like the famed College Street Coffee House *adda* attracts numerous occasional visitors in addition to a permanent clientele.

Our volume is a kind of *adda*: conceived and realized in the *adda* manner and tradition, not at one sitting in a group but individually, over time. The idea came to us during the mid 1980's when the state of Calcutta seemed particularly precarious and a lot of discussions were taking place about the very survival of the city. We decided to follow up many spontaneous discussions, newspaper reports and articles, public meetings and the like, by holding a series of extended conversations with people whose lives were deeply enmeshed with the fate of city. Due to other projects, writing, filming and teaching in India, Tanzania, USA and elsewhere, we could not complete the book in the late 1980's. There are many advantages however in publishing now. The passage of time put the crises of the 1980's in perspective: has the situation of Calcutta ever been other than precarious? Some of what was pressing then seems less so now, some fears and forebodings failed to materialize, others have come up instead. Much of what was said then is valid today. Several of our *adda* partners have passed away, others retired but continue with their work nonetheless. Yet others are still in their jobs doing what they do best. Some have been especially prescient, none have become irrelevant. In every case the ideas voiced here reveal a resilient Calcutta, continuity and change captured in the fleeting moment of skilled conversation. We hope the tone and flavor of voices survive their transformation into print. These pages are witness to passionate, learned, wise, opinionated, exasperating, humorous people who love their city and are not afraid to express their ideas. They do not provide a treatise, a history or a sociology of Calcutta, but they offer something equally valuable and different, a portrait of a troubling, difficult and wonderful city, at a moment in time that may inform all other moments, in the words of a few of its more reflective citizens.

It turns out that all our *adda* partners are men: we did not set out to exclude women nor are women any less concerned with the fate of Calcutta. This is just the way the discussion evolved from one participant in an *adda* group to some one else in another, and the names of particular people came up naturally and consistently. There was no sampling, no attempt to complete anything, nor to represent anyone. There were no interviews and no preconceived questions. The conversations arose from the given situation at the time. They evolved, however, from encounters with and prodding by one avid and irrepressible

Calcuttan, Supreo Bonnerjee, who sadly is no longer with us and *adda* is the poorer for his departure. Political analyst, cultural critic, raconteur, gourmand rolled into one, Supreo-da was our guide and conscience. He suggested some names, arranged meetings with others, and accompanied Lina to some homes and offices where the conversations took place. After a while the logic and energy of the project took over with one encounter yielding another. With one or two exceptions all the conversations we held appear here with only minor, editorial changes.

Another reason for the absence of women may be the circumstances of Lina's research project at the time: she was studying women's organizations in Calcutta (while Ákos was filming in Benares) and conducted extensive interviews with women all over the city. A gender split may also have come about as a result. But *adda* groups tend to consist of men only, especially for the generation represented here. Women, mostly wives, participate on occasion, but according to some aficionados their presence may restrain the language and inhibit the free flow of conversation.

Finally, a word about ourselves: we have been coming to Calcutta and West Bengal on shorter and longer journeys since the mid 1960's, including several stays lasting up to two years at a time. In between we have managed to make shorter trips of 3 to 12 weeks every few years, most recently two months in 2003. Much of our time in West Bengal was spent in the countryside with numerous visits to Calcutta for rest and conversation. We have written numerous books and made several documentary films during these years. Calcutta has never ceased to fascinate us from the very first disturbing and exhilarating moments of our continuing and decades-long encounter.

Lina & Ákos

# Glimpses of Calcutta's Past

## The Shape of the City

Calcutta, more than other cities, bears the stamp of its relatively short history. Barely 50 years old in the mid-eighteenth century, yet its shape, major arteries and distinct neighborhoods, are easily recognizable today. The facts of the city's beginnings are well known and already the stuff of legend. In 1690 Job Charnock, an agent of the East India Company, establishes a British trading post at a site previously used and abandoned by other European traders. There are three villages in the vicinity: Sutanuti, Govindapur, and Kalikata. "Calcutta" is an anglicized version of the latter, which appears, already in 1495, in the *Manasa Mangala* of Bipradas and later, on Akbar's rent rolls in the sixteenth century. Charnock chooses his site for its access to the sea and natural protection (swamps and waterways slope away from a strip of high land along the Hooghly river on both east and west banks). The place is also a prudent distance away from Dutch and French settlements further up the river. A fort is built in 1698, when the East India Company secures tax collecting rights to the three villages.

Although an indigenous trading center with some permanently settled landed families, the area is famous as Kalikshetra (the Field of Kali)—a very sacred place for Hindus where, according to the scriptures, the right toe of the Goddess fell and became a place of pilgrimage. Till today, Calcutta is a center for the worship of the Goddess. Kalighat in the heart of the city is a complex of shrines and halls where acts of devotion, animal sacrifices and pilgrimages are performed daily by hundreds and thousands of worshipers. The Dakshineshwar Kali temple, made famous in the nineteenth century by the devotions of the saintly Sri Ramakrishna, is at the northern edge of the city. Pilgrimage and worship are far more important to Bengalis at the time than the social site of Charnock's city.

Bengal experienced foreign rule before the arrival of the British. Mughals, Pathans, Marathas vied for control here, and Portuguese, Dutch and French traders also staked their claims. The success of the British was made easier by prevailing economic and political conditions: weakening Mughal control and Maratha incursions from the west made it more difficult for Bengal's numerous small kingdoms to protect themselves. Mughal power was exercized through an often independent Nawab in Bengal who held sway over more independent smaller and larger chiefs, kings and landholders (*zamindars*). The historical kingdom of Vanga is known from ancient Sanskrit literature and by the third century BC it is listed as a part of Ashoka's Maurya empire.[1] The later Gupta and Pala empires also extended as far as Bengal but from the thirteenth century to the arrival of the British the entire region came under the often distant Muslim emperors who had to contend with numerous independent, local rulers.

Initially, there is not much to attract people from the countryside to Charnock's settlement. Primarily a sacred center, with some trading by local merchants, but commerce is not an occupation sought by high caste Hindus, and the marshy ground does not provide for large landed estates. The great *zamindaris* are to the north and east. Charnock's spot is somewhat isolated from the principal trading zones of Bengal. Nevertheless, the East India Company endeavors to attract high caste Brahman families by granting rent-free lands. Early reaction to the British is mixed: curiosity while maintaining distance is the best way to describe the meeting between newcomers and locals, but later this ambivalence changes in various ways enabling colonial rule to take root. Soon enough the old landed families from the hinterland begin sending their kinsfolk to set up house in the new town. With a fort, relative security, increasing

---

[1] The Maurya empire extended to north Bengal—Paundravardhana (Rajshahi, Bogura, now in Bangladesh) and Kotibarsha in Dinajpur, most of it in present day Bangladesh and West Dinajpur, a district of West Bengal.

prosperity and opportunities, the British isolate their town from the "natives." Theirs is a core settlement around the fort, with an unplanned "Indian" town growing up around the edges. Beyond the "white" town planned and built in a European manner—monumental institutional buildings and churches—the city becomes a jumble of architectural styles, a maze of lanes, narrow streets and waterways. Nevertheless the striking north-south layout along the river with one major road dominating both sides of the Hooghly defines the city till today. The Grand Trunk Road (vividly described in Kipling's *Kim*) on the west side joins the city with the rest of India. For the longest time only a pontoon bridge connects the two banks of the river, to be replaced by the famous Howrah (Rabindra Setu) bridge in the late 1920's and 30's and two new bridges, the Vivekananda Setu and the Vidysagar Setu, are added later in the twentieth century.

"Social life in Calcutta in the eighteenth century," writes N.R. Ray, "reflects the two-fold process of transformation of a group of struggling riverine villages into a busy mercantile unit on the one side, and on the other, the conflict and adjustment of two distinctly opposed culture patterns." (Ray 1986: 33). Throughout its first century the ethnic composition of the city changes in terms of caste, class and occupation. The riverine villages retreat to the periphery. Trade is attracting more Bengali and north Indian merchants. This influx of people searching for jobs continues today.[2] The 1750 and 1850 maps of Calcutta demonstrate the ethnic composition of the population. The "white" community is housed in Fort William. "Natives" with their acute and confusing hierarchy are lumped together by the "whites." Bengalis, being in the majority, use caste and occupation to separate themselves from other Indians: even now there are caste neighborhoods such as Barabazar, Shankhari-para and Kanshari-para, Jeletola, and Kumartuli. Race and color are used by the British (but not Indians) as criteria for "separate and unequal" treatment of the people they come into contact with.

The source of wealth for Bengali elites is primarily land ownership: the basis of future real estate speculation. The great houses of the landed families become permanent residences parallel to the ancestral

[2]The hinterland to the port of Calcutta was the whole of undivided Bengal, part of Assam, Bihar, Orissa and eastern United Provinces (Uttar Pradesh of today).

village homes in the countryside. Much later these city dwellings will house refugees and relatives fleeing the partition of 1947. With one foot still in the "ancestral home" (*adhisthan*) in the village, the new migrants to the city are motivated by economic opportunity. Population grows rapidly: 10000 people in 1706, 120000 in 1752 and 180000 in 1821. Later generations of migrants are also attracted by a new culture. Early contact with the *saheb's* world is through trade, and employment in the expanding bureaucracy. Ideas and values are primarily Hindu and Bengali. The British make no attempt at this time to change the social and cultural life of the "natives." But the stance of non-interference combined with non-critical attitude in cases amounting to admiration for a complex ancient civilization changes, by the early decades of the nineteenth century, to a contempt for Indian customs.

## Language, Education and Reform

The introduction of English and western education in the nineteenth century creates a new society which combines "Englishness" with Bengali culture. Wealthy families are westernizing their ways bit by bit while remaining attached to being Bengali and Indian. They celebrate the Goddess of Wealth more than the Goddess of Learning and "vie(d) with one another in making a show of their riches through celebration of social rituals like marriages, *sraddhs*,[3] performances like *nautches* and other festivities in which European residents used to participate." (Ray 1986: 45). On the other hand, the Royal Asiatic Society of Bengal is established in 1784, the National Museum in 1814, and in 1816 Hindu College (later renamed Presidency College) which will train generations of future leaders, professionals, and artists. Bengalis come to prize western style higher education since nothing like it has existed before (Roy 1981: 66). From Hindu College emerges the iconoclastic, rationalist, anti-religious movement of Young Bengal, with its journal *Jnananweshan* (Quest for Knowledge). Raja Rammohun Roy, widely acknowledged as the father of modern India, advocates social reform early in the century and in 1829 founds the deeply

[3]*sraddh*: funerary rites

influential Brahmo Samaj Movement, aiming at the reform of Hindu society as a whole. Central to Rammohun's project is the emancipation of women, widow remarriage, and the cessation of *sati* (immolation of widows on their husband's funeral pyre). Rammohun issues a direct challenge to the orthodox Hindu family. The Brahmo Samaj uses education and western influence to reinterpret sacred Hindu scriptures and rituals, and to reform social and religious practices. It challenges Vedic authority, caste ideology, idol worship and the idea of *karma*.[4] But the changes also transform economy and society: class and occupation are used to designate alternative statuses.

Colonial rule requires a competent indigenous workforce and the British purpose in teaching English was, among other aims, to create a cadre of assistants to run the Empire. In the process, the social thinking of those being educated also changes. India becomes united once more but the seeds of anti-colonial and anti-imperial struggle are sown. Education and legislation succeed in imposing alien ideologies resting on concepts of freedom, equality, rationality, progress, and markets—a cultural colonization that creates a group dependent on English language and education for advancement but also finds fertile ground for reform. In this development the Brahmo Samaj was enormously influential since Rammohun Roy argued that freedom depends on reason, individual control and wealth.

While there existed always a constant and sizable group against the British, most people seem committed neither for nor against the British, and, along with the ultra orthodox group and a westernized elite they make up the social composition of the city. Class and education offer an alternative to caste ranking, purity and pollution, as central to a new Indian hierarchy. Social ideals are fundamentally changed by the influence of the Brahmo Samaj, and despite the gradual decline of the movement later in the century other groups adopt the Brahmo social program. While the majority emulate neither the British nor the Bengali elite, it is increasingly influenced by elite ideas. Elite rule does not transform the entire society and

---

[4]*karmaphal*: fruits of work done in one's previous births

age old ways of life based on *Sanatan Dharma* (eternal law) endure, but reforms leave their imprint on society and people. New criteria are used by local people to divide themselves: orthodox Hindus, Brahmos and other reformers, Bengalis, Indians. Anglicized groups sharply contrast with other Bengalis who may take to western education but do not abandon their own values. *Bhakti, ghenna, bhaya* are sustained despite western rationality,[5] and indigenous hierarchies remain present and significant.

The British keep themselves separate from even elite Bengalis, although the Boses, Mulliks, and Tagores invite *sahebs* to the celebration of the annual Durga *puja*. By mid-century there appears a growing disenchantment with the English world. The flowering of culture at this time came to be called the Bengal Renaissance: a Janus faced phenomenon that makes the imperial project possible but is also intent on reforming society in terms of both local and universal, humanistic values. Bengalis also realize that a literature of their own cannot be created through a foreign culture. By the time of the Great Rebellion (1857)[6] considerable and countervailing forces confront the western impact: a reassertion of orthodoxy (paving the way for internal religious conflict and communalism), a movement to return to indigenous roots countering reforms, and caste, language and religion coupled with nationalism and anti-foreign feelings lead Hindu Bengalis to question the very mediators negotiating the encounter between Great Britain and India. Bharat Mata (Mother India) emerges as the sustainer of lives, restorer of lost balance between values and society. India is discovered again. Throughout the century the Brahmo Samaj provides an alternative way of life to Bengalis who remain Hindu but choose to remain outside the traditional hierarchy of caste purity, and move away from convention and orthodoxy.

Rural orthodox families from East Bengal send their sons to Calcutta who come in contact with "*grihastha bhadralok* families and they provide a nucleus of people ready to adopt reform as a means

[5]For explanation see conversation with Radha Prasad Gupta, p. 25.
[6]Also known as the Sepoy Mutiny by the British and the First War of Independence by Indian nationalists.

of establishing their distinctiveness as a social group." (Borthwick 1984: 49). Class, occupation, and literacy become additional, even replacement status-markers, due to the importance of new urban wealth beyond caste and cultural upbringing.

Everything changes after the Great Rebellion of 1857. Growing British distrust shifts to full scale imperialism, departing from earlier paternal in favor of direct rule. Interest in Indian culture declines and accommodation gives way to imposing British ways by force. Among Bengalis there is less enthusiasm for modern, progressive society, but at the same time there is no turning back to a stagnant pining for the past. A new society is being created with the impact of education and universal values pointing toward political freedom and nationalism. The Brahmo Samaj loses ground as a movement by the late nineteenth century: doctrinal splits in 1866 and 1878 weaken its radical reform program but the secular, nationalist, universalist mandate is assumed by several groups, including incipient left-wing organizations.

Significant changes come from another direction, the devotionalism of Sri Ramakrishna (1836–86), the great ascetic of Dakshineshwar and part-incarnation of Rama and Krishna. A passionate devotee of the Goddess Kali, he preaches and practices the unity of all religions (Islam, Christianity as well as Vaishnava and Shakta Hinduism). His most famous disciple, Swami Vivekananda (1863–1902) develops his *Guru's* syncretism into a reform movement, the Ramakrishna Mission (1897). Yet again combining indigenous and foreign elements, Vivekananda embraces Vedanta spirituality, social and religious reform, material progress, and selfless labor for the benefit of humankind.

Although very well known, we cannot leave out the towering figure of Rabindranath Tagore and his peerless contributions: a reform of the Bengali language and a vast opus of works in music, poetry, drama, prose and painting. Many other outstanding figures and achievements should be mentioned, among them the first great novelist of India, Bankim Chandra Chattopadhyay, the theater of Girish Chandra Ghose, the educational ideas of Iswarchandra Vidyasagar. But here the story will be taken up in the first person by the Calcuttans represented in this volume. It is their lives that have been fundamentally changed by the ideas and actions of these giants of Bengali culture.

## City and Nation

In the late nineteenth century Calcutta's old families lose out to ". . . a much larger group of petty proprietors—tenure holders-cum-professionals . . ." considerably changing the cultural and political life of Bengal. A new class becomes influential in the city and its surroundings informing the stratum of society "from which came the early generation of successful professionals in law, journalism, medicine, teaching, the civil and judicial services," a product of the colonially imposed system. (Chatterjee 1984: 13). The anglicized elite of earlier generations can be said to have created an analogous and ambiguous group of middle-class professionals. The decline of the *zamindari* (landowning) strata goes with a loss of contact with the world view of indigenous peoples. New leadership arises from this new, class-like group. Politically this means a challenge to the dominance of the English educated sections of society as the link between the people of the countryside and the expanding institutional structure of the government. Truly local interests were not being addressed but that is about to change. Nationalism and reform converge in new ways in the late nineteenth century. Surendranath Bannerjea (1848–1925) founds the Indian Association of Calcutta and convenes the first Indian National Conference in 1883, two years before the first Indian National Congress session in Bombay. The 1905 partition of Bengal (*Banga Bhanga*) with its attendant trauma kindles the Swadeshi movement led by Bannerjea. Bankim Chandra's "*Bande Mataram*" is adopted by Congress as its National Anthem. By 1912, partition is rescinded and the capital is shifted from Calcutta to Delhi. Calcuttans embrace and Indianize the national movement in earnest. Yet, with the loss of capital status the city's long decline begins. Waves of migration follow partition— at first whole families, later single men from all over eastern India in search for jobs. No plans are made for development. Having moved to Delhi the British essentially abdicate city-planning though urban growth continues unabated with "enclaves" of Europeans, Chinese, and other ethnic groups, a pattern and terms still applicable today. The development of railways and the ease of travel change the pattern of migration and settlement. Bengalis in other parts of India try to adopt the local language and culture but this does not happen in Calcutta: migrant newcomers then and now cling to areas populated by "their own." Manufacturing, engineering, consumer and jute industries draw workers from far and wide without their families and without the possibility of community. "And such people, under the dire conditions of living into which they have been thrust, can hardly become interested in the improvement of their surroundings of their own accord; the task seems formidable; and thus the civic sense, or a sense of belonging to a community tied by unity of purpose, had hardly any chance to grow in a healthy manner." (Bose 1958: 239).

Calcutta, a market, trading, manufacturing, service as well as administrative city by the early twentieth century, sees the decline of the large joint families of the past, the emergence of *paras* (distinct neighborhoods), local and community worship, devotional groups, political and sports associations, each with a different form of integration and a different impact on the locality. The *para*, with its sense of belonging to a community in the city, in a way replaces the village, and embraces different occupational, caste and religious groups. Unlike a village the *para* can be a base for strong intercaste associations. "The term *para* comes from the Sanskrit *palli*, a village. And many of the old quarters of Calcutta like Darzipara, Benepara or Beniatola, Baghbazar or Kalighat were thus centers of a local or parochial patriotism in the minds of its permanent residents." (Bose 1958: 243). Older *paras* change in the second half of the century as the original families sell their houses to the newly rich. The change effects *para* organizations: old Bengali families tend to celebrate family worship privately, but *para* introduces the concept of the *soloana* or *sarvajanin puja* (communal or collective worship), which help, albeit superficially, an integration along new lines. Similarly with political and religious aspects: political loyalties and membership in opposing parties has a negative integrative effect especially in the case of parties with a renewed interest in caste or religious agendas. Such tendencies are more pronounced in *paras* where one or another group predominates, adding a new sense of insecurity. (Sinha 1978: 131).

With the departure of the British in 1912 the well-to-do move south into "white town," while north Calcutta continues to be the seat of the original Bengali settlers. The new division does not rupture the city's social structure, rather it confirms a subtle class-like and status division among Bengalis. Later, the new south Calcutta residential areas of Ballygunj, New Alipur, and the area south of Park Street house upper or middle class, educated, anglicized Bengalis. By 1947, even before the second partition of Bengal and the coming of Independence, the social and cultural makeup of the city changes dramatically. Bengali elites cut their rural ties long ago. Their traditional base in agriculture was given up in favor of urban livelihoods. Many, however, retain a cultural tie with the ancestral house (adisthan or adibari). From the 1930's to India's Independence, we find a dramatic change in the social and cultural makeup of the city. For many the ". . . sources of livelihood, real or prospective, were entirely urban in administration, small trade and commerce, education or the professions." (Chatterjee 1984: 179). There is now a distinct urban outlook, yet "Bengaliness" means different things to different groups.

Paradoxically, the enlightened earlier generations of Calcutta were deserted by their children who time and again discover a different heritage, a process yet again accomplished through English language and education. Bengali and national consciousness becomes a political act—left thinking pervades the city even today. The younger generation which began to follow new socialist doctrines, were the children of the bhadralok elites who could afford the luxury of being politicians. This generation did not ". . . read Tom Paine (nor) despise the Tories, but revered Byron, and rhapsodized about the French Revolution and the American war of independence." (Bharucha 1983: 12). In the process of fighting a colonial war, it rediscovered a lost cultural history. The elite, refined babu or bhadralok (literally, gentlefolk) culture that emerged in the nineteenth century became, at times, the butt of satire ranging between ridicule and respectability depending on a reformist or status quo point of view. Yet, to some extent, bhadralok or babu still characterize a syncretic western/Bengali culture: social programs, literary esthetic standards, values of life much of which finds its ways into modern India, not just Calcutta and Bengal. With the Swadeshi movement, the intensification of the anti-British struggle, Gandhi's initiatives, Congress and nationalism, the fight turns explicitly against colonial rule, sensing a chance to overcome the white man's world and reject the glamor of westernized culture.

The new nationalism of the twentieth century set itself consciously apart from the older elites: no longer a refinement of an earlier culture, yet equally syncretistic. Popular, indigenous literature formulates new ideas of nation, plays, poetry and music rediscover India, and socialist doctrines spread with the success of the Russian Revolution. Tagore's songs and music conferences, folk art and Kalighat paintings—the neo-orientalist school of painting—all deal with Bengali life including the lives of the downtrodden. As Partha Chatterjee notes, "avant-gardism in 1930's literature was accompanied by a new attempt, however romantic and, in the case of lesser artists, even sentimental, to depict the lives of the toiling poor." (Chatterjee 1984: 179). Folk art of Bengal, Kalighat pictures, Nandalal Bose's and Abanindranath Tagore's paintings considered both the positive and negative aspects of Bengali life. The spread of the nationalist movement introduces a social and cultural radicalization, anti-British feeling and a search for alternative, new political ideologies to serve Calcutta and India.

Here we take leave of our glimpses into Calcutta's pasts, and turn to our *adda* partners who are at once interpreters, observers and shapers of the times, events, and ideas Calcutta witnessed during the last century. Suffice it to say that the political transformations of the late twentieth century saw the decline of the Congress Party and the seemingly paradoxical participation of radical political parties in the electoral process. A broad-based Left Front government came to power in the 1970's. Ever since it has been grappling with the difficult problems of refugees and displaced communities, a great influx of people from rural areas and other states, mounting anger and frustration in the city, economic decline due to the flight of capital, the more successful development of other states, labor unrest and a stagnating economy. The trials and tribulations of Calcutta in the late twentieth century are the subject of this book.

*References*

Bharucha, R. *Rehersals of Revolution: The Political Theatre of Bengal*. Calcutta: Seagull Books. 1983.

Borthwick, M. *The Changing Role of Women in Bengal*. Princeton: Princeton University Press. 1984.

Bose, N.K. "Calcutta" in *Geographic Review of India*. December, 1958.

Chatterjee, P. *Bengal 1920-1947: The Land Question*. Calcutta: K.P. Baggchi and Company. 1984.

Ray, N.R. *Calcutta: The Profile of a City*. Calcutta: K.P. Bagchi and Company. 1986.

Roy, S. *The Roots of Bengali Culture*. Calcutta: Firma K.L.M. Private Ltd. 1966.

Sinha, P. *Calcutta in Urban History*. Calcutta: Firma K.L.M. Private Ltd. 1978.

# Radha Prasad Gupta

RADHA PRASAD GUPTA: Bhupendra Nath Dutta studied at Brown University.

LINA: A long time ago?

RPG: Well, forty years. He was the youngest brother of Narendra Nath Dutta [Swami Vivekananda]. I saw him forty years ago, an extraordinary man.

LINA: We were talking about beneficiaries . . .

RPG: The British came here with the obvious purpose of ruling this country. Not for love or even the glory of *Pax Britannica*, just downright trade. After all, trade is politics for money, a predatory phase of colonialism which lasted from 1757 to the time of Warren Hastings. You do not get an idea of what the Indians thought whereas there are 20 shipments of books on what the Englishman thought about India. That rascal Omichand said: "In my forty years of living with Englishmen I never knew that they ever told a lie." When, as you know, the way to Plassey was paved with lies, cunning, deceit, fraud and "divide and rule" as much as force! The *Siyar-ul-Mutakharin* (not very well known) tells you about Muslim India as seen by an anonymous gentleman around 1773. It is an account of how the British looted India and at the end there is an interesting item. There was an international conference at Rome, delegates from all over the world had come to dispense justice among nations. Three men got down from camels and were asked "Who are you?" "We are delegates from India." They were holding the standard of India and then came this Englishman. And he spoke for India, not the Indians!

The British simply arrived one day from nowhere—hymn-books in one hand and a pair of scales in the other—and said, "Look we are very good people, we have come to do some trade and business with you" and eventually when they became powerful they butchered all the Indian people. Warren Hastings, however we might denigrate him, was a remarkable man. He said, we must know the Indians to rule this country. After all, this is a country with a culture, a tradition. Calcutta became first among the Presidencies. The Royal Asiatic Society, Supreme Court of Judiciary, Oriental Studies and so on were established. He also thought it was necessary that the rulers should learn the language of the ruled.

Up to 1817–1818 there was no systematic education. Then Hindu College and Sanskrit College started to teach English. According to a lot of people this was possibly one of the most important decisions during the British rule. Rammohun Roy (who had done Oriental Studies as well as English studies) thought too that you cannot rise out of feudalism unless you are acquainted with western thoughts and ideas. Rammohun knew Persian, Arabic . . . and was an Aristotelian! But it was Macaulay who wrote off five thousand years of Indian civilization and said one shelf of English books is worth all five thousand years of Indian culture, so let them learn English! The main purpose behind teaching English was to create a large number of people who would help, aid and abet them in running the Empire. But there were seeds of change. Once you learn the language, you also subscribe to the thoughts and other things mentally. I have a semblance of a western education. What *I* think is completely different from what a villager thinks. You know, Ramakrishna said, "If a sickly young boy wears a pair of boots he will jump three steps at a time and talk well and eat meat. But if he wears *dhoti* and *panjabi* he'll only sing '*Nidhu Babur tappa*'." Dress is a strange thing. Therefore, to some extent we learnt everything from them [the English]. It could have been through the French or the Portuguese, but it happened to be the British. Whether you talk about Harshavardhan or the Mughals, India is a kind of geographical concept but not a unity. It was the British who united it into a whole. We knew there were Marwaris, Dravids, Keralites—but there was no sense of unity, except through the

*Ramayana* and *Mahabharata* which again have different interpretations!
We thought Ravana was a bit of a grand fellow. The Maharastrians
[in the eighteenth century] thought they were the most victorious,
"a glorious people on earth," while we called them freebooters.

LINA: What about later times?

RPG: Gradually, when people went out into the streets with
processions and strikes, entering a struggle for independence during
the nineteenth century, the Town Hall and other places were sites
of constitutional assaults by Bengalis. They fought for what? Not
for complete independence, but for a share in the government,
equality to the extent of the law, free press, constitutional rights
in Bengali, a role in the government. In those days there was a
saying that "the *dhoti* spread from Sind to Assam," because we were
beneficiaries of English education (the *dhoti* as worn by Bengalis
that is). Nowadays people make the mistake of saying that Bengalis
have lost ground. It's very silly. We were the first to get things and
naturally, we were everything, from Station Master to School
Principal. But now every other region is coming up. You talk about
the decline of Calcutta. Do you consider that the jute of Chittagong
does not go through Calcutta any more? Or that the iron ore of
Visakhapatanam does not go through Calcutta? After all, other
parts of India are being developed.

I spent a great deal of my early life in Orissa. Anyone who attended
high school had to learn Bengali because there were no textbooks
in Oriya nor translations. But you can't expect that kind of thing
to go on: if they substitute Oriya books that is not backwardness.
They are coming up on their own.

LINA: What brought about the change?

RPG: I am not a professional scholar—just a dilettante! The
fantastic thing is they call it the Bengal *Renaissance* which is a
bit of high falutin' nonsense, but there *was* a kind of awakening.
Can you imagine the kind of morass which we had fallen into?
The stories Sarat Chandra Chatterjee wrote about the villages!
The kind of hold the bloody Brahmans had on everybody—on
the women! The kind of nonsense lasting up to the middle of
this century!

The impact when it came completely engulfed the society, secularism, scientific outlook, widening of horizons. This is baffling! Can you imagine how many great people were born at that time? When we were young we were half "foreigners."

LINA: Mentally?

RPG: We didn't know the *Ramayana* or *Mahabharata* well. Up to the 1920's we were talking about Huxley, Joyce, Pound, Faulkner but we didn't know about Michael Madhusudan Dutt. The funny thing is that in the nineteenth century, people like him were the first flush of the impact of western culture but *they* did not lose their national identity.

LINA: That's what I wanted to draw on, that Bengalis . . .

RPG: In a highly selective fashion, they imbibed the best and integrated it into their own personality so that they became better Bengalis, better human beings, better citizens of the world. To give you an extreme example, Ishwar Chandra Vidyasagar never went out anywhere except in a *chadar*, *dhoti* and a *Taltalar chati*[1] even when he went to see the Governor General! Only once at the request of the Governor he wore the *choga chapkan*, a courtly sartorial remnant of the Mughal age. You see, all of the so-called great men except Rev. Lal Behari De and Michael—hardly anybody wore a suit. Bhudeb Mukherjee was a man so orthodox that he did *puja*, and never touched food that wasn't cooked at home. But look at what a *saheb* he was mentally. Ishwar Gupta the poet, may not have had much English, but he was a surprising phenomenon. Though his English was timorous, he was our first poet to live by his pen, created a circle and among his greatest disciples was Bankim Chandra Chatterjee. He was the first travelogue writer. You know people in India either travel because of religious purposes or for study. But to go and see Nature was not done. When Nabakumar went to Sagar Island somebody asked him, "Why are you here?" He said, "I have come here to see the ocean." They couldn't understand him.[2]

---

[1] A kind of slippers with curled toes very popular in nineteenth century Calcutta.

[2] An incident in *Kapalkundala*, a novel written by Bankim Chandra Chatterjee (Chattopadhyaya).

LINA: What set him apart?

RPG: He understood all that! It was he who wrote the first biographies of the poets. Muslims wrote biographies but not Hindus. He was the first *Gazetteer* writer and when he went to recover his health in Chittagong he said "area so much, arable land so much . . . population so much, so many Muslims, etc." There was no public relations department to hand out all kinds of information on a platter. He had to find out for himself. He said things like "the school cost 30,275 rupees, 12 annas and 3 paise. The library has so many books and so many shelves"—how do you think such an inquiring mind developed? He named 22 kinds of birds, it's incredible!

LINA: Anyone else?

RPG: Bankim Chandra Chatterjee: he knew the ignominy of serving under the British. The way in which he was harassed and maltreated! He is probably the most perceptive Indian critic of the British. His "*Ingraj Tattva*" and "*Babu Tattva*"[3] are fantastic. A supple, refined and clinical analysis of the English character. How the Indians look at the English. And even then he acquired all that was good from the West. He might have hated the Englishman but not their culture. He also knew French and was a positivist *a la* Comte. He was also devastatingly sarcastic about the *babus*.

LINA: Which *babus* are you talking about?

RPG: I'm not talking about the *babus* who became Banias and Mutsuddis and made a fat lot of money betraying the country and spreading the *babu* culture with wine, women and song. I am talking about the new breed of Bengali who were educated. Even among them there were some who were not very happy when their countrymen acclaimed them as great scholars, until many got the *dhobi*-mark[4] from the *sahebs*. At one point Vidyasagar said an interesting thing about Raja Rajendralal Mitra: "Rajen is a very clever fellow—he goes and tells Englishmen 'I don't know English

---

[3]Essays published in *Bangadarshan*, a journal published and edited by him.
[4]Washermen mark clothes with a special indelible ink indicating individuals or families.

but I know Sanskrit.' Since he speaks marvelous English, the Englishmen think that if this is what he calls 'poor' English—his knowledge of Sanskrit must be vast!"

Bankim babu in his "*Ingraj Tattva*" said, "I'll give you a speech, please applaud me. I'll write essays, please appreciate me. I'll go to my own society, *ingraj ami tomake pronam kori* [Tr. Englishmen, I salute you], I'll be your bond slave." There was this kind of weakness but generally, the great men were extraordinary in their integration of their own national culture with highly selective, discriminating assimilation of the good aspects of foreign culture. The only exception was Michael Madhusudan Dutt. Early in his life he revolted against everything—his country, his parents, but realized his error later, the wheel turned a complete circle for him. He wrote:

Oh mother Bengal
I have traveled here and there looking for treasure
But there is so much treasure here.

He introduced blank verse into our literature. He made Ravana the hero. He said, "I love Ravana, he is a great fellow. I hate Rama." Until the end he had sideburns and he went to expensive salons. He was a fashionable hedonist.

LINA: When did he change his name?

RPG: When he became a Christian. He would give a guinea in those days for a haircut. Sidewhiskers, muttonchops, three-piece suit, watch-fob and chain and drank like nobody's business. When he was dying, the man who had taught him Sanskrit and all that said, "Michael, for God's sake, you are spitting blood. Don't drink anymore. You'll die." He said, "Look Pandit, I love you, I respect you but if you are going to tell me to give up drinking, I am not going to see your face again." And he drank himself to death. There is a very interesting cartoon section done in *Sanibarer Chithi* [a satirical paper whose name means "Saturday Post"]. It spared nobody from Jibanananda Das to Tagore—all the great writers. They published a cartoon in which Vidyasagar was shown in dinner jacket and Michael was shown in *dhoti* and *panjabi*. One was a *pucca saheb* and the other was a true Bengali. The futility of trying to create great literature through a foreign medium . . . I may be a little prejudiced about Indo-Anglian writing, but I don't think it can ever attain the kind of excellence if you compare the poetry Sakti Chatterjee writes with that of Nissim Ezekiel.

Bankim Chatterjee was once asked, "Why are you so upset if somebody eats with knife and fork, wears a dressing gown and eats off plates?" He said, "Look, you can buy those for four *annas*. They are not suitable for this country. What is the point of aping them? Go for the deeper things."

LINA: What of today?

RPG: I know so many people who don't know their own mother tongues. The bloody Doon school *wallahs*! I am all for a spotlessly clean bathroom. I think a bathroom should be as clean and nice as a room of worship in a house. But you scholars of western culture shouldn't be seen in a perfectly knotted tie or a jacket with a shoulder for which you have given 13 "trials" [at the tailor's]. If you tell an Englishman "You are wonderfully Gaelic," he'll probably throw you into the English Channel and a Frenchman will probably slit your throat. Totally chauvinistic! Nobody wants to lose his own identity and to be known as a man of another country. But this is what is happening now. Just see Michael, Bankim, the fantastic cultural efflorescence! They took so many things from the West like satirical writings; take Bengali prose, a *parvenu* compared to prose. in Orissa. I know Oriya and have even read a sixteenth century Oriya book. Bengali we speak in the colloquial way but when we write we use chaste Bengali—nowadays that's gone, though some people still write it. Our prose was created at the turn of the century. Before that, prose was confined to letters (very stilted prose), legal documents, accounts. The missionaries also had a great hand . . . Carey, Marshman, Ward. They didn't want to create another *sastra* but something that would be intelligible enough, like translating the Bible. If you write some high faluting' nonsense, no one will understand. They were selling Christianity to the heathen. So they wrote short sentences.

The Bengali of the Pandits began from the left hand corner of the page and ended on the next page. I give you an example of how writing helped in the simplified, evolved modern Bengali. Before Bankim Chandra, there was no such thing as the novel. It was he who adapted that medium with *Durgeshnandini*. *The Last Days of Pompeii* prompted him to write *Rajani* but it's not a half-baked, bastardized version of English and Bengali. It was a hundred percent Bengali novel, in masterly style. My own idea is that in only one sphere this didn't work and that was in the sphere of painting.

LINA: That remained purely traditional? Like the Kalighat style of painting?

RPG: Yes, yes . . . the concept of identity, the concept of specific nature. Regional schools were there . . . like Kalighat. They were unlettered people. There was also what Mildred Archer and others called "Company painting." Who were the Company painters? The Company painters were Indians who were taught to paint mainly in watercolor on paper. And they were asked by the *sahebs* to paint all kinds of arts, crafts, people, sex and so on. The bloody English always wanted their own bloody dogs, horses and flowers and of course national history. From there arose the Kalighat School of Painting which adapted the western techniques of painting in oil. Pure watercolor. You got Puri, Madhubani, Tanjore. Any painting done under the shadow of a temple is religious painting. But in the 1830's . . .

LINA: *Babu* culture again?

RPG: Apart from *babu* culture, you know jockeys running a race, shooting a tiger, and later *babu* culture. The commentary on the Elokeshi[5] murder case, anything sensational was depicted like that. But the academic painters, no matter what these people say, the founders of the Calcutta School of Arts and Crafts said, "We don't want them to be copycats and mimics of western paintings. Let them do their own painting." The concept of national identity came much later with the *Banga Bhanga Andolan*, the partition of 1905.

You know Abanindra Nath at first started painting Persian, Rajasthani, Japanese and Indian painting, and created a synthesis.

---

[5] A sensational criminal case about Elokeshi, a young married woman, who was seduced by the Mohanta or head of Tarakeshwar, a Saiva monastic center near Calcutta. When her husband found out, he killed her. There was a criminal case in which both the husband and the Mohanta were punished, for separate criminal acts.

I have left out an important thing! There are some barristers, some civil servants and others who turned into *pucca sahebs*. In the hot summer with 180 degrees Fahrenheit in the shade, wore a three-piece suit, took a walking stick and went on a morning constitutional. They had some justification: unlike Bankim Chandra Chatterjee, others were blinded by the brilliance of western culture. Here are people of a small island in the sea and all the *"Sasagara Prithivi,"* the ocean bound world, they have conquered! How have they done it? Through their culture and look at where we were. We have been dedicated to the Astrological Almanac, the bloody priests, old women. We were caught in a hopeless morass. Never visited four miles beyond our village, therefore, they discarded everything and became *sahebs*. Satyajit Ray's father had written a poem called "Cry Baby." He talks about the mighty cry-babies and among the mightiest was *"Booth Saheber bachcha"* [Tr. "Mr. Booth's baby," thus an English baby]. When he cried no one could hold a candle to him. They criticized, but they knew their Milton and Shakespeare.

LINA: What do you mean?

RPG: I am not denigrating anything and this is a slightly delicate thing. We went to Orissa, a highly civilized place. Enormously subtle people, magnificent culture, but we Bengalis looked down upon them and never tried to integrate with them. We are so close! We went to Bihar and never got integrated with the Biharis because (again treading on rather delicate ground) culturally compared to Bengal, it was a bit of a . . . you know. But the Bengalis who went to Uttar Pradesh, particularly Lucknow, became Lucknow-*wallahs*. Because they met their match there. But not everywhere. Not decadent, but . . . if you read any book on wine, you'll see that the world's greatest white wine is from a very large grape. A sweet, heavy, honeyed wine. The grape gets rotten, the new skin is formed—which is fully enriched with sugar and they call it "noble rottenness." Similarly, decadence has also a noble rottenness: the music, culture, calligraphy, how you wear your perfume, how you dress.

LINA: You talk about those who imbibed the best of British culture and maintained their identity; you mention the creation of *babu* culture, moneyed people, traders, but the rest of the people? How did the rest of the people fare?

RPG: I will tell you . . . moneyed people, as you call it, the *babu* culture. If you go to north Calcutta—you will find Corinthian, Doric, Ionic, pillars—family histories will have salt trading behind them or Banias, that means they got their money from trade or from being a middleman. Their attitude towards the *sahebs* was naturally one of *bhakti* (devotion). Between 1810 and 1830 was a great phase and all these Basaks and Mullicks, Tagores and Roys, invited the British to their houses during Durga *puja* and gave more respect to them than to the Mother Goddess, who after all, could not do much for them. Maybe after you die she might help—but not in this unfortunate, imperfect world.

The albino gods and goddesses were important. These families ran through their fortunes by the end of the century. And what about ordinary people? Bengalis are very stubborn people, culturally that is.

LINA: Yes, I noticed!

RPG: You will never see—hardly any of that among Bengalis—I'm not naming any community. People wearing floral dressing gowns, smoking a pipe. "Yes darling . . . oh mommy, oh daddy . . ." that kind of thing doesn't . . . Also I'll invite you home, I'll give you the kind of food we eat, and not Welsh rarebit or Yorkshire pudding and some tepid tomato cream soup. The point is . . . these people make the same mistake. Ordinary Bengalis have always been very stubborn. They went to school and all that sort of thing. Read up to a point. You see, 1817 or 1818 to 1856 (when the universities were started), then schools started. Bengalis went to school, learned something, to my mind, they were very peace-loving people. They are/were not interested in the future of India or the future of mankind. I think their attitude was a compound of three things—one is devotion (*bhakti*), another is hatred (*ghenna*), the last is fear (*bhay*). For *bhakti* see Satyendranath Tagore's "*Bharatvarshiya Engraj*" (The Englishman in India). He was Rabindranath's elder brother by about 19 years [born in 1841, and the first Indian member of the Indian Civil

Service]. I don't see why there should be any question that the Englishman has conferred great benefits on us. Look at what we had in our anarchy—the Pindaris, the Bargis, the Thuggees. Bankim Chandra Chatterjee had written that after 1757 came an era of great anarchy. Mir Jafar smokes opium and sleeps, the Englishmen write dispatches and collect the paddy revenues. There is no peace in keeping paddy in a barn. Your gold in the chest at home or even the child in the womb of the mother is not safe. Karl Marx said that in order to exploit the people of any country you have to open it up first. Good things come out of this: one is English education, second the telegraph, and third the railways. Marx himself in his letters in the *Herald Tribune* said this. In order to exploit the country you have to open it up. By building railways you do a lot of things.

LINA: How did the people react to this?

RPG: The ordinary Bengali said we are happy under this regime: at least there's some peace and quiet. The second great unifying factor was the loyalty to Queen Victoria. She wouldn't die and things wouldn't change. In 1839 when Emily Eden (she was Lord Auckland's sister, a painter and writer) was here and Victoria became queen she called the young queen "a charming invention." Now no dramatist could write a scenario with a better symbol of unity for people who were dominated by a foreign nation, than the queen. If she was not there you would have to invent her. The Africans called her the "Great White Queen." Particularly we Bengalis . . .

LINA: Associate her with the Mother cult?

RPG: With the Mother cult! I sometimes feel why hasn't she become a god in the new pantheon like *Santoshi Ma*. Whether she was deified or not she got far better, far greater respect from the ordinary Bengali. I have five or six publications from Battala.[6] They say, "We have nothing to fear in this world so long as the Queen is there. She will save us from everything." These people are not aiming to be Rai Bahadur or Khan Bahadur, just sheer outpouring of heartfelt loyalty for the queen. In 1875, when Edward VII came as Prince of

[6]Bengali press and publishing houses in the beginning were located in that area.

Wales, there was an interesting paper called *Basantak*, which means "fools" in Sanskrit. A highly sophisticated paper. We had two other comic magazines, one was *Delhi Sketchbook* (1860's) and *The Indian Charivari* (1870's) from Calcutta. There was a cartoon in *Basantak*: a housewife saying to her husband in typical Bengali, "The ways of the crown prince are like those of the *pandas* (priests) at Kalighat Temple." The husband asks "Why?" "Because whatever you ask him, he says it's his Mother's wish!" says the wife.

After 1858 when India became part of the Empire (of course, Victoria did not become Empress of India till 1873) everything was tightened. They had gotten the biggest traumatic assault during the rebellion of 1857 and at that time "loot" became an accepted word in the dictionary. Secondly, "nigger, dirty and black nigger" was endlessly repeated. Edward VII, Prince of Wales, had written a letter to Salisbury (who became a minister thrice like Maggie Thatcher) "that just because somebody is black why should our people call them dirty niggers?"

LINA: What were the consequences?

RPG: Racism is bound to become state policy. When only 10000 people with the help of 50000 soldiers rule a country—unless you behave like god and create a distance you are in trouble. If an ordinary man stood before the great Lord Curzon's seat at Keddlestone he must bend as if he were before God. Edward Lutyens' "saracenic capital of Delhi" was also like the center of the universe. Of course, the poor fellow couldn't live there more than 19 years.

These fellows terrorized the Indians in such a way. Suppose a *Sadar Wallah*[7], a young fellow, is going on a horse, the Indian must stand aside but if he does not salute him, he'll get down and whip him; if he salutes, he may be whipped for being "familiar."

LINA: Do you think the common man took to this culture out of fear or . . .

RPG: They had to earn a livelihood! Don't forget that we are only talking about Calcutta because the rest of the world does not matter.

---

[7] A high official at the District Headquarters.

There must have been hundreds of people who had never seen a white man.

One Oriya, the famous novelist Phakir Mohan Senapati, said there are some Bengalis who keep governesses and send their daughters-in-law to Bethune College to learn English and appoint *chabuksowars* (horse tamers) to make horses walk in the *dulki* style, like *memsahebs*. One great difficulty of the Bengalis with the *sahebs* was the language. Language was a great barrier. The average Bengali almost died a little for fear of speaking English to a *saheb* whose accent he didn't understand. Lots of funny stories—some true, some apocryphal. I'll tell you a true story from 1925 or 1926. Indians met Englishmen in half a dozen places—in the court, in offices, and on playfields: cricket and football. There used to be a cricket match called the Bengal Schools vs European Schools. The European schools were all *sahebs* and some were great, playing even against Australia. There was a young boy named Chone Majumdar, 19 years old, short chap, dark, who even failed to enter school. Practically unlettered but a marvelous natural player. He played cricket and he beat all those mighty bowlers (English county cricket bowlers) to a pulp and scored a century. Stanley Jackson was Governor then and he was the captain of England in Test cricket against Australia in 1903, 1904. He said: "Where is the boy gone—who could dance on his feet, had a sharp eye, cross bat cricket, I want to talk to him." Somehow the boy realized this and ran away, locked himself in the WC. People were waiting for him. Somebody yelled at him to come out and he did like a sacrificial goat. After that, any time he was scoring in the 90's he would throw away his wicket and go away lest he be caught and forced to come out and talk. There are many stories of this fear. The job depended on speaking properly.

LINA: You said that the common man did adapt some of these ways and the intellectual elite imbibed some of the best but kept some of their own culture. In looking at today's Calcutta, what happened to Bengalis? What do they look to? The nineteenth century? Do they look again to the West? The country of the big cities? Is there a Bengali culture outside of Calcutta?

RPG: I am not being chauvinistic. I've been to Bombay, Delhi, Madras. Delhi is a hothouse flower and under government aegis you cannot create a culture. Bombay is too commercialized and English oriented. But here in Bengal, you have the right kind of orientation, political mind. But because of the numbers of the lower middle-class people being very vast—they are in a sense useless compared to the more practical people in Delhi, Bombay, and other places. They know the iniquities of Englishmen, they know that there are still racists in the UK High Commission. But they are culturally cosmopolitan.

LINA: A carry over?

RPG: A carry over—but only about half a dozen people write in English, all others write in the vernacular. Take Bishnu De, Sudhin Dutta [Bengali poets who came after Tagore], their poetry was full of great mythology; as much of Roman as *Ramayana* and *Mahabharata*. They know that you have to be a citizen of the world. You cannot live in isolation. My own objection is that we know only a little English. How wonderful it would have been to have a German or French perspective.

LINA: But being citizens of the world is that going to help? Does it mean giving up some of their own identity?

RPG: I am trying to say that we'll never let go of English no matter how much you talk about it—English must be there otherwise our tenuous ties with the universe will be gone.

LINA: They say Bengalis or Calcuttans are cosmopolitan or citizens of the world—yet, at the same time, people are beginning to be concerned about a Bengali identity. They still keep the language, but feel that many things are changing. Totally new values, that contradict perhaps some fundamental Bengali values; there is the family and then there is community at large.

RPG: I tell you, we have pride in our language but nowadays, pride is more present in Bangladesh. But you know, the old family ties like the joint family . . . there are joint families in Calcutta still, with 110 people living in them. They have their joint club, own cricket team, own institutions and meetings—cooking rice and dal together in the communal kitchen and nowadays they have permission to cook other things separately. Tati Sen's house in Baghbazar is like this. I still hear of families of about forty people living together with apparently no discordant note. But these are exceptions. You have nuclear families, but nuclear families does not mean, according to my reckoning, that you care for too much privacy and opt for loneliness. You try not to intrude on other people's privacy. Can I come on such and such a day? You telephone and ask. I have three brothers here and one sister, they drop in any time they want to. Our society has amorphous family ties, though we are not eating from the same kitchen we are not lost. The values are there. Eating-wise, Bengalis are very stubborn.

LINA: Would you say that Bengalis are more chauvinistic within the privacy of their family? In their community? Is there more of a core Bengali identity within the family?

RPG: Within the family means a minor casteism. This miniscule casteism in Bengal is not very perceptible. For example, in Haryana, in the Jat belt, there are two things which will not happen in Calcutta: we will not vote caste-wise and we will not kill people to prevent cow sacrifice. Can't speak for others but my relatives visit, so do friends, many more friends than relatives. Family ties yes, but attachment to certain friends is stronger. Bengalis *are* chauvinistic.

LINA: They are chauvinistic and at the same time they are cosmopolitian.

RPG: There is pride, but before they used to say "*Ure, Khotta*[8]." Now many wouldn't. In their heart of hearts, but not use them.

LINA: How different are today's Calcuttan anglicized community from that of the nineteenth century?

RPG: Not just a Bengali anglicized community, there is no alternative to English so far as the entire country is concerned. You have to learn English if you want to secure a job. Hence the proliferation of English medium schools has been fantastic.

[8]Pejorative terms for Oriya and Hindi speaking people respectively.

My wife was telling me (she is a school teacher at the Bow Bazar Loreto School) that she met a woman somewhere. She's not a great one for cosmetics. She's got a Nivea cream [a popular cold-cream] and something like that . . . some powder to dab on in the summer and a cake of soap. But this woman had a fantastic array of perfumes, etc. And she said, "Our own smuggler gets us all this and also Scotch." Mind you not whiskey, but *Scotch!* Very innocently she said, "*Accha!*"

LINA: Have you written something that's still available?

RPG: I've only written one book, *The Sounds and Cries of Calcutta Streets*. Do you read Bengali?

# M.J. Akbar

LINA: Is it a waste to have a seminar on Calcutta, since you ask "Why Calcutta?"[1]

M.J. AKBAR: I don't think it's a waste but I think sometimes academic interest can be purely academic.

LINA: I could say the same about journalism.

MJA: Sure. You can take the study of Calcutta to an extreme and get lost in preconceived patterns. There is a law of perception which is accurate for journalism and for more serious things like academics: you perceive what you want to see.

LINA: Are you talking about subjective reporting?

MJA: The subject of subjective/objective reporting is a very difficult one to define.

LINA: It is easy if one has a strong ground in ethics and morality.

MJA: But without a strong ground in ethics, I wouldn't expect a good journalist to emerge.

LINA: You can be a reporter and be biased.

MJA: I think the bias of academicians has been one of the greatest punishments this country has had to suffer. Particularly western biases, since I flirt a little with history. It's not only western historians who are biased. Indians are too. They mold facts exactly as they want to preach: colonialism completely reinvented facts. I

[1] In 1987, Lina organized at Brown University a small faculty seminar on Calcutta.

am a little terrified about what Brown wants to do with facts about Calcutta.

LINA: I can tell you! I have always been interested in Bengal and after this work is finished I'll continue working in Bengal.

MJA: That's you, but what about Brown?

LINA: It's not Brown as such—it's just five people who have a common interest and this is a way for us to communicate in an interdisciplinary way.

MJA: What aroused your interest in Calcutta?

LINA: In the 1960's, I was trying to go to Sudan and the Middle East and I wanted to study identity and Islam. At the University of Chicago, most of the professors I had worked in India. I felt if I wanted attention I should come to India. So I came in '67 but I was only an undergraduate. I got interested in Bengal. One person who colored my imagination about India and Bengal was Gour Kishore Ghosh. He welcomed my husband and myself with open arms and an elaborate meal. I understand this happening in my country but to total strangers! I did a study of Muslims in Bishnupur and later of Hindu ritual and symbolism in life cycle rites and wrote several books. My interest in India has been strong because it's a challenge. Even when I finish I don't think that I'll have totally understood India. So Bengal/Calcutta society represents one more community for me to understand and to compare with others.

When *The Telegraph* first came out, I was happy that there was an alternative to *The Statesman*. I found *The Statesman* representative of a generation rather set in their ways. I was in Calcutta; I wouldn't have reacted as strongly elsewhere.

MJA: In the first editorial I wrote, I said I was not sure that I could have brought out *The Telegraph* from any other city.

LINA : There is an audience.

MJA: But before the audience there is a group of people who can actually sit down and create a newspaper. A newspaper is not created by the editors alone. You're right about the new mindset of the newspaper. One of the reasons why that happened was because we consciously went to the younger generation and the paper was both written by and for them to a large extent. When you take up a newspaper you have to know from which point to enter the family. A newspaper is very different from even a magazine and the difference can, in fact, be pinned down to the logic of marketing, at least in our country. A magazine is something you can pick up arbitrarily. All people who sell magazines get a general sense of what their circulation will be but it's different for a newspaper. A magazine is also different because the male buys it and there may be elements in it he may not want to share with the rest of the family. He may read it himself, there may be a pin-up. He always has the privilege of not showing it to the rest. A newspaper is essentially a family product. Slips in under the door when the family is asleep and is picked up. So you can't afford to take the liberties with a newspaper you can with a magazine. If you turn off the decision maker of the family for a particular reason, you lose him. To enter a family is a critical decision and you have to figure out the vulnerable points of entry.

LINA : How do you enter it?

MJA: I had been reading *The Statesman* for 20 years and found that it had got caught in a groove which it had cleverly converted into the image of respectability. It was a kind of confidence builder for the insecure. The comfort of familiarity. Even when it wandered into questioning a policy or a decision it did it in a set way. You could see this was a mind which had stopped thinking for a long while but was being read because it was a historic institution. When we decided to challenge it, I wasn't just challenging another newspaper. If all *The Telegraph* managed to do was to become as good as *The Statesman*, why should anybody stop reading *The Statesman*?

The first priority was to be different. Many people have complimented the paper for a difference in layout. That's only cosmetic. It's a difference of content and attitude. The right to believe that leisure is also part of the daily mental need of the individual. There is a place for the explanatory article, the relaxed piece, a bit of wit and the report which doesn't begin and end with "she said," "he said." We introduced a great number of things which in five years *The Stateman* is imitating. Curious that the competition has made the front-runner imitative. Even simple things like the use of the byline, the nature of the headline. The other day I was joking with our staff Deputy Editor: I had given him a headline which he thought was unusual. An interview-based story on a policeman who'd almost been shot—so the headline was "The full story in Handa's[2] words"—not a sharp headline. By mentioning Handa and making it a first person story we were exciting interest in the personality: the reader will respond. The editor said it's not done, but I said, of course it's done. Sure enough, soon *The Statesman* had exactly the same headline in the context of someone else. Once you've broken the mold, people tend to follow.

LINA: I thought one of the differences between the two newspapers was that *The Statesman* used to give a bare report and you were left with a dry story with no narrative description, the paper not really telling you anything. *The Telegraph* ended with a strong stand. I wondered if that was something that was needed in Calcutta for Bengalis.

MJA: And people have appreciated the fact. There are dangers that the reporter might overdo it. He might concentrate so much on the stand that he might forget the content.

We had no tradition, so we couldn't keep it. But we kept the respectability through a strong commitment to accuracy, not that anybody can be accurate all the time. We kept a strong image of the paper and allowed (within that) a leeway for the individual to flourish. A complementary role. The institution had to flourish with the cooperation and talent of the individual and the individual had to be allowed to flourish for the strength of the institution.

To get back to the original point: how do you get into the family. I felt *The Statesman* had become not a family newspaper but a head of the family newspaper—paper that only the decision maker, the male decision maker in the family was reading. So I said, appeal to the others. I said get through to the young, the wife, the children. In the beginning we used to be sneered at. They said "children's newspaper." I didn't mind. The first thing the establishment does

[2]A very senior Indian Police Service officer serving in West Bengal.

when you accomplish something and there is competition, is sneer at it. Today they're losing circulation and trembling.

LINA: How do you deal with society's values, tradition, problems in the city?

MJA: Problems in the city are the most obvious area for a newspaper. I think we've done more to protect the city's environment than anyone else. In the last two months we have had major victories through our campaigns. One is the Rawdom Square Project, which has been stalled. A park in the heart of the city which the government had handed over to the Birlas to set up another theater complex. Destroying every bit of green in the city. The government became very hostile to us. Mr. Basu [the Chief Minister of West Bengal] abused me personally and the paper—because there was inevitably corruption there. Corruption I didn't care about, but how can you destroy what little greenery there is in the city? There's no excuse any more. It's the last city which can afford this—it's been much raped. And the second one was the cemetery which the church was handling. Both these projects have been stalled.

LINA: That's one way that you deal with problems.

MJA: That's a real way. Identify problems and solutions. You're right about the feeling that Calcuttans seem to have given up.

LINA: It's like they're waiting for someone else to come and do something.

MJA: I think the newspaper has a very real role to play in the atmosphere of apathy. We have to take the lead even if the people aren't taking the lead. I used to get phone calls from readers. We were going through a bad phase with the government harassing us, so I told them, "Why don't you get into the streets and protest?" People weren't willing to do that. They want the projects to stop but they're not willing to do anything about it. But I think they're grateful.

LINA: But the sense of values is not something that the paper picks up on.

MJA: Values have to be common to every newspaper. You have to have a certain commitment to your readers. I don't think *The*

*Telegraph* is any better or worse. I think we put extra effort into investigative reporting: the reporting we've done on these financiers and crooks, the Handa story. Other papers have refused to touch this story because a particular financier has bought all the manuscripts. He's even sat in this chair trying to do the same to me.

LINA: What about an article on high-rise buildings? My concern is about the two-story house which was replaced by a 12 floor building without provision for parking, water, garbage collection.

MJA: I'd like to leave you with one thought. An interesting thought that comes from living in the city. In the 60's the concept of living in Calcutta was living in a nice one-storied house. In the 80's that has become a multi-storied house. The unique conversion of this city to apartment living is fascinating. These tall apartment buildings have become, in fact, vertical *paras or mohallas*. This is not true of Bombay for example, where neighbors don't really know each other. The building in which we're staying, I would not want to leave it. Although the company is ready to give me a house with a garden, I won't leave it because my children were born there and I have a lot of friends. Just like in the traditional *mohalla* where I was born and grew up, when we could walk into anybody's house and come out of anybody's house; the only boundary line was that of the *mohalla*, if the child went outside that, people would worry. Otherwise, people assumed that you were around. At dinner time you'd check at whose house the child was. The 50 families who share this building have religious differences, regional differences, but there is interaction.

LINA: You are one of the few who expressed it this way. More noted the loss of the horizontal *para* and community.

MJA: I think what is happening is that flux and change is taking place but people aren't recognizing it. Maybe in five years' time it will be a commonly expressed experience—at the moment it's just being experienced.

LINA: Why are people against vertical living?

MJA: They see it as a collapse of their sense of pride.

LINA: A collapse of their sense of numbers?

MJA: Bengalis are very conservative and this is also a sign of mental laziness. They fight against change much more than they pretend to. They are not revolutionaries; they are basically conservatives.

LINA: This generation?

MJA: No! This community which is created by the British Empire. By the Permanent Land Settlement system.

LINA: I find this generation very contradictory.

MJA: They pretend that they want to be the leaders of the Paris revolution but in their heart of hearts they just want *rosogollas* from their mothers.

LINA: I had a conversation with some people, one said that Calcutta used to have a central core, and another said a ring of villages. Now Calcutta itself is breaking into an inner core and an outer core: the inner core is non-Bengali and the outer core is 60 percent Bengali and further out in the suburbs.

MJA: Non-Bengali again, mostly.

LINA: And the person said, "If I was a non-Bengali, I would be worried about being surrounded." I brought him the fact that the *Amra Bangali* Party was a total disaster.

MJA: You must remember one thing about this community. Any community which is so fixated on the idea of property cannot be revolutionary.

LINA: Do you think that they have an idea of culture like the nineteenth century did?

MJA: That was a flowering which took place in the post-British period. A major embarrassment. Bengali leadership of the nation is coincidental with the British because Calcutta was the capital. Therefore, the people of the Raj became the major influence on power. Their power was an appendage to British power, never an independent power. Whereas most other power centers in this country have had independent political powers created out of their own strength. Created through conquest, armies, etc. The Bengalis never had an army. An army of bureaucrats. A *babu* country.

# Satindranath Chakrabarty

LINA: What's happening in Bengal/Calcutta since Independence and why are people, Bengalis in general, not addressing issues which affect the family-values, belief system? I am talking about the middle class, not the upper-class *sahebs*. Are these the responsibilities of the middle class? Which year did you join the Communist Party?

SATINDRANATH CHAKRABARTY: I joined in 1949. In my college days—40's to '45/'46—I was a Kantian Vedantist. Gradually, I developed an interest in Marxism, and to the extent I could read Marxist classics and interpretations of Marxism by writers from the Soviet Union—during World War II they sold books by the millions, they were dumped here on a mass scale. Because I don't know German or any other foreign language, I had to depend on second-hand interpretations.

LINA: What made you join the Communist Party? Was it a reaction against the British?

SC: Originally it was, then, somehow, during the war days the Communist Party was a part of the national mainstream and did many good things, e.g. famine relief and many other social services.

LINA: What did replace the Community Party?

SC: The secretary at the time was P.C. Joshi and to my mind he was the ablest, most patriotic of all the communist leaders. His thesis was important: that the communist movement must be integrated with the nationalist mainstream. Therefore, apart from political movements, he was the originator of things like the Indian

Peoples' Theatre Association (IPTA), and all these cultural artistes were at the time communists or fellow travelers, and because of that, the Joshi Movement helped Indianize Marxism in a way. Later Marxists did not go for this, they were doctrinaire, they did not seek to integrate.

LINA: That is against true Marxism.

SC: To my mind it is possible—it was done by Mao Tse Tung in China. "I want to marry the universal truth of Marxism to the concrete situation in China." And that he did to a very great extent. Anyway, because of my Communist past, I didn't pursue my scholastic exercise. I stayed in politics on the whole and therefore I wrote many articles in journals. Current topics—Stalin's theories, criticism of one of my teachers who criticized historical materialism.

LINA: So you were politically active and that is where you made your career?

SC: I couldn't make a political career because of my philosophical training. I was born in an epoch when the national stalwarts were present. Nehru was there and the national movement was not stagnant. The nationalist movement created a sort of ascetic morality and the original communists till 1950 or so were not out for self aggrandizement—many were self-sacrificing. The communist stalwarts were all the sort who lived simply, had not much money. After the 1950's they joined the elections and obtained seats in the assemblies. They became a force. Now they are the ruling party in West Bengal, Tripura, Kerala.

LINA: Has it helped the people? Do you think the Communist Party of India in the 30's and 40's *vis-à-vis* the people in this city was different than today?

SC: The leaders now are victims of circumstances in the sense that while fighting capitalism, they have imbibed all capitalist values. That is, they are after money, careers, stabilizing their own men (nepotism). There is corruption. They talk of the vices of capitalism but the party itself thrives on these "vices."

LINA: What do you think is the problem with Calcutta? Is it too political?

SC: To my mind—when I was young, Calcutta was a decent city despite the fact that it was a colonial creation of the British. We carry forward the legacy of Partition. That is the most important historical factor. Because of the Partition of India and West Bengal, so many refugees came over since 1947. Then there was the Great Calcutta Killing and riots, the famine. So the social fabric was really destroyed by (1) the partition, (2) the influx of refugees, (3) . . .

LINA: Migrant laborers . . .

SC: Laborers were there—but the partitioned state had to accommodate millions of refugees. And they are truly the alienated. They could not be rehabilitated in a proper manner. That constituted a great strain on the economy of West Bengal. And the politics of West Bengal revolved around that problem. The refugees grabbed land and in a way developed the suburbs of Calcutta. At the same time there was a large concentration of people. Colonies developed in a haphazard manner. No minimum amenities.

LINA: I heard they improved *bustees*, and the water and sanitation problems?

SC: Peripheral. Instead of ordinary toilets, we have scientific toilets. But then slum life hasn't been remodeled. In any slum you'll find people bundled together—husband, wife and children. No separate bathroom. Their lives are absolutely different—even from that of the lower middle class. Amenities have been provided to some extent but they do not constitute any fundamental improvement so, to my mind, the post-war Calcutta changed fundamentally because of the refugee influx. It constituted a great strain on the economics, politics, culture and morality of entire Bengal. Added to that, after Independence, was the planned "development" of this country. One peculiar phenomenon of West Bengal was that, during the British days, West Bengal didn't develop an entrepreneurial class because of the land tenure system of the Permanent Settlement. The landed interest in rural areas received a fixed quota of rent, the land was tilled by peasants who had to pay *khajna* [revenue on land] to the landlords.

LINA: Why didn't they have a sense of investment?

SC: Because it was a life of ease. Money flowed in—they started schools. Excavated ponds. Built temples. But this class of *zamindars* did nothing to radically reform the land, augment production, introduce new technology. They amassed wealth, purchased houses in Calcutta and stayed here. We are all middle-class people and if you trace the history—we are all children of the Permanent Settlement system. My grandfather's father held some land and lived on it. Then because of certain factors, his son went off for English education and then his son joined a profession. So, many professional people like doctors, lawyers and clerks, etc., are coming out of that Permanent Settlement system. But they all cast aside the land. And what professions were they in? Either doctors, or lawyers, or clerks, or serving in British courts. You won't find a Bengali industrialist. You won't find a Bengali who had a lot of land and contemplated using tractors. No enhancement of production. That line, Bengalis were never accustomed to.

LINA: It's as if they despise it.

SC: Then again, for *bhadralok* and ordinary people—the term is there—*babu* class. This didn't happen in other parts of India—Punjab, Bombay, the Parsi community, etc. So there is this difference between the Bengali set up and that in other states: (1) the refugee influx; (2) the paucity of land; (3) the paucity of industries—Bengalis have no industries. At this time something happened—namely, the development of the Indian economy. Planning was introduced not only on the basis of private enterprise but also in the public sector. In basic fundamental industries, the state must interfere. The state pumped a lot of money into the economy. Doing that opened up opportunities for contracts.

LINA: Bengalis took up contract working for Marwaris?

SC: Also independent small contractors. Avenues opened up for different kinds of middlemen. If a factory purchases different things, I appoint you and then you appoint others to get them. *Dalal* or middlemen. This way new openings became available, which were mostly unproductive. Salesmen, middlemen, *dalals*, black marketeers; paucity of goods but flow of money. Productively, the Bengali economy didn't develop but there were unproductive expansions: (1) refugees; (2) Bengalis having no other skill, owning no industries. Bengalis acting only as clerks, lawyers, and doctors—mostly unproductive—you can say, tertiary sector jobs. Not primary or secondary.

LINA: They don't have the entrepreneur spirit but one thing did develop in Bengal—the arts, literature.

SC: The Bengali middle class, children of the Permanent Settlement, imbibing British ideas (Calcutta was a city where English education started very early). The Bengali middle class took to English education whereas the Muslims did not accept it. Because of cross-fertilization we have a tradition of our own. Bengali is a rich language. We have our own folk songs, folk music, and dance tradition. Because of cross-fertilization—new ideas from the West and our own indigenous ideas came together. The nineteenth century was a century of genius so far as West Bengal was concerned. All sorts of ideas—social reform movements, religious movements, debates—if there was any golden age in recent times, it was the nineteenth century. On the plane of ideas, the Communists did not give any new ideas.

LINA: So how are they maintaining this city?

SC: What happened is that Calcutta is suffering from "giganticism." It's too big. It can't accommodate its sewer system built for a population of 10 lakhs[1]. Now with the outlying areas occupied by refugees and all that we have a population of 100 lakhs or 10 million.

So, per square mile it has the highest density of population (in the world). The sewer system is at least 70 years old. But you can't shape it, because of the influx. This is the mischief this Communist government has done—and where my criticism lies. So it developed in an unplanned, haphazard manner. So many people came here and were allowed to occupy land forcibly and this has been legalized now. Refugees have been settled. But then, no planning took place. And because of the accretion of wealth in so many hands, you can just pay the Corporation and construct houses illegally. Bengali political parties did not emphasize planned development at all. The Congress was there when there was an imaginative chief minister,

---

[1] 1 lakh—one hundred thousand.

Dr. B.C. Roy. He couldn't think of such huge numbers of people in Calcutta and started satellite towns. He started Kalyani (a satellite town in Nadia district). And because of his initiative we have Durgapur, Digha. The positive things, he did. During the Congress regime, he was the topmost in this respect. There is such a large population but the electricity production has not kept pace with the growing numbers. For the last ten years there have been tremendous power cuts, load-shedding for 12–13 hours, shortage of water supply, sanitation problems.

What we Indians lack, despite the political movements, what we lack is collective action and discipline.

LINA: Is it because of the breakdown of the family? Loss of values?

SC: I feel there is less of values because of disruption in the social system. Village life was disrupted. Millions uprooted from the soil. Living the life of animals in refugee colonies for many years. No organic tie between man and woman. Victims of exploiters/money lenders. So many factors. The social fabric was destroyed and values distorted. The emergence of black markets and parasites started. The growing *bustees* or "slumization" of Calcutta. Rash Behari Avenue was one of the finest roads thirty years ago—now it has become a slum.

Calcutta could be saved if we had a master plan. But there is no such plan. And, because of our false sense of democracy. If you've read Gunnar Myrdal's *Asian Drama*, he emphasises the situation aptly—he says that the Indian state is a false state. On paper it arrives at many decisions but cannot implement a single one because of franchise.

LINA: On the issue of lack of discipline. In Hinduism, discipline was always embedded in the family.

SC: But we had a national movement stretched over a 100 years.

LINA: But you had leadership and that national movement was a temporary one.

SC: The communist movement is 60 years old in India—in West Bengal, and Communists are known for their organization and party discipline. It's a monolithic party. But in society they can't take any decision. Why? The chance of adult franchise and the existence of plurality of parties and social forces create a situation where you can't take a quick decision. There are too many bidders. Congress says they'll do this much and if you want to bid you'll have to say you'll go further. When the streets were occupied Congress supported it, when the Communists are in power—Congress opposed it. Eviction of hawkers and all that. Why didn't they (the Communists) remove the hawkers from the start? Humanitarian considerations were there but the material considerations were stronger. The election agents work as party cadres! Because of this anarchic situation and lack of discipline Calcutta is in a bad way.

LINA: So what's going to happen? Are people moving out of the city?

SC: But West Bengal is so small . . .

LINA: The people who are most affected are the middle classes. The lower classes are here for temporary jobs. They don't have homes, schools and children to worry about.

SC: Also they (the unorganized sections of the people) have no awareness at all. They are the majority. They feel this is their destiny and they can eke out an existence.

LINA: The middle class will lose out. There will be 3–4 percent upper classes and the middle classes will move out to the districts and satellite towns.

SC: There is racketeering in land sale.

LINA: Everyone is selling their homes!

SC: They can't maintain it. Near the railway station, you have three famous men, three brothers, and after their demise their children left, rented the houses. Now, if you have to whitewash the house it will cost you 5000 rupees. You'll have to procure masons and all. But the son lives in Bombay. He is not interested. So the rooms were partitioned. Now you have shops there. Every bit of space has been utilized and in 15 years it will pass out of their hands. If you want to purchase a flat in Calcutta now, because of the racket—for 1000 sq. feet you'll have to pay 5.5 lakhs. Middle-class people have no chance of purchasing! For example, when my son was here—

this is my house (my father's house since 1937). On the first floor is
my doctor brother and my mother. I have three rooms on the ground
floor. A drawing room (*baithak-khana*), etc. When my son joined
Jadavpur—there was a problem of accommodation. So we gave
him this room. My wife had one and I had one. Very difficult. I
told him if he stayed he should rent a flat. He appointed *dalals*. You
can't find a house on your own. In Regent Estate—not a very good
locality—he found a two-room apartment house. They charge 2000
per month and 12 months' advance! When enquiry was made about
purchase of an 800 sq. feet flat—very small rooms, one verandah,
toilet, kitchen—would cost 3.5 lakhs!

LINA: These are problems that happen in all major cities. The way
they happen in Calcutta is interesting.

SC: My point is—who are now owning flats? Non-Bengalis. Bengalis
purchase, but the next generation can't maintain. Maybe the top
level of 4 percent and those below the poverty line—these will be
in the city. The middle class will be driven outside the city into
the suburbs.

LINA: A circle around the city. What about the sense of culture?
Do you think what they call Bengali culture today, corresponds to
your sense of culture? Of course, when we talk about Bengali culture
we are talking about middle-class culture. The culture formed here.

SC: There has been a plethora of cultural organizations—so many
drama groups, cultural experiments, films, there is a quantitative
increase. But qualitatively, no.

LINA: What about revolutionary theater?

SC: All superficial, catering to the taste of the middle class again who
idolize revolution. They can't make revolution—mimic revolution.

LINA: What remains in Calcutta that is positive today?

SC: Positive is the fact that urban anonymity is not too advanced.
There are still *addas* and chats at the local teashops. Religious
congregations, meetings. Parties where you have heart to heart talks.
In Delhi you won't find it. It's more drab in that sense.

LINA: Do you have a group that you have *adda* with daily, here.

SC: Occasionally. We are organizing a meeting for someone who was a victim of the Communists. Four years he spent fighting the politicization of Calcutta University and then retired. But we are giving him an ovation. He was the Vice Chancellor [the effective presiding officer]. We'll meet tomorrow and arrangements for transport will have to be made. We meet occasionally and discuss things. If you have a party (political) you have to do these things. If you have religious feelings you can go to Ramakrishna Mission. There are talks daily on various subjects, biology, the *Gita*, Ramakrishna.

LINA: Do you go?

SC: I don't. Occasionally, for a talk that I have to give! Recently I haven't on account of my eyes.

LINA: Is there hope for Calcutta?

SC: I am very pessimistic because with hope you can't deal with politics.

LINA: I don't think the CPI(M) can do anything.

SC: The CPI(M) is a replica of the Congress. It has no life force, no ideal, no idea for leadership.

LINA: How about a new party?

SC: No sign yet.

LINA: There was the *Amra Bangali* but people didn't respond to it.

SC: *Amra Bangali* will cut no ice because it has no economic or social program. Bengalis (it must be said to their credit) are less chauvinistic because of our nineteenth century tradition.

LINA: But for how long. What about all this sale of houses, etc.? Will that create/continue with existing chauvinism?

SC: There is chauvinism but not really of the aggressive type—the vulgar type. You talk to a Bengali. They have anti-Marwari feeling. Very strong. They hate Marwaris. You talk to a Bengali—he will exaggerate his importance by recalling the past. Glorious culture. That sort of tendency.

LINA: But they don't use it to fight.

SC: Even here, the communal feeling—relatively speaking, is not so high. That is because of our liberal culture promoted by nineteenth century stalwarts. Not a "Renaissance" of the European variety but still a great one. So, in a desultory way I have answered you.

# Satyesh Chakraborty

LINA: An urban planner, you are also a renaissance person, a geographer, a quasi-anthropologist, a politician . . .

SATYESH CHAKRABORTY: I'll put it this way Lina, I'm a geographer by profession and I have to study urban geography. I was brought into planning by geographers and then I had to dabble in policy making. So in a sense, the image you have of me is correct. But I prefer to describe myself as a management specialist: how to manage a city.

LINA: Since 1947, how has this process of managing the city changed?

SC: In 1947, I was a sixteen-year-old kid and I came to Calcutta in 1944. Since then I've stayed here almost continuously, except for short absences when I've been out of the country. So I've grown attached to the city. Emotionally, it's a difficult city to live in, but it's also a rewarding city with its intellectual focal point. But if you talk of managing the city: in 1944, the Southeast Asia Command was operating from Calcutta. The Japanese were on the Burma Frontier, Netaji Subhas Chandra Bose was a hero of the nationalist movement. All these things taken together meant that the city was geared to meeting an emergency and had done very little to accommodate the events which were to come shortly. In 1944–45, we still believed that India would attain independence without partition. In 1947, India was partitioned and as far as partitions are concerned, Bengal was destroyed in 1905, 1912, 1947. And this was handled in such a fashion, that people came without property unless they managed to smuggle in some! So we have people of limited means flowing into the city—occupying whatever space was available, in unauthorized ways. City managers couldn't extend services to them because their occupation was not legally valid.

LINA: If you extended services to them it would mean approval?

SC: As a matter of fact, when I was a member of the State Planning Board between 1972 and 1977, around 1974, we raised this question, saying that it is an accomplished fact of life that the refugees have come and built up their small houses. So why don't you recognize it? So what we call *patta* i.e. giving record of rights was issued only in 1974–75. As a political decision maker, I personally validated the historical fact which originated in 1947. It took so many years. Why did it take so many years? The first reason is that Calcutta received an influx of population bearing an imprint of a culture that was not heard of. Refugees from East Bengal were rural. Calcutta has always received people from East Bengal, not Bangladesh, but they belonged to the upper echelons of society— the landed gentry who came here with education, participated in the urban culture and carried back a list of elements of Calcutta urban culture into their respective home districts. But this time we got really rural people. This raises a distinct hypothesis. Suppose we had a similar influx of people from rural West Bengal, would the impact have been the same?

As a social scientist, I believe it would have been the same. I shall tell you why. I notice that the culture of Calcutta has little linkage with the culture of rural Bengal—east and west doesn't matter. And the culture of Calcutta imposed itself entirely on the rest of Bengal. Is it not a question of bringing in culture from the rural areas, giving it an urban interpretation and giving it back? What happened in the process—the refugees in Calcutta and the old Calcuttans . . . although I am technically a refugee by virtue of my history and of my family, I rather belong to the old Calcuttans because of the urbanite values which for generations our families, parents, received through education in Presidency College in Calcutta and so on. So I, as an individual, was a product of the interaction of the landed gentry and the urbanites of Calcutta, and when I came I found no difficulty in getting a niche for myself.

Now, in terms of the physical size of the responsibility, failure was bound to come in terms of sanitation, sewage, garbage clearing, conservation services—on every front they failed. From 1960 onwards, some attempts were made to improve the city, but between the planners and the execution of plans there was a hiatus. First, say the Calcutta Metropolitan Planning Organization (CMPO) was up only for the purpose of planning, without any promise or guarantee that the plans so formulated shall be executed. So in 1967, when the Basic Development Plan was produced—there was a wonderful approach, nothing else. When the Calcutta Metropolitan Development Authority (CMDA) was created in 1970, they were exclusively implementers and not planners. So the implementers without any reference to the Basic Development Plan concentrated on physical development and that is still going on. The fault is this— the role of the city *vis-à-vis* the reform of its location was an element of clouded understanding among the intelligentsia in India and Calcutta. The superposition of the role of a British imperial city upon the rest of the economy was accepted as something normal and wasn't examined in terms of its implications. So they thought, Calcutta was rendering good service to the region. That it was not doing so came out in the post Independence era. So now Calcutta is referred to in various quarters as a "siphoning instrument of British imperialism," "burden of a private city"—this kind of description is only just coming up. Only during the 1970's does the intelligentsia in India start to examine the historic role of the city *vis-à-vis* the region of location. Before that, it was taken for granted that Calcutta was doing a great service to the rest of the country. Therefore, this hiatus between the planners and the implementers is a national thing. In 1972, we who belong to the planners' group are unhappy, so around 1975, again as a member of the planning board, I had power and access to decision makers of the CMDA—to impress upon them the need to re-examine the Basic Development Plan. They did it. They found out that many of the premises are no longer holding good. From 1965–66, West Bengal was going into an industrial slump which has become a permanent one. That assumption was not there in the Basic Development Plan. We had to take note of that fact. So, the CMDA was now constrained to identify employment

generating schemes instead of physical construction schemes. There
were other mistakes. For example, the role of a development agency
and the role of a city government, and the linkage between the two
was not examined, even in 1975. So, CMDA created the infrastructure
for the municipal government, and the municipal government found
that the technology introduced by the CMDA was unmanageable
in terms of the training of their own personnel. So the municipality
started to protest—refusing to take responsibility. And the World
Bank was very unhappy. So we had to tell the World Bank that the
responsibility of identifying the need of a city should not be that of
the planners or that of a development agency independent of the
municipal body. This identification would have to be done by the
municipal body. An agency may come to create that on behalf of
the municipality. So CMDA has now changed its role.

Calcutta Municipal Corporation Act of 1981 accomplished
that—now CMDA is trying to strengthen its planning capacity.
There again we are about to make a mistake. If the municipality
doesn't realize its own role as a planner-developer, then anybody
trying to assist them in planning will be like appointing a tutor for a
boy who is reluctant to learn. This is happening now. The municipal
government is not seeing the importance of developing the city as
planned. I hope that by the turn of this decade, they'll learn that
they don't have a choice because the repayment of loans will start.

LINA: Where will the money come for the repayments?

SC: That's a problem. Say in Tollygunj, Jadavpur (in the south
suburban area of Calcutta)—here the refugees settled. The CMDA,
under the advice of the World Bank laid expensive underground
sewage systems for them. After having done that, the Corporation
of Calcutta was asked to take it over. Calcutta Corporation said: "I
have got to make house connections, otherwise this system won't
operate." But whose house is it? Because they were occupying the
land illegally.

LINA: They were *bustees* [slums]?

SC: Not *bustees*, but middle-class houses and the title of the land was
under dispute till 1974-75 when we had influenced the government
of West Bengal to give them *patta* (title deeds). After doing that

they found out that evaluation of the value of property will be so much that the resultant accrual on the terms of tax liabilities would not be affordable by these small house owners. So the source of money for repayment is from property tax. Where the property owners don't have the money to pay—what they can afford to pay is insufficient to take care of the debt servicing. Will you buy a very expensive record player or a record player you can afford? The cost element wasn't linked to the social conditions of payment. This is a problem the Calcutta Corporation is facing.

LINA: But all these problems are not just the refugee issue?

SC: Up to 1970 the intelligentsia, including the urbanites, took it for granted that the city is fulfilling its role in its area of location. This was seriously challenged in the 1970's.

LINA: And that was not done through a major revolution but just advice.

SC: Then comes the idea that the planning must be linked to need and the people who execute the plans. Refugees complicated the situation. When it comes to rent payers and non-rent payers, there is a difference. Non-rent payers are primarily refugees whereas rent payers are normally old urbanites.

LINA: If I get you right, between 65–70 percent of the people don't pay taxes?

SC: Yes, 70–75 percent. You see the difference between the rent payers and non-rent payers was here from before the influx of the refugees. But the non-rent payers at the time were migrant laborers and related to the production system that the city was maintaining. They were legitimate so the Calcutta Corporation had decided that the *bustees* should have proper water supply. But when the refugees came, they did not come in response to the demand of the economy in Calcutta. They came and had to seek entry. Where the up-county laborers live in a *bustee* there is no protest, because they are needed by urbanites. Maybe he is a Gujarati Marwari, or a Bangal. But when the refugees came, they are unattached. They have come to secure a position and they had to find a niche in the economy. So refugees felt neglected but they were large in number!

This conflict between the rural culture and the urban culture has been the nature of politics in this part of the world.

LINA: When does politics become realistic with regard to the problems that politicians have created in this city? It's uncontrollable!

SC: Well, the politicians have their two feet on either side of a crack and it's widening into a chasm. In terms of democracy and voting power the non-rent payers outnumber the rent payers. In terms of economic clout, political clout, it's the other way around. So the city manager will not have to reconcile the two, but the city managers in India have never been given the power to secure conflict resolution between interest groups.

LINA: The majority of city managers are rent payers and Bengalis?

SC: Well, Calcutta Corporation Staff Recruitment was such that Bengalis got in. For example, in 1935–36, Subhas Chandra Bose was the Mayor of Calcutta and said that anybody who has participated in the freedom movement, for independence of India, shall have a berth as an employee in this Calcutta Corporation. This is the employee situation.

LINA: So the majority are Bengalis?

SC: The effect of having Bengali majority staff in the city government's role—you see, the Bengalis in the 1901 census accounted for something like 75 percent of the total population of Calcutta. The others were up-country people, British, Hindi and Urdu speaking population, Marathi, Gujarati, truly an Indian metropolis. In the 1961 census, the Bengali speaking population accounted for 48 percent of the total population; 52 percent were non-Bengalis. And the relative incidence of Bengalis has declined still further by now. What does it mean? The immigrant population who are non-Bengalis are getting their hold within the city. You think of it, they must be getting a shelter, and the city size hasn't really grown (except Salt Lake which isn't part of the Calcutta Municipal Corporation). As far as the Municipal Corporation is concerned, its territorial jurisdiction has expanded over the urbanized area, but as far as the old Calcutta of 1931 is concerned, a territorial development hasn't taken place. So, migrants must have replaced Bengalis who were the house-owners. Now you have a Bengali employee in the Municipal Corporation. What will he do? He will try not to use the instrument of the municipal government leading to the displacement of the Bengali house-owner. For example, valuation of property does not go up to the extent it should (to protect kin or friends). This is being taken advantage of by other successful users of land also who are not necessarily Bengalis. So, the compromise has come at the level of the state legislature where they have said that the increment in the value of propery can't be arbitrary like 5 percent for 5 years. Which really means that the rate at which the economy is going and the property values are going have no relationship with the rate at which the recorded property valuations are going. The gap is increasing. Say BBD Bag [formerly Dalhousie Square, the heart of the business and administrative district]. If you want to buy 720 sq. feet of land there you have to pay 5 lakhs of rupees minimum— but you may end up paying 15 lakhs (5 lakhs will be recorded and 10 lakhs under the table). But when you go and examine the Calcutta Corporation records you'll find a 25000 or 30000 rupee recorded. The value is an infinitesimal fraction of the cost of maintaining that property.

LINA: So who are benefiting from this?

SC: Property owners and . . .

LINA: This must be obvious to the government.

SC: But property owners have the economic interest in their power and the non-rent payers are often also property owners. The fight is between the poorer and richer property owners and the compromise is all against the city government. All would like to undervalue their property.

LINA: So what really loses out is the city government.

SC: Shall I give you an example of how the loss may come? The city government up to 1968–70 thought that the displacement of Bengalis will come through outright purchase of land or buildings. By 1970–71 they noticed that the land was sold on condition that the owner shall get a flat in the building. So high-rise buildings came up. Immediately Calcutta Corporation created a new department for high-rise buildings and tried to impose all kinds of restrictive measures completely ignoring the fact that Calcutta's territorial jurisdiction or geographical area is not going to increase—you have to go upwards.

LINA: There are problems with that—

SC: Yes, but you have to compromise. You can't avoid the problem by denying it.

LINA: You think building high-rises work?

SC: People talk about typical Bengali culture that is springing up here—some with disdain and some with enthusiasm. Politicians with enthusiasm, because they think it's time for the new protelariat, a new person who is more ideologically oriented, doesn't have middle-class hang-ups—even though they might be middle class. Education is not a very important component either in this middle class. This is looked at as an alternative to decadent middle/upper-class inheritors of values from the nineteenth century.

Say early nineteenth century, when the city of Calcutta was small and the ratio between the rent payers and the non-rent payers was much better, we find the development of a kind of culture which we describe nowadays as decadent culture, like keeping mistresses, having erotic festivals, gambling and entertainment. From the mid-nineteenth century things became rather difficult and English education spread. This produced two things: a modernizing village which started thinking of including western values and the revival of classicism. Looking back into the roots of India was one product. Looking forward to Europe was another. And they brought in new art forms—modern theater, etc. An alternative to the "nautch-girl culture" and the theater culture. Now, when the partition of Bengal came up around 1905 this modernization, nationalistic element got the leadership. And that is the point of *baiji* history where "nautch-girl culture" was looked down upon. It was no longer an alternative. Victorian prudishness comes in. I'm not using prudishness to show how they behaved. So this modernizing elite went on developing this art form in various ways. By 1930, the situation of the Empire in India had become more difficult. The nationalist movement was strong and the socialist thought came up as an alternative: now the problem was that the values of socialism weren't seen as relevant by the workers—so-called proletariat—but were again seen by the modernizing elite and this is the middle class and lower middle class, whose leadership was again absorbed by the upper middle classes. So, they started playing a role of substitution action on behalf of the people. In the nineteenth century they were less concerned about rural people. My readings and research tells me that the *bhadralok* did have a concern for the maintenance of certain values.

. . . Let us take the traditional theater *jatra* which had no proscenium. There was a space around which the spectators sat and the actors came there through the audience. In 1937, I remember I was taken to a *jatra* which was either *Chand Sadagar* or *Mahisasur Badh*—religious themes. *Jatra*, which is an indigenous art form, comes to Calcutta and the indigenous linkage with the past is retained. Now, go to a *jatra* in Calcutta. It's totally different. They are talking about social problems, they no longer talk about religion.

# Sunil Munshi

LINA: How are contemporary issues taken up by political parties? Any changes?

SUNIL MUNSHI: Yes, there are changes from the earlier days. After all, the Left parties have the power, so the issues tend to be much less controversial.

LINA: You mean they are not as stern?

SM: You don't see movements, processions and demonstrations or public meetings like earlier days. Meetings do take place you see— there are a lot of seminars, discussions, group meetings of many organizations in which problems are discussed. The problems with the people running schools on the pavements, the problem of squatter colonies—these problems are discussed with the government and some steps are taken. The concern for these people in the political parties, I think, is still there, though the expression may be different.

LINA: So, bustees can remain under terms of bustee improvement in the given social services, water facilities, etc., but what about the squatters? They are not recognized yet by the local government.

SM: No, they are not recognized yet. Squatters are a very serious problem—it is a kind of a vicious circle! But the influx quota has gone down. I think that you have read the book Under the Shadow of the Metropolis?

LINA: Under the Shadow of the Metropolis? Is it a CMDA book?

ANOTHER VOICE: She was asking what you have published and I was telling her about your book Metropolitan Explosion.

SM: It is a book about 40000 squatters. The flow of people coming and staying on a pittance, has in some instances, gone down. There is massive relief operation going on.

LINA: I must confess that the Left Front government in Bengal did improve the rural areas, that no other government could have done as good a job in the rural parts of Bengal. I lived in Bengal for six years totally, and I see the change in Bishnupur as a result of the Left government. But what about Calcutta? I think that Calcutta's condition is worse.

ANOTHER VOICE: In fact the West Bengal government has diverted more funds to small town improvement than to Calcutta. Almost everything was concentrated on the old Calcutta in earlier days.

LINA: How do squatters manage?

SM: There are two types of squatters. First are the squatters who sleep on the pavement, they have a small room, a very small *paan* shop—a cigarette shop, they can possibly sleep there but 2, 3 or 4 people cannot sleep there, so they sleep out on the pavement but they have that shop, it is kind of a very small shelter—in one small room, for 15–20 people. They actually come and stay. They keep their things there and at night they sleep outside—this is one kind of squatter. The other kind is the one who builds a kind of temporary structure on empty land or on the canal banks.

LINA: How many years can you stay on a plot of land before you can claim it? I understand that in Delhi people will buy these farms outside of Delhi and worry about the guard who is hired to guard the farm. The owners give one day off out of the week so that he can go somewhere and then come back. In this case, one day of the week the guard does not sleep on the land. If he can prove that he consecutively slept for a whole year on the farm—he can claim some sort of squatter rights. Do squatters here have such rights?

SM: Yes, there is a limit but I can't tell you the exact situation. It is a legal matter. Here the people stay mainly on government property. It's mainly government land that the squatters appropriate and if the government wants to clean up the land they have to remove the squatters. You can't satisfy all the needs for Calcutta's environmental improvement, widening of the roads, and at the same time protect the squatters.

LINA: Where are the squatters coming from? In the *bustee*, I understand there are people who have a job and have a place to sleep but do they all come from the rural areas?

SM: Yes, but squatters are mainly West Bengalis. There may be some who are East Bengalis but the overwhelming numbers are West Bengalis. Mainly from the 24-Parganas. The book *Under the Shadow of the Metropolis* has these details. Right now there is a problem in Palmer Bajar in South Beliaghata where there are squatters beside the canal; if the government wants to deepen the canal, they have to be moved. The government is thinking in terms of giving them alternative shelters in Sonarpur but they don't want to go!

LINA: Now, what happened to Gariahat Road? I think that is disgusting! All of those shops on Gariahat, you cannot walk there. The pavement shops have destroyed the place. In 1967–73 I used to love to walk up and down Rashbehari Avenue and now it is painful. It is difficult with all the little shops plus the generators—why can't these be cleaned up?

ANOTHER VOICE: It is a kind of squatting and the problem of the unemployed people.

LINA: But it is squatting. How about creating a market somewhere in . . .

SM: It doesn't help, there have been a number of markets created in other areas, but another lot will sit on the pavement—sheer demand for livelihood. These squatters, on the canal side, the government offers them land in Sonarpur or Haltu—but they have already given up some sort of a means of livelihood in their native place. They make cardboard out of wastepaper. That's the cardboard they dry right on the asphalt roads. That is their means of livelihood. If they go to Sonarpur they cannot do it. Also, being right inside a big city there is always some way or other that they can be employed and get a meal.

LINA: What about coming back to the second part of our conversation. We have talked about the refugees, the labor migrants and so on, if we look at contemporary Calcutta, how did all of that impact the social side of the city?

SM: The city is currently changing as far as I can see. One of my students is doing her Ph.D. on the high-rise buildings in Calcutta. She is trying to see what was there before the high-rise buildings went up.

LINA: This should be a very controversial study when it is published, I can tell you that now!

SM: Who are the occupants? How do they use the various flats, where did they come from, etc. There are about 250 or so high-rise buildings—beyond sixth floor the building becomes a high-rise. There are additional taxes on them. High-rises have extra taxes for safety conditions, fire escapes, etc. What my student has seen is very interesting, that high-rises are coming up mainly from the central business district of Calcutta towards the south, Park Street, Camac Street, Circular Road, south of Circular Road, both sides of Amir Ali Avenue, mainly in the south up to the Lake and the railway lines. The high-rise buildings have probably changed the composition of these neighborhoods' small communities. For example, if you go to Ballygunge Circular Road and Gurusaday Road, that whole area has changed. Mostly Marwaris live there now. I have seen, but I have not been able to go through, the entire list of occupants that my student has compiled but I have seen that 80–85 percent are non-Bengalis. So can you see the total change that has come about as a result of these high-rise buildings? The social composition is changing very fast in some areas of Calcutta and not as fast in some of the areas of north Calcutta or in Jadavpur, etc.

LINA: Would you say that the families in north Calcutta are solidly Bengali? How would they react to the selling of mansions and building high-rises?

SM: In Salt Lake, the properties are getting transferred to non-Bengalis very fast. The changes in Calcutta proper are going more and more under the control of the moneyed people. Working people, not just working class, but working people, including the middle class, are forced to move away from the city itself.

LINA: Well, is it because these Bengalis controlled the city's property in the past?

ANOTHER VOICE: Yes, and they are going out of the city. I think that this is happening in all of the metropolitan cities of India.

LINA: But I am interested in Calcutta, because I think it is more extreme here. In Madras, there is the sense of the "son of the soil" policy, you cannot buy land unless you are a Tamilian, born or brought up in the town.

ANOTHER VOICE: So Salt Lake began with middle-class Bengalis but with a trickle of non-Bengalis. It is changing though. Why do Bengalis allow this process to happen and why don't they do something? Why don't they react differently? I do not know who should do that. That is the Bengali culture.

LINA: You mean being tolerant and cosmopolitan and allowing changes to take place?

ANOTHER VOICE: You can say so possibly.

SM: They are more *Indian* than Bengali—this is the one city where chauvinistic, communal forces are less. Uttar Pradesh, Baroda have riots every week and but not in Calcutta. In fact, Bengalis are proud of it.

ANOTHER VOICE: If you talk to some of the Bengalis they will say that some of the non-Bengalis are buying up the city. They have money power. The Bengalis don't want to make it an issue of Marwari and Bengali—it's an issue of money or class which is correct.

LINA: Let me give you my assessment. When Independence came, there was India and there was Bengal and I think Bengal was still inward thinking—I mean Bengal was not really outward oriented in the sense that Punjab or Maharastra was. Bengalis were more in tune with the language, with the society and so on, they saw themselves more as Bengali than Indian. Now that has changed in the sixties and seventies. What happened is that they look at India and West Bengal and the many changes that they cannot cope with so they move into a community, into a *para*. In the seventies and eighties even the concept of *para*, of caste, breaks down and they go even more into the nuclear unit of the family, so it is OK to be in the city such as Calcutta because what counts now are immediate family values. Where you can preserve Bengali values, Bengali language and so on. At a general level they are not chauvinistic . . . but they are chauvinistic within families because they still prefer to see their children married to Bengalis and not to Marwaris.

ANOTHER VOICE: *Ananda Bazar Patrika* has supplements on how Calcutta has changed socially, culturally. Different writers have written on this, Samaresh Bose, etc. All the writings are not good but they are interesting.

LINA: Oh, I interviewed Samaresh Bose. Interesting to see how newspapers report on the concept of culture and the city of Calcutta.

ANOTHER VOICE: Yes, a study of social and cultural changes in Calcutta is so interesting.

LINA: See, that is why it is easy for families now to sell a mansion. When a family had a mansion for many generations they sell it and move on. It's not just moving out of the house and buying a flat but it is a symbolic move identifying more with the nuclear unit of one's immediate family.

ANOTHER VOICE: There is an economic base, most of these families at one time or other were connected to land, but today that land base of the middle class is gone. Hardly any middle-class family has land. Actually the source of income from land is gone. That part of the income which came from the land is gone. Different family members earning from salaries and living together in a joint household tend to cause more social tensions.

LINA: But it is not only the economics of those family members who do not work and expect to be maintained according to tradition that creates this change. I think when people move out they also adopt a totally different lifestyle—new values. They emphasize the nuclear family, children's education. So that the changes that we see are not superficial. It is not about living in a high-rise vs a mansion, it's really more of a structural change. What is the role of big families today? Like the old Calcuttan families— what role did they play in dealing change or is it that they didn't have an impact at all of that?

ANOTHER VOICE: No, but the old big families are mostly broken up.

LINA: They don't have any leadership in the community, symbolic or otherwise?

ANOTHER VOICE: No. No leadership. At the time of Independence you could see that these old families had power. Our mayor Kamal Bose belongs to a big family but today you don't have that leadership any more. There's an interesting article. A person did a statistical exercise on family life and social structure of Calcutta (J.L. Berry), a factorial ecology of Calcutta. On the basis of 1961 census data, he statistically analyzed the social structure, whether the city could be analyzed broken up into units—big, small, nuclear, non-nucleated families etc.

LINA: Well you can say then that Bengal compared to the rest of India has the most modern and advanced concept of a state. That it transgresses all cultural, traditional barriers to progress . . . by this I mean that the individual thing gives way to universal . . .

ANOTHER VOICE: What you just said Marie Seton, a film critic and Satyajit Ray's biographer, told us long ago. Calcutta, from the point of view of the economic situation is backward, but from the point of view of cultural values, it is the most European city in India. That is what she had said.

LINA: But, for example, Satyajit Ray's notion of Calcutta and Mrinal Sen's idea of Calcutta differ. Satyajit Ray comes from that nineteenth century social reform extension of the Brahmo Samaj—very *bhadra*, calm; Sen is more dynamic, current, aggressive, political and for him Calcutta is a vibrant city.

ANOTHER VOICE: Have you seen any of the films by Ritwik Ghatak?

LINA: They're the best. My husband works on films in anthropology and he did three documentary films in Bengal. In Ghatak's films, well . . . I went to a film conference once where they spent four hours discussing one shot, about the refugee family and the girl who dies of TB [*Meghe Dhaka Tara*].

ANOTHER VOICE: Ritwik brings out clearly what happened to Bengal as a result of partition, actually the whole phenomenon of middle-class women working. The first time I came here was in 1948, that was just after partition. I am a Gujarati, born and brought up in Bombay, studied in London. I have been in Calcutta continuously since 1952. You hardly saw any women in trains or buses. Absolutely out of necessity they started to work.

LINA: Refugees. But how does that contrast with what the Brahmo Samaj did for women to enable them to come out in society— they worked and they moved about but not because of an income.

ANOTHER VOICE: You see, they did look after the women of lower classes—widows' "Homes," etc., but that was with an attitude of charity. Well-to-do ladies doing something for the good of their poor and unfortunate sisters. The ones who actually ran the schools and homes were the more affluent Brahmo women, Lady Abala Bose, women of the Tagore family. It is true they were pioneers in the field of women's education but it was like a women's movement up to the fifties, confined to a small section of the educated. The refugee women came out of sheer necessity and the women's movement changed character.

LINA: Shall I just ask you a last question? . . . I am keeping you. People talk today about political culture in Calcutta.

ANOTHER VOICE: Political culture, *bhadralok* culture is an extension of nineteenth century landed aristocracies.

LINA: What about Calcutta culture vs the political culture people talk about as being different? I think that one can understand what political culture is, maybe, but Calcutta . . .

ANOTHER VOICE: I think these are mixed to a great extent. Calcutta culture cannot be separated from the political culture of Calcutta.

LINA: OK, so you are looking at the more holistic picture.

SM: I don't think that you can create separate entities of Calcutta culture and the political culture of the city. Unless you speak of an upstart culture which belongs specifically to Calcutta. You can call it "disco parlor culture" but that is not Calcutta culture.

ANOTHER VOICE: No, it is the kind of culture that is different.

LINA: But I think that by Calcutta culture maybe the emphasis would be on the urban scene.

ANOTHER VOICE: Let us see what are the impressions of Calcutta culture. By Calcutta culture you would possibly mean the expressions in cultural activities, which may not be directly associated with culture but it is there in real life. In cultural functions, programs, theaters, films, libraries, discussions, cultural exhibitions, book fairs, the arts . . . all of these have been going on for a very long time in the city. But because of the intense politicization of the middle class there is a political culture of Calcutta.

LINA: Oh, I see, but it is not necessarily the same thing. A politician or a political leadership need not emulate and nor take in all of the Calcutta culture?

ANOTHER VOICE: It doesn't.

LINA: It doesn't, so they are parallel to each other. Some overlap but not entirely?

SM: No. Some overlap but not all. Actually the political culture of Calcutta you can date back to the early forties. The Indian Peoples' Theater Association, The Progressive Writers' Association, The Antifascist League, etc., saw the merging of the two cultural currents.

Even now, from the point of cultural content, people queue up for particular films and programs—this has something to do with the general politics of each individual, it's difficult to explain. People in Calcutta have been very intensely associated with politics all of their lives, for generations, you can almost say from 1905!

LINA: That is why it is so difficult to rule Calcuttans and Bengalis in general, you know, they are all fired up and they are all ready to march and to take action any time.

SM: They are different, yes, it is true but there is an area where they overlap. More than in any other metropolitan city. Delhi culture is different from Delhi political culture.

LINA: Punjabi culture or universal culture?

ANOTHER VOICE: There is no universal culture there. A superficial metropolitan air expressed in functions and theaters.

LINA: I heard it said in the past that in Delhi you can't have *adda*— and you starve for conversation. You run to Calcutta, and then after two weeks of extensive hyperactivity you run back to Delhi to rest for a day or two.

# Gour Kishore Ghosh

LINA: What happened to Calcutta's universal thinking? What's the Bengali emphasis now?

GOUR KISHORE GHOSH: I'll tell you my opinion about this. Before Independence, Calcutta had a cosmopolitan character. It was the capital city of the British Empire at one time. Bengali culture, including the "Renaissance" period, was evidence of this. Despite Hindu-Muslim riots, until 1946, Calcutta was a cosmopolitan city. After Independence, Calcutta has become a provincial big-town in all respects except the creative fields. In forty years the Bengali mentality has changed, something that causes people like us, who are of two worlds, great pain. It surprises me, how could this have happened so rapidly?

Before, Bengalis were unified in a manner of speaking. There was a single center, Calcutta. Now there are dual centers: Calcutta and Dhaka. The Bengali language is also changing, the national language of Bangladesh is Bengali—not of all Bengalis. This brings a sense of loss. In the Dhaka-centered culture, Bengali is the only language. But in India, Bengali is one of our 22 languages. This brings about a change in the psyche. When a person's mind is strong, this strength allows for broadness of mind and vision. This attitude is the one we are calling cosmopolitan. During the entire nineteenth century in Bengal, this had been cultivated.

But as we are moving away from it, we are becoming rather parochial in our attitudes. It is coming up from our subconscious.

LINA: Only the Bengali aspect is being emphasized versus the rest of India?

GKG: You can't pinpoint it as being against India. Although Calcutta is being bought up by non-Bengalis, the old Bengali liberal attitudes die hard. There is no equivalent of the Shiv Sena like in Bombay, who say "Bombay for the Marathis!" There was an attempt to create a party called *Amra Bangali* but it failed. Politically, Bengalis reject parochialism but the ordinary Bengali feels that [Calcutta] was discriminated against by the Center. They fought for independence but did not receive their just rewards. In all fields they feel discriminated against. In the area of education in all-India competitive exams, Bengalis aren't faring too well. Big Bengali businessmen are facing losses and lockouts. Huge numbers are unemployed. All this is working to make Bengalis feel threatened and defensive or hostile. This is the change in the Bengali psyche before and after Independence. A cumulative reaction.

LINA: I talked to a man from the *Amra Bangali* group and he said he was surprised that though Bengalis number only 46 percent of the population of Calcutta and are being forced to sell their property to non-Bengalis, they are not ready to reclaim Bengal. He said that they weren't claiming Bengal for Bengalis only, not a "sons of the soil" policy. They were urging people to invest in Bengal. Put back something of what they took out of it. I had thought that Bengalis were internationally minded, but I get a sense of parochial attitudes.

GKG: Circumstances are pushing them.

LINA: But the people of this city are becoming apathetic. Is this a political, economic, demographic phenomenon?

GKG: They are not as apathetic as you think. How do you think their reactions will be expressed? In political movements? The effect of events on cultural reactions takes time and are difficult to monitor. Human beings have two currents of motivation: political, including economic, and individual creativeness. In 1988 the political flavor is not so strong. It has subsided.

LINA: Because people are satisfied?

GKG: Not at all. They may have thought that political agitation alone is a futile exercise, and the youth of today are probably undecided about whether they should place their careers above political agitation. When you first came to Calcutta, it was at the height of political movements, the Naxalite period. The best youths in 1967–68 were taken up in the global wave of youth power. I was in the US at the time and had seen how anti-Vietnam feelings were expressed on campuses across the country. Stokeley Carmichael and then the hippies. This is not there now in America. Bob Dylan, Joan Baez, after twenty years have gone a long way from the earlier protests. They have turned to different creative ways of existence. There is a change in attitudes and activities. Also in West Bengal. But the situation is different across the border. They are caught in tremendous political turmoil. One of the reasons why politics is so low key here now is because the radical party is not in Opposition. The Marxists are in power. Ever since Independence (Congress was in the Opposition after 1967), when the Congress came to power in West Bengal, the Marxists were in Opposition. There were agitations, movements about unemployment, unions, education, women's rights. When the Leftists came to power West Bengal was badly off in almost all fields—economically, educationally and even emotionally. You'll see that my son is allergic to any kind of agitation, he lacks faith. People of his generation don't really respect their father's generation. There is a different value system between the ages of 20 and 35: young men have become apathetic. Women are not that badly affected. Even twenty years ago, they were the most oppressed. Even the few opportunities they receive are seen as progress by them. The males feel, however, that there is no future for them.

LINA: I think males feel that they need a bigger future because society still sees them as supporters of an entire family. Women's position is still to supplement the husband in the family.

GKG: In our traditional Bengali family women had a definite place, in some families, a dominant place. In some, not in the public field, their position was absolutely zero. Except teaching, writing, etc. Now you can hear their voices. Even in the midst of unemployment six out of ten women would say they have a future, only two out of ten men would say that. This is the attitude you can see for yourself. This then is a picture of people's mentality in Calcutta at present. What are your other questions?

LINA: In anthropology we study culture, people's systems of belief and values. Up to about the 1920's we have an idea of the kind of values Bengali people in Calcutta had. It's clear that the family was the center and even if there was some embedding in western culture, there was a strong sense of identity with Bengal, whether linguistic, kinship, household customs, community, and *para* (neighborhood). These, obviously, have been affected. Were westernization and modernization at work or were wealth, greed, population movements and migrants from other parts of India responsible? I personally feel a sense of civic responsibility is lost in Calcutta.

GKG: The things we call values in my generation are not the same for the next generation. Yet the gap is not a tremendous one. Take something like friendship, or respect for parents. These are values. Respect for parents, if you take it at the personal level, the more westernized the person, the bigger the gap, what is known as the "generation gap." The educated, who are not very westernized or English educated, who work as clerks or teach, not necessarily at any elite school or college, these people's values haven't changed all that much. Whatever has changed took place in the city, much less in the villages. Even in the city, the westernized aspects register more change. Political activism brings about a kind of camaraderie and affection. Solidifies friendship that still exists. But personal friendships are not that confined nowadays because of circumstances. School friendships and so on don't last that much. I have seen signs that friendships are not as enduring as before. Think of the *para* or neighborhood. Even now, in the older areas there are *paras* and in each *para* the teashop is the center of all activities. The verandah was another site for meetings, chats in the afternoon. Now these two things are shrinking. The musclemen (*goondas* or *mastaans*) are using the spots, seeking to control them. Before, students, clerks and everyone went to teashops, now these are used by rival street gangs.

LINA: Kinship ties then, have given way to political ties?

GKG: To power, as it were. Another thing in Calcutta that destroys the *para* is the multistoried building. The unified sense of neighborhood is destroyed. In times of danger or need, the people of the neighborhood rallied around to help but in a multistoried apartment complex nobody knows each other.

But there are two kinds of multistories. Four-story houses on "estates" and taller ones. The former are built in rows and they maintain some elements of kinship. You have common *pujas*. If you go to Salt Lake, in every "Block" you will find a community *puja*. It's not like before—meeting all the time, but at least sometimes everyone gets together, some communication. The people in the housing complex I live in still find it possible to discover a bond of fellow feeling and kinship.

There are quarrels but they are usually resolved. If anyone falls ill or there is a death in a family, everyone rallies to help. Enemies are forgotten. The apartment complexes have two effects—the new atomized western family relationship found in skyscrapers and community ("modern") form of *para* culture in the four-story housing complexes.

LINA: But something has been lost.

GKG: In a *para* if anything happened people came at once to see and resolve. This inquisitiveness is less.

ANOTHER VOICE: As a matter of fact, in the old *para* in which we grew up, it was very difficult to start smoking [cigarettes]. Some one or the other was bound to notice.

GKG: You could not smoke in front of an elder.

ANOTHER VOICE: Now if you tell kids not to smoke before you, they say "Who are you to tell me what to do?". Even if we were not related, we called elders *dada* (older brother), *kaka* (uncle). In this age of multistoried apartments, even if a man dies, no one cares, no one bothers to go to his place.

GKG: The closer to the soil you live, the more the chances of maintaining neighborhood ties.

ANOTHER VOICE: The higher you go, the more alienated you get, the less humanity you have.

GKG: That's true. I think there is a difference between a horizontal culture and a vertical one. The horizontal one is not like the *para* of old, less noisy and more freedom: live as you like—yet a friendly concern. Once vertical, people stand in lifts without speaking to each other! Peculiar. You can stand and carry on a shouted conversation with someone else on his verandah.

LINA: How about immigrants? All these laborers coming into the city while middle-class Bengalis are moving out?

GKG: I have said that Calcutta was the capital city during the days of the British Empire. At that time people from different parts of India came to Calcutta. Those who came then have become Calcuttans proper. That is one difference between other Indians and Bengalis: the former have less linguistic chauvinism. They usually learn Bengali, not vice versa. Therefore, conflict over language is not something common. No linguistic problem really. For about two to three hundred years people have come to this city: Marwaris, Parsis, Biharis, people from Lucknow, from Gujarat, and Tamil, Telegu, Oriya speaking people. Quite a few generations. No one forces them to learn Bengali, therefore all their characteristic cultures make Calcutta a multilingual cosmopolitan place. Biharis are mostly Hindi speaking, Muslim, backward and fundamentalist— they live in different pockets of Calcutta. The Gujaratis live in other pockets. They have the money. Go to Bhowanipur, you'll find Gujaratis, Marwaris everywhere. They are enterprising and they have the most money, but for Gujaratis, Bombay is the "capital," for Marwaris, it is Calcutta.

LINA: So are you saying that immigrants affect Calcutta?

GKG: They are watertight. Not much communication. Recently many cultural associations, theater groups have been formed and there is some interaction in the last 15 years and this is gathering momentum.

LINA: But this is an upper-class phenomenon. What about the rest?

GKG: It's like Karachi. It's a Sindhi city with immigrants from UP, from Bihar, from Baluchistan, then Afghans, and troubles have increased. This hasn't happened here.

LINA: Is it the tolerance of Bengalis, or their strong government?

ANOTHER VOICE: It's a part of the education we inherited from our forefathers. The Bengal Renaissance emphasized the importance of being introduced not as an Indian, but as Bengali.

GKG: What about the "uneducated" and the non-literate?

THIRD VOICE: If you read the *Mangal Kavyas* you'll understand that our tradition is that of Satyanarayan/Satyapir. It's a combined culture that Bengalis care about. We are not that intolerant of one another.

GKG: Bengalis are by nature tolerant.

ANOTHER VOICE: Bengalis were the first of all the Indians to take to English. True, we've had riots and tensions but nothing major. Apart from the one exception—the Great Calcutta Killing of 1946—which was instigated by people from outside.

GKG: In 1956 and 1964 there were riots as well, but not major, nor localized.

ANOTHER VOICE: Even in the Naxal period when it was easy to mislead people and lead them astray against their wishes, even then it wasn't possible to make the Bengali provincially chauvinist. Even when Mrs. Gandhi was assassinated and people started attacking Sikhs everywhere, nothing happened to them here.

GKG: The Sikhs publicly stated that they were secure in West Bengal. That was because of the administration. There are three contributing factors: tolerance and this translates into politics too, and third is the Leftist government. They are touchy about this.

THIRD VOICE: But even during the Congress regime when Prafulla Sen was the Chief Minister, there weren't any communal riots. It's not the Leftists only.

GKG: Whenever there have been communal riots, there has also been outcry against and shame about such behavior.

ANOTHER VOICE: Shall I say something? In other states, Hindus and Muslims go to separate schools, their languages are separate and different, but here, everyone reads Bengali, and reads Nazrul. The chances of friendship are greater. In other states, before going to college, the chances of Hindu-Muslim friendship are rare.

GKG: There is another factor. This tolerance has a source: Hinduism
. . . the religion, philosophy, and attitude towards life have to do
with tolerance. A wider concept ingrained in people. Even a person
without education, a non-literate, has a value ingrained in him.
You'll notice that there are common traits from an upper-class
Bengali to a peasant. There are petty things about Hindus, but also
a broadness.

ANOTHER VOICE: Hinduism is the only religion, if you can call it a
religion at all, which has followers who do not have to even believe
in God.

GKG: It isn't monocentric, rather multicenter. The tolerance comes
from this.

LINA: But you can't say the same thing about Madrasi Hindus. The
Tamils are different, and the reason why orthodox Hindus in India
can't relate to Bengali Hindus is because of the latter's tolerance.

ANOTHER VOICE: I am a non-believing Brahman, even so I am
acclaimed as a Brahman. But in no other part of India do you find
beef-eating Brahmans! Not even fish-eating Brahmans.

GKG: Bengal has always been dissident. Even our system of
inheritance is different from the rest of India.

LINA: Do you think in the next decade or so, you will see an inner
core of Calcutta which is not necessarily Bengali? Or even if it is
Bengali it is not the one that counts, since they are the people
who have really changed. Then you'll see an outer circle of Bengalis,
moving out to the suburbs. Eventually this will create friction.

GKG: Calcutta is a city of Bengalis. They have a sense of belonging.
A sense that this is our city. Marwaris have more or less taken this
to be their economic base. They come from Marwar, live there but
invest here. Now of course they are diversifying. The Birlas are
going and the people who have come from UP and Bihar (Hindus
and Muslims) know they have to live in Calcutta because they have
to earn money. But they are the people who have no real sense of
belonging. Every amount of money they earn here, they send back
to their homes. Poor and middle-class Marwaris who have small

earnings also put away their earning. The Tamils, Telugu, (the Oriyas have almost the same culture as Bengalis), Marathis don't really have a sense of belonging to Calcutta. In New York, people of different cultures have come together—as in a crucible, and have developed one sense of culture—"New Yorkers," so everybody tries to make the city work. In Calcutta people exploit the city.

LINA: Do you write about this as a journalist?

ANOTHER VOICE: Ninety five percent of our pavement dwellers are from outside. Laborers from Andhra, Bihar. They come here, don't pay a paisa municipal tax . . .

LINA: As a poet and journalist, do you bring this up in the papers? As a Bengali concerned for your city?

GKG: I can't tell you what will happen but I can tell you what is happening. The Bengali who has a sense of belonging to the city is getting pushed out. Those who stay have no sense of belonging.

ANOTHER VOICE: You won't find rickshaws in any other city in India. But you can't get rid of them. Nobody cares, or will make the effort.

GKG: When I left this paper for a short while and became an editor for another, I was obsessed by this issue. We write in the newspaper but not systematically. And so it made no impression on our readers.

LINA: I interviewed Aveek Sarkar and I got the impression he was concerned about Calcutta and the identity of Bengal. In the papers he runs, this has been on the agenda.

GKG: There is often a fear that such finger pointing can kindle parochialism that may turn nasty. Maybe I am doing injustice to the Calcuttans and Bengalis—but fear and discontent are easily inflamed. It seems that this city was created so that people would earn a livelihood. That's why Bengalis first came to this city. To earn a living they came to the city from the village, lived in a Mess (a boarding house), sent money home. Gradually they settled. If the country had not been partitioned, this process would have continued. Because of partition, a large number of immigrants entered the country and the city was stretched to its limits. They came as survivors, without anything. Like Bombay—there the

Marathis are evident only in the political and cultural field. We have the same city for earning and culture.

It started with earning money but some Indians/Bengalis/ men of the world born in the nineteenth century added cultural themes to Calcutta. Village culture was too rigid—they could be excommunicated for their liberal ideas. In a big city there are advantages. They added a cultural dimension.

# Samar Bose

SAMAR BOSE: I've spent about ten years with the Calcutta Metropolitan Development Authority. What's happened to the city has affected many people in many ways, particularly Bengalis. For example, I myself came from East Pakistan [Bangladesh]. I have lost one home, this is my second home and I would not want anything to happen to this city. Emotional aspects should be left out when it is the question of a city.

LINA: How about the problems of the city?

SB: Don't you think that New York, Tokyo have similar problems? Bombay?

LINA: Bombay is facing the problem now but in the next 10 to 15 years it will get to the point where it expands to satellite cities. But what will happen to Calcutta?

SB: It is a matter of degree, not mind. We have this problem in all big cities. There are certain areas where Calcutta is improving faster than Bombay.

LINA: Water supply?

SB: Calcutta is better than other cities of India: our per capita availability of water is 40 gallons per head per day which is quite high.

LINA: It never went down?

SB: We did hit the bottom with 22/23 gallons per head but not now. In the meantime we have increased the capacity of the Palta

Waterworks, the Garden Reach Waterworks. We are setting up a new one in Baranagar.

LINA: What about electricity?

SB: Temporary dislocation. Cable faults, mechanical problems—we have more electricity than we need! We produce more electricity than we consume.

LINA: Drainage is a problem.

SB: I met a gentleman from Moscow. He said he left his luggage in Moscow because it was flooded. The point is that all cities plan for development. They take an average rainfall and build their system—they take into account the maximum rainfall possible when constructing the drainage system. You live with it. Western cities get snowbound in winter.

LINA: I am not criticizing in asking the question. I wonder about planning for the growth of the city. What is being taken into account? Is expanding satellite cities going to help problems of overcrowding? Also, people come back to the city: is that a problem?

SB: Let's come to the historical part of it. The British chose this place, the worst place they could have chosen, but they had strategic reasons. They wanted the river as a barrier to the Dutch, French, Portuguese, on the other side. The drainage here is very poor. I tell my British friends next time you want to colonize a place, please ensure there is good drainage. Really, they took care only of the European part of the city, but what about the "native quarters"? That is one reason we are having so many problems! The shape of the terrain, the slope of the land, everything goes against natural drainage and there is a limit to which you can improve matters with artificial drainage, pumping, etc. Expensive. The World Bank people had made an estimate—they would require 12 hundred crores (12 thousand million) rupees in order to have proper drainage for the metropolitan area. Fantastic! The maximum investment made by the CMDA for drainage is about 200 million. You have to live with waterlogged shoes. Well, really, low lying areas get waterlogged and stay waterlogged for several days. That's a hardship but just because I don't want to get my shoes wet I can't afford to spend 12 thousand million rupees. There are certain things you have to accept!

LINA: How about Salt Lake? Were arrangements made?

SB: Yes, it was built for the better-off upper class, and the sewers and drains are bigger in diameter. They calculated the maximum rainfall. But you can't dig up Calcutta and do that all over the city.

LINA: They did it for the Metro!

SB: And at what cost? To what benefit? According to their projections, 1.6 million people will travel every day, 365 days a year. The capacity of city transport, trams, buses is 3 million passengers. The demand is about 6 million so there is a 100 percent overcrowding. By the time the Metro is completed the demand will go up to 10 million. You have to move faster and faster to catch up.

LINA: Did Calcutta need a Metro?

SB: The Americans said yes, the French said yes, the British said yes, and we said yes. There is no other way we can even touch the traffic problem in the city. There is a circular railway project. It's stuck halfway because there is no space available through the port area. This was the answer. There's no doubt about it. When completed it will benefit 1.6 million passengers. Save them time, save the environment. It's an impossible dream that Calcutta will one day be free of water. Come to think of it, I have lived in Calcutta for the last 30–40 years. It doesn't trouble us for more that 7 to 10 days a year. June, July and August. Have to grin and bear it.

LINA: What are some of the other services the Calcutta Metropolitan Development Office has in mind for Calcutta?

SB: It's a long story. Goes back to 1970 when it was set up. It identified only four major sections in the beginning: traffic and transportation, water supply, sewerage and drainage, development of the township.

LINA: Transport they have touched upon. Drainage is an impossibility. Development of new areas besides Kalyani and Salt Lake . . . are they envisioning others?

SB: Others that have practically come up are Baishnav-ghata, Patuli beyond Garia. Blocks have been sold out, they will now start building houses. They have also opened up the east Calcutta township. That is behind Kasba, behind the Eastern Metropolitan By-Pass. Beyond Dhapa. They had another township project at Kona in Howrah. That hasn't come up yet.

LINA: Does it harm the Calcutta Corporation to have more of these townships incorporated into Calcutta, or is it better to develop those areas and keep them under a separate municipality? What is the benefit of bringing them in other than for the vote?

SB: It can work both ways. Two or three years back they incorporated three municipalities into Calcutta: Jadavpur, Behala, Garden Reach. The argument is that they are adjacent to Calcutta and when you are planning you have to do so for the whole metropolitan region. There are several jurisdictions: Calcutta Electric Supply Corporation (CESC) and the State Electric Supply Board (WBSEB) supply power to the greater Calcutta area, and the State Electricity Board has jurisdiction throughout West Bengal. But it is a mixture. They give power to the CESC also. It is a political decision to bring municipalities within the Calcutta Corporation, or to separate them. An unpopular thing to do except as a vote getting device.

LINA: You bring a group of people into the service who will vote for you if you give them something.

SB: Three municipalities were incorporated but Salt Lake was not. Salt Lake is adjacent to Calcutta. There is no justification for it to be a separate entity but because the middle class and upper middle class live there, no interest was taken in it. But even then, local people do want a local administration.

LINA: How are decisions made?

SB: You pass a bill in the Assembly and it is passed by the elected representatives of the people.

LINA: Kalyani did not acquire the status of Salt Lake. What happened?

SB: The infrastructure was not built and it is about 45 km away (further than Salt Lake). It is only ten years ago that the railway was extended to the town, till then the station was 5 km from Kalyani. Take a rickshaw to come to the station, get to Sealdah Station in Calcutta, and then get to work. Also, on the other side of Kalyani— the other side of the river—there is a municipality called Bansberia. An industrial town. One bridge would have made it possible for people of Kalyani to work in Bansberia and come back. A dormitory town. But this wasn't done. Now a bridge is being built and when that is completed things will improve. The CMDA has built a Barrackpur-Kalyani expressway which will relieve the strain on the existing road and help in its development. Kalyani must have its potential developed or people must have access to those areas and be able to come back. But Kalyani didn't have anything. People couldn't go out and work, they had no opportunity for work in Kalyani. Difficult. The selection of the site was wrong. Planners with their pencils and paper will identify all sorts of areas, but nothing will happen.

LINA: During your term with the CMDA what were some of the projects which were started and which have been completed? The other question is how much has transportation like mini-buses helped develop Calcutta?

SB: In this situation, any contribution helps.

LINA: No, I'm talking about long distance buses which go beyond the limits of the city, bringing people to work here and also enabling them to go outside the city to work.

SB: There was a time till 1960 when Calcutta only had state buses. But with population pressure, they had to concede to private buses. Then they found people are willing to pay slightly more in order to be able to travel. So the mini-buses came up. Police said that auto-rickshaws cannot be allowed to operate in Calcutta. But the pressure was such that they had to concede. And they will expand.

LINA: Who uses the rickshaws? The upper class and middle class?

SB: It's not for the poor. Minimum is one rupee and from Tollygunge to the Esplanade it is Rs 1.50, pretty expensive.

People talk about decentralization but nobody means business.

Salt Lake came up 10 to 12 years ago, even now the Departments of Fisheries, and Education are located in Writers' Building or in the central business district. Why? Tollygunge or Dum Dum could be very good centers of development, but they aren't serious about decentralization. There seems to be no compulsion.

LINA: Why?

SB: Calcuttans are tolerant. Calcutta is a tolerant city.

LINA: Tolerance is working against development at times. You'd think that planning for Dum Dum and Tollygunge would be important: a lot of people live there who work in Calcutta. They could provide a good area for hospitals, schools, instead of coming all the way into the city. There are very few offices in Salt Lake.

SB: There is a great deal of resistance on the part of many to move out. Once they start operating from Salt Lake or wherever they'll find it is alright. The CMDA has built a 10-story structure in Salt Lake with the idea that everything will move there but even today after eight years the head office people don't want to move out.

The CMDA has made some contribution to renovating old schools, building new ones but they don't run them. The Ministry of Education and the Calcutta Corporation runs them. When the CMDA was started, it began as a funding organization. They would collect the funds and give it to various groups. Collect the money from the World Bank and others, and give it to the local agencies for development according to a plan developed by the CMDA. The octroi tax was imposed not by the CMDA but by the government of West Bengal for the benefit of the CMDA. Fifty percent of the collection would go to CMDA. CMDA would also get some funds from the State Government, some from the Center, some from the World Bank and distribute it to local agencies like the Corporation, the Municipality, etc., for construction work according to plans prepared by the CMDA. There was no accountability. The results were not coming, the completion certificates were lacking. But in 1977, when the Left government came into power—they are great believers in the philosophy of decentralization—they initiated a process that CMDA will only do the planning and some monitoring but actual execution will be done by the local body: Calcutta

Corporation—a swing of the pendulum. Except for some central projects and inter-municipal projects, the CMDA distributes funds to the local bodies. But this time there is a little bit of difference because the projects are sponsored by the municipality. The local municipality says, "These are the projects which we want to take up." The CMDA says, "OK, here are the funds. You complete it."

LINA: I think Calcutta Corporation will eat up CMDA.

SB: The CMDA has no *locus standii*. It is an outsider. The Corporation is the owner of the city. We can't do anything on our own. It has to be sanctioned by the Calcutta Corporation.

Some of the projects which have actually been completed since I joined are some flyovers—Brabourne Road flyover, Sealdah flyover, a pedestrian subway in Howrah, the new road—Eastern Metropolitan By-Pass, the Barrackpur–Kalyani Expressway. Apart from that about 30 roads have been widened: Diamond Harbour Road, Sarat Bose Road. On the traffic and transportation side, there is some improvement in the circulation system. Water supply—we have set up the Garden Reach Waterworks, increased the capacity of Palta, and Howrah has also come up to some extent. Sewerage, the less said the better because except for increasing the pumping capacity of the pumping stations not much has been done. But the greatest achievement of the CMDA was in slum improvement. Not a relocation or urban renewal project—we are not demolishing the slums and we are not housing people (we did try that experiment and the displaced didn't come back but there were lots of legal difficulties—they occupied their allotments and rented them out again). It's the question of slum improvement. We provide water supply, sewerage and drainage, electricity, convert the privies into sanitary latrines. Formerly there used to be bucket latrines which had to be cleared manually.

LINA: What's the difference between a slum and a squatter's settlement? You don't supply all these amenities to squatters?

SB: A "slum" is a reorganization, a legal term. *Bustee* and slum are the same. The Calcutta Corporation has a definition for a slum. It must have mud walls, its structure should be thatched or tin. Can't be two-storied, and must be registered with the Calcutta Corporation. There are about 300 slum clusters in Calcutta. Squatter's colonies are just places occupied by people.

LINA: It's a problem here in some areas. Eventually if left for a long time, a squatter's colony can turn into a slum?

SB: Worse than a slum. Only point is whether it is a private or government property that is squatted on. But it is not recognized or registered as such.

LINA: It's easier to break the squatter colonies without any legal problems but it is difficult with slums?

SB: You can't remove slums. They are as good tenants as I am in my own house.

LINA: What if they decide to improve the slum and build buildings?

SB: They can't do that.

LINA: What's the problem with improving the aesthetic aspect of slums?

SB: If you have a multistoried structure you no longer have a slum.

LINA: Can you upgrade it?

SB: Who does it? The city? The slum dwellers are not the owners of the property. A recent amendment has made some the owners of land but otherwise there was a landlord with the right to the land. The slum dweller was renting a structure built by an intermediary: it was a three-tier system. Landlord, *thikadaar*,[1] slum dweller. Nobody could interfere with the landlord's right to his property. If the slum dwellers want to do it themselves they have to be owners of the property. Secondly, there is the question of money. It's expensive. Why did they give up the idea of re-housing them? Because of the money. The CMDA annual budget for slum improvement when I was there—was about 80 million rupees only.

---

[1] A type of middleman who leases the land from a landowner and rents it out to others.

# Sunil Ganguly

SUNIL GANGULY: I am basically a writer—I write poetry and fiction. I also work for a newspaper—*Ananda Bazar Patrika*—a Bengali language paper. The house which publishes it has other newspapers and journals, like *The Telegraph, Sunday* in English and Hindi papers like *Ravivar*. I work with the literary weekly *Desh*. I grew up in this city though I was born in a village in what is now Bangladesh. We immigrated during the time of the partition.

LINA: Do you consider yourself a Calcuttan?

SG: Now I can claim myself a Calcuttan, but most pure Calcuttans do not consider me a Calcuttan. They still treat me as a refugee.

LINA: How many generations before one can become a Calcuttan?

SG: At least three.

LINA: What are some of the issues you find most interesting? Do you deal with social problems of Bengalis?

SG: Of course. I write about the modern period, the situation around me, the people I meet every day. Social problems crop up all the time. I have seen very poor people, lower middle class, and middle class. I think I've just moved a way up into the middle class but I was born in a poor family. I know how the lower middle class lives.

LINA: How do you bring this concern into your writing?

SG: In literature it's not a case where I write to make people socially aware. Essentially you write about life as it is—the problems of life. When people read a novel or a poem, they enjoy the music of the language. But underneath every story or poem there must be a social reality. This is also felt by the readers.

LINA: How do people respond?

SG: Here people are very conscious. For instance, if I attack any social taboo or religious practice in one of my writings then immediately a lot of letters come to me and are published in journals. Some people support me, some don't agree with me. There are always people who are against any criticism of religion. Here we have many problems, but to me the most urgent one is the problem of religion, the tension of communalism, also among Hindus there is still casteism.

LINA: Do you think that caste is still an important issue in Calcutta?

SG: Not in the city. But if you go out into the villages, yes. In Calcutta also, all you have to do is scratch someone and you'll find he's "Brahman" or something.

LINA: So caste has not really been replaced by class.

SG: No. In arranged marriages, they still consider caste. You can see the "matrimonial" ads in the newspapers.

LINA: Do you do contemporary writing?

SG: Yes, I mostly write autobiographical work, my experiences. I have written historical novels also, but mostly I write about contemporary times. Two of my novels have been filmed by Satyajit Ray, *Days and Nights in the Forest* [*Aranyer Din Ratri*] and *Pratidwandi* or *The Adversary*. In both I have described the lives and problems of young people.

LINA: In looking at Calcutta in the nineteenth century, *bhadra* society, the culture which emerged then incorporated the best of British and Indian society, discarding some of the more strict traditions reflected in Bengali society. Later, in the 1920's and 30's, things changed. Some of the changes had to do not just with economics but with people developing values slightly contradictory to their culture.

SG: Yes.

LINA: Would you say that western education and a new kind of professionalism brought change?

SG: Calcutta was one of the first places where English education came into India, so people around this new city started to get ideas from the West. Also, in the very beginning, people got so westernized that they forgot about their heritage. Later there was a realization that it was good to get the best of both worlds. That's how the culture developed here. About our literature: it is very fortunate that at the very beginning the standard was very high. Bankim Chandra Chattopadhyay, our first novelist, a great novelist, set standards which people subsequently sought to follow. Now with the media explosion, there is "trash" in magazines, potboilers—still literature has a good standard not only by Indian but by world standards.

LINA: You don't think that people are moving away from Bengali as medium of communication?

SG: There is a section of our people who want to hold on to English education only. But that is a minor section, the upper classes. Not the middle class, about three to four percent not more.

LINA: How much power does this three to four percent have on determining policy?

SG: At least about two percent migrate to other countries. Until now this has been the trend.

LINA: I talked to some people from the 3 to 4 percent group and one thing that struck me was that while I reacted strongly to what was happening in Bengal and to Calcutta, they say that it is good to have universal Indian identity. Identification with Bengal and Bengali doesn't really matter. Then there is the middle class complaining about how fast things are moving. People talk about a "Calcutta culture" which I never heard of before.

SG: Calcutta culture was labeled the "*babu*" culture of the *nouveau riche* in the nineteenth century. The new generation of rich people acquired some western knowledge and ideas and also had a fancy for wine and womanizing. Now you cannot label anything as "Calcutta" culture. It should be Bengali culture. In Bengal, the *nouveau riche* are aloof from the mainstream. They don't contribute at all. Their eyes are always on the West and they try to send their children to the West.

LINA: Bengalis move out of Calcutta: I understand that 46 percent of Calcuttans are Bengali and the rest are non-Bengali.

SG: No, it's good that Calcutta is metropolitan and the population is mixed: I appreciate it that there is no "sons of the soil" attitude. There has never been a language law in the city. In Orissa and Bihar there have been incidents but not in Calcutta. Never a language riot though there have been communal riots.

LINA: Are these people who share language and culture?

SG: Well, most of the Muslims lived in separate parts of the town. Even in modern buildings like this one you will rarely find a mixed population of Hindus and Muslims. A Muslim friend of mine tried to buy a flat in this apartment block and was denied, but the committee would take a Marwari.

LINA: I'm surprised they allow a Marwari.

SG: They would allow a Marwari grudgingly—but they'd allow a Marwari. Maybe there are some residents of the building who work in a Marwari firm. But religious bias is so strong. This grew after partition, because the refugees here (I am a refugee) are still very anti-Muslim. A section of the refugees mixed with the Muslims, mind you but I find that many pure Calcuttans, 3 to 4 generation Calcuttans, have never had Muslim friends. Interaction between Hindus and Muslims is very little.

LINA: In the last fifteen years there haven't been many riots.

SG: 1964 was the last big one. But there is tension all the time.

LINA: Now there is tension among all the ethnic minorities.

SG: For instance, if there is a football match between Mohammedan Sporting and Mohan Bagan or East Bengal [popular Calcutta sporting clubs]. Afterwards there's bound to be a clash and it may take a more serious turn.

LINA: Are you concerned about the out-migration of the middle classes into satellite towns? The sale of old houses and the building of high-rise apartments?

SG: I am personally very concerned about this. All these beautiful mansions sold and demolished with match-box houses coming up. Anyone concerned for the city should be sorry about that. For a long time the corporation or the municipality was suspended and there was a minister of the government who looked after municipal affairs. So they didn't bother. Most of these buildings were demolished and sold to non-Bengalis. Declining old Bengali families are forced to move out of the city. A sad state of affairs.

LINA: Is there a law to stop the tearing down of buildings? I feel that some of the problems of multistoried buildings are not addressed by the government.

SG: There is no proper planning. These high-rise buildings grew up haphazardly and now the city fathers are thinking about restricting high-rise buildings. But it's already too late. So ugly. At one time Calcutta was called "the city of palaces," but no longer. Many Bengali families have become poor and are unable to maintain their ancestral homes and are forced to sell. I know a family on Lansdowne Road—now Sarat Bose Road—who owned a beautiful house, the Bhowal Sanyasi family home. In East Bengal there was a small *zamindari* called Bhowal, the site of a famous case about 40 years ago, "the Bhowal Sanyasi case." Many books have been written about it. The Bhowal Sanyasi was a prince or landowner (*jamidar*) and was supposed to have been killed by his wife and his wife's brother. He was cremated. After twelve years he returned as a *sanyasi* and claimed that he had escaped, become a *sadhu* [mendicant, holyman] and come back. People thought he was an impostor but he seemed well rehearsed—even knew of certain marks on his wife's body. The case went up to the Privy Council in England. The *sanyasi* won the case. Anyway, that house was very beautiful, and now it's been demolished.

LINA: It's not just demolishing a mansion but a whole way of life, and a class. The concept of *para* is destroyed by high-rise buildings.

SG: In north Calcutta there was a building which was so big and sprawling that they needed a small train to travel from one part of the building to the other, now it's no longer there.

LINA: Do Bengalis feel affected by this?

SG: You see, Bengalis write letters to the newspapers but do nothing about it. Is it in their power to stop it? A particular person or group can't resist but the government should take action to protect some historical buildings. But they were careless and busy with infighting.

LINA: What if you had a political party that addresses issues like a return to an awareness of who you are, a pride in the language, and policies which protect Bengali rights. Is that possible?

SG: There is a trend among Bengalis: the educated Bengali will not utter that "I am a Bengali"—by nature they are universal types, they think about the whole world. I have a theory that the whole world won't care about Calcutta but Calcutta is caring about the burdens of the whole world. Talk to an ordinary Calcutta man. He'll discuss Vietnam, South Africa, Ethiopian famine but not the condition of Calcutta.

LINA: I used to think it's because of apathy or an expectation that something better will happen soon. It's like they're waiting for leadership. And I don't see another renaissance in the near future.

SG: No, I don't foresee one either.

LINA: At the same time there is a liveliness. You are writing, there are theater groups, painters.

SG: Culture sometimes thrives in poverty. Because the upper class, the rich, don't care about culture. It's mostly the middle class.

LINA: The repository of "Bengaliness" remains with the middle classes and yet they are not in a position of power.

SG: But politically, especially after the coming of the Marxist government, the middle class has something to say.

LINA: What can they say that will change the situation?

SG: If you go to the villages, I think lots of work has been done by the political parties. Now almost every village has a political consciousness. They know what is their right. In other parts of India they do not have this consciousness.

LINA: I find it interesting that many people say that Calcutta would not exist unless it's run by a Marxist government, yet I don't think the Left government has addressed some problems but the Congress (I) would not do that either.

SG: Actually there is no hope for the Congress here, now. There was so much infighting and bad elements in the party that people have got disgusted. And unfortunately, there is no alternative. The Left is strong and they have shown for the last ten years that they can govern and hold on.

LINA: Are you working on a novel about Calcutta at present?

SG: I am working on a big novel now—it has a simple name—"The East and the West," *Purba Paschim*. It has three levels of *purba/paschim*. In the first part there is the division of Bengal into East and West. I have described the conditions, the migration of Hindus and also of Muslims. In the second part is an eastern hemisphere and western hemisphere division. In the 1960's, many of our bright boys and girls migrated to the West leaving their parents here. Believing like Rimbaud, that they would come back with gold and make their parents happy, but many never returned. There is a third kind of east and west. I think in every individual's mind, there is an east and west, philosophically speaking. The center is Calcutta, but the novel goes to Dhaka, England and America.

LINA: In looking at two or three generations you are bound to be looking at changes in the city as well. Will you include the breaking down of houses? I feel that when you break a building you lose a sense of community, *para*, you move from a horizontal *para* with events, *pujas* and communication to a vertical one.

SG: You are very right. I feel I have lost contact with the people in the streets. I don't hear the sounds of people talking, the peddlers— once I come up to my floor I am unaware of what goes on outside.

LINA: If residential planning were different would there be less antisocial elements?

SG: You can think of these houses as villages.

LINA: Yes, I have never associated Calcutta with fear, though I am a woman and an outsider. In Delhi, after six pm, I would not walk outside. I used to take music lessons in Kalighat and return home by tram at eleven at night and never feared anything. I had a sense of security and it had to do with Bengali attitudes towards women. But now I am not so sure.

SG: It's not so bad yet. There are some notorious localities but otherwise it's not bad.

LINA: Hungerford Street, Camac Street, I don't recognize: they are like little Marwari islands. They have changed a lot in ten years. I have been coming here since my undergraduate days in the late 1960's and if you do that you are more aware of change than people who live here. Are you involved in theater?

SG: I am not involved in the theater. I go to see performances. We have a small group called *Budh Sandhya: Budh* means "Wednesday" and the whole meaning is "Wednesday Evenings." That's when we meet—the *Budh Sandhya* Club. Mostly writers, some singers, our wives, some artists. We stage plays once or twice a year to raise money for social work—we give money to the Cancer Research Institute at Behala, to the Ramakrishna Mission Hospital, and to a small school in Bongaon—a border town near Bangladesh. We insist on staging original plays. We raise a sizeable amount of money because many famous writers take part in the acting. It's always "house full."

LINA: I went to see *Raja* yesterday but I couldn't understand the audience's reaction. They stood up but didn't clap.

SG: Perhaps because it's a Tagore play. In the Santiniketan atmosphere they usually say "*Sadhu,*" or something like that [i.e. call out "Good! Good!" in Sanskritised Bengali and not applaud in the borrowed English style].

Have you seen *Bela-Abelar Galpa?* It's on at the Academy of Fine Arts. It's a very well acted play and deals with the problems of the city. The debate between the Leftist and the others is always there in this play. And the disillusionment of our Marxists. The group staging it is called Chetana.

LINA: Is Badal Sarkar still playing?

SG: Now he doesn't believe in staging plays on a fixed stage. He doesn't even want to sell tickets. So he has become a *sadhu* of the theater world. He sometimes plays to a very small audience. He puts out a box and you pay whatever you want. I knew him very well at one time. These days I don't see him but I've heard about his disillusionment.

LINA: I heard that *Raja* is about more than the forces of good and evil: it deals with the political structure engulfing the individual.

SG: I think that is stretching the play too far. But it is about the dual aspects of personality. Dual personality.

LINA: In Calcutta, you can't be bored.

SG: There is a new art gallery called Chitrakoot where artist have showings.

LINA: I remember Sunil Das, Sarbari Raychowdhury.

SG: One time there was an environment of literature. At the time in which I came here, as a boy, I saw other people writing.

LINA: You don't think that Bengalis have become callous?

SG: Bengalis have always been callous about certain things and also upright about others.

LINA: Yes, but if you scare them a little and tell them that they'll have Hindi instead of Bengali, you'll have a riot. If you tell them that they can't read Tagore, they'll react strongly. My feeling is that Bengalis have a level of tolerance and if you go beyond it they blow up.

SG: Some foreigners who came here said Bengalis were too tolerant. They have such problems, but they take it. In other countries people may not. Here they write letters and talk about it, but they don't organize.

LINA: They'll argue for hours about garbage, they'll go out to eat *paan* and spit it out and go on! I can never relate the reality to the conversation.

# Calcutta, 1986-88 : A Photo Essay

# Samaresh Bose

LINA: Your life is writing political philosophy. How come?

SAMARESH BOSE: Calcutta is the hub of political interest in the eastern zone, more so than the Hindi speaking belt. Left-minded.

LINA: Were Calcuttans always "Left" minded or is it a recent phenomenon?

SB: From the very beginning of modern politics, it is hereditary! From Ishwar Chandra Vidyasagar on. In the nineteenth century, when people couldn't think of widow remarriage, Vidyasagar was the first person who declared that there was nothing in the *shastras* forbidding widows to marry. There were two parties involved and his opponents on this issue were strong. Rammohun was another pioneer who fought against *sati*. Vidyasagar declared that he would rather be beaten to death by the Calcutta populace than give up this fight! Harish Mukherjee had a paper *The Patriot*—he lived in Bhowanipur [an old south Calcutta neighborhood]—and it spoke out on behalf of the Indigo peasants. You can understand that Calcutta had a reputation for fighting against injustice. This ultimately culminated in the Left movement. Gandhi was not successful, particularly in Bengal. I cannot say why. The anti-British movement was launched by the terrorists.

LINA: But don't you think people think of Gandhi as a "Left" person?

SB: Gandhi was not a Leftist. He was typically a supporter of non-violence. Bengalis were not for non-violence. Once upon a time I was also a Left-minded man and a member of the Communist Party of India. When it was banned I was in jail. I never got my job back. I didn't remain with the Communist Party, and now I am thinking that we should focus again on Gandhi. I think that Gandhi had something others don't. He is the only leader of modern India whom millions of people came to. Leftist parties never drew millions. He was a real Indian who never thought of other countries—while being on good terms with Tolstoi and others. He had another philosophy and saw India by traveling. It wasn't all from books. Didn't go to museums and libraries to know the country. Non-violence and love are the ultimate keys. Without them, we may get something temporarily but for the future we can't make a great nation by violence. Today I feel Gandhi is more necessary to us, given the world's situation.

LINA: People say that no other except a Left party can run Calcutta.

SB: I think a party other than a Left one can do something for Calcutta. It is its power structure one has to see. Perhaps one can say there is not much difference between Leftists and the Congress Party. A major difference is of course that the Leftists are concerned about their party and the Congress is less so. I don't think that people are very much Left-minded. This is the first time the Left Front has been in the country, this is the first time the people have seen some money. When Congress was in power for a long time, in the countryside villagers were poor and depressed. I don't think this is so much a question of political ideals or consciousness. It's not really party ideology at work.

Now the Leftists are thinking that if we could have worked more successfully in the villages we might have had more influence. Now, since they're in power they're fighting for *Panchayats* and have captured most of them. They know that the party is getting a bad name because the *Panchayat* leaders are getting money.

Everybody knows in the village that during floods, when people suffer, their leaders get money. The "cadres" travel on motorbikes and live in good houses. The poor remain the same. But you can say that the Left Front has done more than the Congress in the villages. They have created the party in the villages and Congress can't fight against them now. They don't believe in the Congress. People only think about what they're going to get. It's not an ideological fight, but a question of give and take.

LINA: How do you deal with all this in your writing? What do you have on Calcutta?

SB: On Calcutta? I have written a novel about Howrah: *In Search of an Unshackled Land*—about a fourth generation iron worker who became a big fighter, well respected in his area. He became an MP [Member of Parliament] and forgot where he came from. From a poor beginning to a workers' leader and a house in Delhi with a green carpet, all else is forgotten. When the party declines to give him another chance at nomination, he is frustrated and begins to think. His grandfather is still alive, living in his old style. This is when he begins to search for his roots.

Another novel that I wrote about Calcutta deals with three generations. The father was a Gandhian, then became a Congress supporter, went to jail, became a Marxist, and a Communist. He had ideological differences with his father. His eldest son also became a Communist but ultimately the Communist father and son have fights. The father is a Communist minister but there is conflict between the father and son. The son loves a girl who is with his father's party and she believes the party comes first. She said that the party is bigger than love.

That's the tragedy. My Communist friends were upset. The Communist father was criticized by me. He could not explain the millions of rupees he spent! These questions were brought up in the novel. Though there is a difference between the Congress and Communists, I do not see the differences very clearly. What's the difference between Left and Right now?

Gandhi said that the middle class thinks of change but not really revolutionary change. The middle class seeks to optimize its position. The same character I see in middle-class Communists or Congress members.

LINA: Who is thinking about Bengali culture, traditions and values?

SB: I don't think that they seriously believe in revolution. CPI(M) leader Sundarraya was a member of the Politbureau. He had a difference with the party about organization. In his last few years he was frustrated and was not in a high position in the party. At the Boat Club in Delhi [scene of large public meetings] it is said that at least ten thousand Calcutta people attended the meeting. I don't believe it. I think it's a pity that they're thinking of going to Delhi to make a party at the Center. The people of India are not Communist in their mind.

LINA: Maybe that's why the meaning of "communism" is different here.

SB: CPI(M) cadres here are very involved in Durga *Puja*, Kali *Puja*! How is that possible?

LINA: Because they are Bengalis first and ideologues second!

SB: First they are Bengali Hindus and then they are Communists! Janaki Ballav Bhattacharjee was a scholar of Bhatpara and he was a Leftist. I asked him one day, "Janaki-da, how are you a Leftist? I heard you're being nominated by the Left party. How? You are not a Communist!" He said, "No, but I am a Hindu Communist!"

This gentleman is now dead. He was a professor at Calcutta University and a Sanskrit scholar. I asked him what he thought of Vidyasagar and he said he thought he was a "loafer." Apparently, he was in love with a widow and wanted to marry her, so he fought for that cause. What should I say? Calcutta looks like a city but people are not modern. You go to any Hindu or Muslim house and you find that they are living and thinking in the same old way. There is no modernization. It's like a village inside the city.

LINA: You think that all these non-Bengalis in the city will not change Bengali values?

SB: This is another tragedy of Calcutta. One-third of the property in Calcutta is owned by non-Bengalis—particularly Marwaris and Rajasthanis. They don't bother about West Bengal. But they're buying and Bengalis are going outside the city to the suburbs. A specific class of people.

Suppose you bought a flat for 2 lakhs and I gave you 10 lakhs for it, you can't resist. So you sell and move out because you get eight thousand rupees a month from the bank. This is why Calcutta is going out of Bengal! One-third of its owners are non-Bengalis. They're typically businessmen.

LINA: One day you'll wake up and discover that the middle-class Bengali is gone from Calcutta. Only lower-class Bengalis, Biharis, and Marwaris will be left.

SB: They are the people who will improve Calcutta. Kalyani isn't developing (though Salt Lake is) because of its position. There are antisocial elements, the police aren't strong. Nobody is interested in Kalyani now. Salt Lake is nearer and is more popular. Bidhan Ray's dream has faded. There (in Kalyani) is a university, and a few factories but that's all. If they do construct another bridge it'll change. At present, the North 24-Parganas and Nadia district border on Kalyani and all the bad things of these districts happen in Kalyani.

LINA: Can you write about all these things without getting into trouble with the government? Is there democracy in Calcutta?

SB: If I have a reason to criticize Jyoti Basu, I can do it.

LINA: Recently there was the Bofors case in New Delhi and *Indian Express* [powerful national daily] exposed it. There was so much trouble with the government, I wonder how free one is to express oneself.

SB: Here too—if the CPI(M) cadres and the party want to they can impede your work and activities. I am Samaresh Bose living in Calcutta. Say I lived outside Calcutta and I was a critic of the party, I'd have a lot of unhappiness in my life. I cannot say that we are enjoying democracy in a deep way.

LINA: You can still write.

SB: Yes, they criticize me but they can't beat me or drive me away from my house. I write in almost all papers. Even the CPI(M) daily *Ganashakti* is sent to me. They are trying to have me write in their paper. I asked them, "What should I write in your paper. What I'll write will go against you and you won't publish it."

They say, "Why will you write against us? Once upon a time you were a Communist. You can criticize us, but you must do so truthfully."

They say they are doing something for the poor. But they are doing nothing.

LINA: Why have Bengalis become so apathetic over the last 25 to 30 years? They don't seem to care—they see the city falling apart but they don't do anything.

SB: They are idle—not regular in going to office. The government is facing this problem too. Take the example of Tamil Nadu's Chief Minister who threatens her people to come to office in time to work. Janaki has announced that she'll give money to 10 lakhs of people. I don't know where the money will come from. Janaki is with Congress, the widow of Ramchandran.[1] Yesterday he was a critic of India's government, then Ramchandran said that the government was doing the right thing in Jaffna and the people believed him. I can't understand how a man like this can be a leader of the country. When he died many people committed suicide. We, Bengalis can't think like this, it's not good. The Left Front will remain in Bengal. They are going outside Calcutta.

LINA: What can the Left Government do to induce Bengalis to protest against conditions in the city seen much of a reaction to the deteroration of Calcutta, not written comment much on corruption, the sale of historic sites, such as the attempt to sell off the old cemetery for example. What can the CPI(M) do to make Bengalis really angry? Would they use newspapers, theatre or literature?

SB: I don't think they are going to do anything. "Anti-Congress" is a strong tradition which includes pro-Subhas Chandra Bose attitudes. Congress did the wrong thing—they didn't do their job and are suffering today. They are fighting each other openly which the CPI(M) doesn't do. These people can't be respected. That's why Jyoti Basu has a place. He is a moderate person. He isn't a typical Communist—a "London" person. A member of the Communist Party from Britain, knows about the parliamentarian way. That's why people are willing to vote for them. The cadre system seems to function. The Communists know that ideologically much of it is a sham, but they are doing it.

[1] The famous film actor who became the Chief Minister of Tamil Nadu.

LINA: Are you going to write a novel that looks at contemporary Calcutta?

SB: I have written *Bibar* and *Prajapati*. The latter was not really obscene but I was charged and acquitted honorably, after 18 years! I say one thing with these novels. I found that they brought the Congress and the Communists to the same platform against me. They know very well that I don't find differences between them, well, there are differences. The Leftists are clever, they know how to organize. The Communists have their money—they are leading their own sweet lives.

LINA: *Babu* communists? I wish some of your novels were translated.

SB: I wrote some books on politics and the social life of Calcutta.

LINA: Do you write poetry?

SB: No.

# Surajeet Ghose

LINA: How long have you been in the publishing business? What is your thinking about publishing?

SURAJEET GHOSE: Actually, our publishing house, Proma Prakashani is very typical of its kind. It originates in a little magazine in 1978, called *Proma* which means "*prakrishta gyan*" or "real knowledge"—a Sanskrit word. We have a board of editors—Arun Mitra (who won the Sahitya Akademi award), Samik Banerjee, Dr. Pabitra Sarkar and myself. We are from different disciplines. Pabitra is basically a linguist, Samik is in film and theater and Arun is a famous poet and French scholar. Our main objective was to publish a bi-monthly paper which will carry serious articles on various topics, literature, linguistics, anthropology, sociology, economics, everything other than day-to-day politics. Maybe political philosophy but not current politics. Not party politics, nor sports or typical commercial films. Other than that we'd concentrate on normal areas everywhere. That's why we selected a different cross section of people as editors. I was editing another periodical *Satabhisa*; because of my young age I could do more. Editing was divided equally amongst us. If you are aware of Bengali little magazines—you may hear everyone trying to define a little magazine by its incapabilities—a magazine which comes out irregularly, shabbily. But at least three of them *Bibhav*, *Samatat* and *Proma* are not defined by incapability. We should define ourselves by our capability. That little magazines are irregular is because of other problems. We can make it regular, worth reading and we can improve the printing. Little magazines have a bad habit of not paying authors. Because our resources are less, whatever small resources we have for our space, our paper supplier, binder, designers—we extend to our writers. We started to pay a nominal honorarium after a year.

LINA: How much do you pay for an article?

SG: At that time 50 rupees. Which is nothing. What happened is that after a year and a half, we evaluated our resources and we decided we could pay the writers 150–200 rupees for an article. At that time the suggestion came from Samik Banerjee, "Unless you can pay them their full money, for an article say 500 or 1000 rupees, like *Ananda Bazar* does, it hardly matters whether you pay them 50 or 150. It is either an honorarium or the full money."

Rather than increasing by a little, you go on publishing certain books which commercial publishers will not take. We should get those books in print right now so that later when a demand is created, the books will be in print. This is how we started Proma Prakashani.

LINA: What about the content? Is there a focus? Is it mainly Bengali oriented? National?

SG: It started with an international focus, the first book printed was a translation from French. A biography of Mayakovsky written by Elsa Triolet who married Aragon [the French Marxist and Surrealist poet]. The book was banned by the Russian Communist Party because it speaks of Mayakovsky's personal life and suicide, etc. It's still banned. It exposed his love affairs, etc. In the Mayakovsky Club you'll never see a photo of the lady he loved. Then we did full translations of Brecht's songs and poetry by Alokeranjan Dasgupta. Then we did Bengali translations of Surdas. It was the five hundredth anniversary of Surdas and so our first publications started from translations. We did Greek plays, Aeschylus, Euripides, Sophocles.

One point was that the person translating must know the original language. Not English. Must know French, German, Greek, etc. Fortunately we have good translators. Alokeranjan Dasgupta for German, Arun Mitra for French . . .

LINA: The international is one facet, what about your commitment to Calcutta and Bengal?

SG: Later we came to something different. We found, particularly in Bengali, a rich culture of Bengali short stories and poetry. But nowadays no publisher ventures to publish poetry or short stories. They publish novels or travelogues. I don't have to make my livelihood from this, so we do poetry. Out of the 75 books we've published, 30 are poetry. Important new writers from Calcutta and its suburbs publish with us. Even an established poet—Sakti Chattopadhyay. He said in a recent interview in *Ananda Bazar* that nowadays in Bengal, the only publisher of poetry worth mentioning is Proma Prakasani.

LINA: You're investing in less-known people.

SG: Ones not patronized by the commercial houses. We did so with short stories.

LINA: Do they sell well?

SG: No. That's why commercial publishers are not very interested in these books. If they'd sold 5000 copies each, they'd be interested. But they sell a maximum of 1000 over two or three years. From the beginning, the name of our magazine and publishing house was famous for its literary and non-literary articles. So our books were on things like the revolutionaries, struggle for land, Lenin's plan with all the original references. On the literature side, we have Bishnu De and Sankha Ghosh on Aurobindo, Sisir Kumar Ghosh on Tagore's China visit.

LINA: Do you find the contents focusing more on Bengal?

SG: Yes, now I am going to specialize even more. Pradip Sinha is preparing a book about the metropolis of Calcutta, on the typical urban attitude of Calcutta. He has written three important books on this subject in English. Now he's trying his hand in Bengali. Pradip is also doing something for our magazine, the difficulties of doing historical research in Calcutta, the bad aspects of it, the wrong concepts, what our forefathers did, what's happening today.

LINA: Are the readers changing? Do they want more commentary on politics?

SG: Actually, building up the people's taste mostly depends on more powerful media—TV, radio and the press which has a wide circulation.

Particularly *Ananda Bazar* exploits the taste of the public. Also *Jugantar*. They have made things cheap and flashy. That's why no good articles are written. They are only full of information. No interpretation lucidly presented. Analytical articles are disappearing. The problem is that we cannot change the minds of people overnight but if small papers like us don't go on fighting against this trend, then a day will come when no taste will exist at all. Those who want to sell are doing well.

LINA: What happened to the Bengali mind?

SG: Nowadays there has been a degeneration. I can remember roughly 3–4 years ago there were special *Puja* issues. Out of five novels of *Ananda Bazar* publications, four novels were on wife swapping.

LINA: Were they popular?

SG: Very much. But how can all four writers write on the same topic in the same year? Samaresh Bose, Sunil Gangopadhyay, Buddhadev Guha, Shankar—all famous writers. Possibly they were told by *Ananda Bazar* that this is a subject that people are taking an interest in—write novels on it. It will cover the market. I'm not sure but these surveys must have been done otherwise such coincidences wouldn't occur. Once Lionel Trilling said that we don't really know what these little magazines do. We can never know that until they cease to publish. They create some discomfort to the establishment.

LINA: Do you think that the media and politicians are determining the values of society?

SG: It is in the hands of newspapers and the TV.

LINA: A warped, unacceptable sense of values. People are being judged by Hindi film stereotypes.

SG: The middle-class Bengalis have a conflict. They want those comforts but cannot deal with dramatic changes in the family. They want the best of both, a peculiar combination.

Once we felt that we were failing to run our publishing house.

So we should make a few popular books to fetch us money to be invested in other areas. When I did that, I chose novels written by Sunil Gangopadhyay, Asutosh Mukhopadhyay, Prafulla Ray, Mahasweta Devi (her main publisher was Karuna Prakasani, but now I'm the main publisher). She is associated with us from our first volume. She wrote the first story in our first volume—"Behula" and I have published her best short story collections. Seagull does good work. My previous co-editor, Samik is working there. Very knowledgeable boy. Sometimes we differ in ideology but he was very competent.

LINA: When you take a manuscript what is it that you look for?

SG: Basically I am not very interested in printing novels, rather serious books.

LINA: A novel could be serious.

SG: Yes, but to keep the stream alive my first consideration for selecting a novel is whether the title will sell. But I am very particular about the content. Popularity can be achieved by so many things. I have never yet printed a novel which can be called sexually loaded. Sensuousness is not wanted. Have you gone through the novels of Samaresh Majumdar—he is very popular and he was capitalizing only on that point. In our country there is a peculiar problem after Independence, from 1947 to 1987. From only one university we have gone to eight in West Bengal. Rabindra Bharati, Visva Bharati, Burdwan, Kalyani has two campuses, North Bengal. They give so many MA degrees but what about the secondary, and primary education in the state? They haven't changed all that much. So, with the basis of an MA a person will say I won't go for a pornographic book. But he is not being tested by serious books. He is interested in books which have good print, good covers. It's for a certain class and it's easy to capitalize on this section. Because of their weak foundation they'll be quickly interested in these books.

LINA: So you have a particular sense of ethics and morality. That is yours. But is it a part of a larger group?

SG: A similar question was asked recently about whether Bengali writing or films have changed from their traditional concepts or whether they still retain them. In my opinion, all those basic values being followed by my parents have changed a lot. Basically, after the Second World War, we were exposed to world literature even more. Our literature has changed. Our egos have changed, as have our priorities and sense of values. We were discussing a personal issue and Supreo-da said that marrying too many times was not acceptable. Even my daughter said this, she said, no it's not good and I wanted her to examine her reasons for it. By and large, Bengali society is conservative. Still attaching value to education, to marrying only once, post-marital, extra-marital relationships are basically not acceptable. This is not just me but basic to all Bengalis.

I could have shown you our publications. I don't have a shop. Round the year we sell to the booksellers. Our agents in College Street are De Bookstore, Subarnarekha, Saibya, D.M. Library, Aparna Book Distributors.

LINA: But the majority of your readers are within the state? In Calcutta and the surroundings?

SG: Not just Calcutta and its surrounding area. My books are read in north Bengal and Assam, Kachar.

LINA: Do you as a publisher see yourself as a repository of values? Something which theater does to some extent? Not newspapers, cinema. And do you see politics as a destroyer of values?

SG: Values are not just conformation and that nothing should change. Where you have individuals there will be change but I believe that changes happen in society all over the world, no one can go on with his values as it is. Things have to change. You must have watched many changes in peoples' attitudes to divorce and separation. What it was in 1967–70 and now.

LINA: It's more acceptable but what disturbs me is the apathy of Bengalis that I see more now than I did in 1967. They recognize it but don't do anything about it. Apathy gets translated into self-centered, self-motivated life cycles, individualism. The famous Americanism "What's in it for me?" You tell them to come to a demonstration, but they won't, they've lost a sense of community.

SG: They are not saying it in articles because they are not accepting it, but in stories, yes. This observation is true of novels. Dibyendu Palit is a good example. Last year the *Jugantar* novel was a good example. Once Gour Kishore Ghosh was an important novelist of this type but not now. He's too frail. And writing conscientiously is a strenuous activity; that's not Sunil's problem.

LINA: Is there hope for the younger generation?

SG: At one time Samaresh, Mahasweta were excellent. Gunter Grass came last year for one year and at the end of his visit he was introduced to some writers. Actually he didn't want to meet anybody until he was leaving. One of them had produced 250 novels and Grass refused to meet him because he thought someone like that would have to be low caliber. It was harsh but you understand what he meant.

LINA: But most writers today have another profession. Totally unrelated to writing like Sunil.

SG: Sunil's isn't totally unrelated to writing.

LINA: Like Mani Shankar

SG: That's true. But Sunil is Senior Editor of *Desh* who does nothing but write. That's ideal.

LINA: Do you think this addiction to writing which I associate with Bengalis is gone? That people write to survive or just to write. There was a period in Bengal when people just wrote. It was like a disease.

SG: That's still there. But in the old days there was almost no chance of earning any money from writing. Whether you were successful or not.

LINA: Most writers come from comfortable backgrounds.

SG: Yes, but now even a middle-class writer with good contacts can earn their living. There is a woman about 26–27 years old and writes very good poetry and is the wife of a good student, who became a branch manager of the United Commercial Bank at their foreign branch in Hong Kong. They have a five or six-year-old daughter. They invited me to visit their house when he was here from Hong Kong. I asked, "You aren't taking her [the wife] away?" He said, "I will, this time I have a good flat." Sometime later I met his wife at the Book Fair. I asked her, "You haven't gone to Hong Kong?" She said, "No, but can you organize a school or hostel for my daughter?" I said, "Why?" and she said, "I've decided not to go to Hong Kong."

LINA: As a writer she has to stay here.

SG: Her husband said, "If you want to be here, be here. If your writing is important . . ." But does the question of divorce arise? It is all reported by her. She wants to be alone, self-dependent. I asked her, "How can you do that. You haven't earned anything, you are not in service." She said, "I have been assured by *Desh* and *Ananda Bazar* that my writing will be printed continuously." By freelancing, she has shown me how you can live by writing. She showed me all 100-rupee checks, 16 in number. Sixteen hundred rupees! I said, "This is fine, but where is your writing?" She said, "I earned this by writing." I said, "No! You are a very good poet. Gardening, and how to do face masks is not what writing is about."

# Badal Sarkar

LINA: Did you give up CMPO because you objected to their plans? When did you start writing plays?

BADAL SARKAR: Not really. I loved town planning because I was an engineer, not because of my own wish, but because my parents wanted it. I hated it, but town planning made me interested—my own love. When I was working in CMPO I had great hopes, I also loved Calcutta. I thought I would remain on this job. It didn't happen, so after trying for about three years I gave it up. It had nothing to do with theater at all. *Bhoma* had been written much after that. It wasn't "development" but "planning" with which CMPO was concerned. When *Bhoma* was written—from experience—I could see contradictions in the whole development plan, so these things came out. There aren't many ties with my job in CMPO. Of course there are certain things. While working with CMPO I could see many things happening to which I reacted quite strongly. This is also there, but there are other things as well.

LINA: Did some of the things you reacted to have to do with a loss of Bengali values like family, people, community, a sense of neighborhood or *para*?

BS: I don't think in that language: I'll tell you how *Bhoma* was written. It was not written straight on—beginning and ending. Usually when I write plays I write very quickly: in six or seven days I finish. But *Bhoma* had been written in the course of three years. Without any intention of writing a play. Anything I reacted to strongly, in the positive or negative sense, I put it down almost like a diary from time to time. Because I was involved in playwriting and theater for a long time *Bhoma* came out in the form of a character, the color and speech of a character. In *Bhoma* I began with a color, there was nothing on its left. I did not arrange how to distinguish a line spoken by somebody and another by someone else. The characters were not there—absent, just the division of the lines. Another way of structuring a diary, a three-page scene would come out, then after 6 months another two to five-page scene. The concept of *Bhoma* was only one of the themes. I went around the country, I saw the conditions. The phenomenon of *Bhoma* was in a particular scene. Then when our group was searching for a new play I read out these lines, and I asked them to write scenes. Not many did, my present wife did and some of her scenes got into the play, not a whole scene. I started putting the scenes together, then *Bhoma* became more prominent.

The things I reacted to were very much a part of the process— the community, its structure, the person in society. That's the link in a way. And the growing contradiction of our attitudes from the top government level to the bottom, because I'm very much a part of that. My person is in *Bhoma*. That's why *Bhoma* begins with— "Though the lives I have come to know today, yesterday I did not know . . . Now I want to tell others who do not know even today (like me yesterday)"—that faithfully represents the way I felt when I put together the things in *Bhoma*.

LINA: So *Bhoma* was for you not necessarily a character, an incident, or a place. A combination of all that put together?

BS: As a matter of fact, I used the name "Bhoma" but talked about "Bhomas" in the plural, not "Bhoma," the person with a definite identity. I heard very interesting stories about Bhoma which I didn't use at all. Because I was interested in the phenomenon, something apparently quite unrelated to Bhoma is also there, for example radioactivity. But to my mind there are different facets or aspects of the same poison in society.

LINA: Is this poison, apathy on the part of Bengalis or is it political, economical, or historical?

BS: Historical, political, economical, social, everything. Total nature.

I would put my finger on the order of society. At present we can call it the capitalist society. But it doesn't mean that the socialist society is excluded from the poison. It takes a different shape. Maybe it gets redefined a bit but it's still there. The total problem is not solved yet. But definitely the structure of present society is the root cause, although it did not come out very clearly then. I think for every starvation, for every injustice, there is somebody or other who stands to gain whether that somebody is aware of it or not. That's what my experience tells me—if Bhoma starves, I do not even know him. I know nothing about him, maybe that's why I get a plate full of rice every day. But I'm not aware of it and have no reason to feel guilty about it. Or rather, I don't feel guilty though there are reasons unknown to me for feeling guilty—as a matter of fact there are many such recent ways where I want to arouse a sense of guilt in myself and in others. Because maybe, so far as our middle classes are concerned, a sense of guilt can be translated into a kind of motive force or energy which may take action to change the present order of things.

LINA: You talk about guilt, but what about responsibility?

BS: It's a process from guilt to responsibility. If I go on eating, thinking all the time that everything is all right with the world because I'm eating, then the awareness that other people are not eating is not there. But if the awareness comes then maybe a link also comes—is there a relationship between my eating and other people not eating? If there is a link, there is a sense of guilt. Not the kind of primary level guilt—I begin to starve and then they will eat. It's not that simple. But something is wrong, when some people will have to starve because I know that there is no reason for anybody to starve and I can support that by facts. Say for example, there are countries where wheat is burnt, farmers are paid subsidies not to cultivate. But the fact remains that every four seconds one person is dying of hunger in this world—see Ethiopia . . . the famine. At the same time I've seen pictures in the newspapers . . . in London, Ethiopian figs are being imported.

LINA: Vegetables too . . .

BS: This is happening all the time. Famine here, drought there, people starving to death and we know of many other expenditures. In Calcutta there are festivals, security for VIPs, the underground railway—everyone complains about it—because the building is too slow, causing lots of trouble for Calcutta citizens. Nobody says that it is a criminal project. Less than 10 percent of the underground water is tapped yet we are spending so much money on the underground railway. Here is a link with CMPO knowledge. When I was in CMPO, the chief traffic engineer was drawing up the plans and estimates for the underground railway. Then it became bigger. At that time it was in an intermediate stage of planning and I remember I was chief town planner—I had a discussion with the chief engineer. At that time the total estimate was only one hundred crores—now already they've spent more than one thousand crore rupees and it is not even half done. He calculated that the running cost alone to break even—they'd have to make the minimum fare 85 paise. At that time, the minimum bus fare was 10 paise. So the running cost would have to be subsidized and what about all the work undertaken for the capital cost? From that moment I knew it was criminal. And now it is one thousand crores you can imagine how much the actual cost will be.

LINA: Who is paying for it now?

BS: We go on taking loans, and add to it that for every 100 dollars of loan from America or anybody we have to repay 60 dollars immediately to service our own debts—I'm giving you back-dated figures. Now we must be paying 70 dollars and when we come to the absurd situation of repaying 100 dollars for a 100 dollar loan— that means complete political subservience. Now it is political subservience—though not complete. It is happening, we are blind to these things because we are deliberately kept blind.

LINA: You are not keeping your audience blind!

BS: I try not to. First of all we have to find out if there may be two sets of government statistics. One set is always projected through the media and the other set through official papers; a person who wants to do research will find that the agricultural products of India have doubled since Independence. Statistics show a great advancement. There is another fact, since the census of 10 years ago the number of agricultural laborers has doubled. Everybody knows that apart from the beggars in the street, the agricultural laborers are the poorest in the community. Not only below the poverty level but often below the starvation level. I've been to the villages, I've been to their houses, talked to them, I've seen the vacant look in their eyes. I've tried to calculate—not arithmetically— how they keep on living. Their income and the times they don't work: I asked them, "What do you eat?" The answer is the little snails in the ponds and such. So there are two sets of facts. Read *The Statesman*—every day they praise the underground railway and criticize the fact that it's too slow, nobody says that less than 10 percent of the water is utilized. Nobody talks of the implication that agricultural laborers get jobs for 150 days out of 365.

LINA: What you do is like an anthropologist who collects facts and creates something around them?

BS: Not that process. I don't collect facts with the intention of writing a play. Looking into the facts some things come out, inevitably. I don't call myself a writer. Other people know me as a playwright. I call myself a theater man. And I read newspapers, books. I talk to people and I go to the villages as much as possible. I try to reason. It's all there. Sometimes almost accidentally . . . things match. If the consciousness or awareness of facts is there within you and then you write something, these things are bound to come. Meena, my wife, is writing plays and I find newspaper clippings for her about women's issues. Day before yesterday, there was the news about malaria, and the village witch doctor said it was a spirit so the whole village was abandoned. Religious observation and superstition are also there—connected with *sati* and bride burning. Meena either puts them in a file (she's not very regular or systematic) or she keeps them around. But when she writes a play they come out very strongly. Her attitude is from the woman's point of view. It's almost the same process as mine. It's not as if she's collecting these items like an anthropologist to be used in a future play.

LINA: What about your play *Procession*?

BS: The same process: Young boys dying every day is a part of our experience. Particularly in the Naxal period. Police cordoning off young people and shooting them dead. We lived with it. As for the old man, losing his way and trying to return, that's our own story. Those who have managed to conform, maybe the majority, are the middle classes with jobs and positions—building a house, buying a refrigerator, a car. They are content. But there are others, maybe the minority, who are not at peace. They don't want to go back to their old home yet they can't find their way. That's our own story. So it's quite normal that it would come out. When I wrote *Michil*— the last lines are: "So I am following you. I am supposed to lead, but I'm following you." That's personal in a way. At the same time it is the situation of the middle class.

LINA: The middle class in Calcutta is fading away?

BS: In which way?

LINA: In numbers, in holding of important positions, economically.

BS: I don't know about that. It depends on your definition of the middle class, how large is the group? What's the range?

LINA: I think we agree about the middle class. I know the community you're talking about . . . the professionals, skilled, white-collar workers.

BS: Not clerks. When I say middle class I mean middle and lower middle. The term "middle class" in the western sense is quite different from the term we use here, and I don't think their number is decreasing. What is happening didn't happen before. Say a factory worker, illiterate or practically illiterate, and a middle-level peasant owning not a large tract of land, maybe illiterate, will try to save whatever money they can to educate their children so that they don't have to work in a factory or till the soil. They are joining the lower middle classes. Maybe they go to school finally and increase the number of the unemployed, so I don't think they are decreasing in number. I can't support my statement by statistical figures but this phenomenon I know is happening. When I went to the villages, anybody having a little means—even the non-Bengalis coming from impoverished places, Orissa, Bihar and UP to pull rickshaws— try to save money to build a hut, buy more land to cultivate. They will spend on their children's education so that the children don't have to pull a rickshaw. They will pull a rickshaw even when they are seventy. So what about those children? They don't want to do the same job as their father did, they are gradually trying to get into the lower middle classes. It is a very rare phenomenon here for a middle-class person to accept the job of a laborer. He will remain unemployed—and a parasite on society and his parents!

LINA: When you direct or write a play, what is it that you hope will come out of the play other than guilt and responsibility?

BS: I talked about guilt and responsibility but in a reversed way. Not intending to do that, it has happened that way.

LINA: Reading *Bhoma* one questions what is the government's responsibility towards the people. What's one to do?

BS: Yes, that's the basic attitude. Searching for Bhoma is really searching within you. Why search for Bhoma? It's a question about whether I have to do something about this world. The present state of things—whether I have some responsibility for changing or whether I should go on conforming to the present sate of things. Ultimately it's my own self interest. Even if I have at job, I try to get a better job or move to a higher position in the job. The room at the top is always in front of the middle classes, but there is also the awareness lurking behind that my son may not get it. That insecurity is bound to be there. As a matter of fact, there is a joke. A businessman said, "The money I have amassed will take care of the next seven generations to come." His wife started weeping, so he asked, "What's the matter?" She said, "What about the eighth?" There may be an infinitely small minority of the middle class which would be aware of the middle-class values and long-term self instinct. Because ultimately I believe, every person works for his or her self interest. But it's a question of self interest and wider self interest. Short-term self interest and long-term self interest. And quite often the short-term interest is the long-term interest. Society is like a staircase—we are always told to go to the next higher step and not to look below, because we'll feel dizzy. But we also know that the higher step also means somebody going down. Maybe I'll go down— we are also aware that as a class we cannot go up, it's impossible. Then my self interest is to demolish that staircase and do something else. That's the long-term interest. But if I try to do that, I cannot try for my promotion. I have to go on with my job but the rest of my time will have to go into something else.

LINA: Who is your audience?

BS: It has a history—it has been the middle classes of Calcutta, the lower middle classes in particular. Because of the street theater movement, different people have called it different things. I use one term now, another at a different time. I have written a book called *Third Theater* in English. You can get a copy from me if you want. I have one in Bengali with more theory which evolved from my practice. Form-wise, we do not perform on the proscenium stage. That we left in 1973. We perform either on the floor of an ordinary room with people sitting where we want them to sit, or in the open air. But that is only one part of it, form-wise. That's not the philosophy of it. The philosophy is free theater. That means the payment of a certain amount of money is not the condition for entrance to theater. It must be voluntary. Even in our Calcutta theater where we had to spend money to hire the hall and some other expenses, we always had our ordinary lecture room which was much cheaper than any regular auditorium. But even there we had a convention of everybody paying a donation of one rupee to get in, and if we came to know that even that one rupee someone could ill afford, it was free. There was a donation box if anyone wanted to pay more, most people forgot anyway. In 1986, you must realize that one rupee is cheaper than the cheapest film ticket and even our audience laughed and said when are you going to make it at least two rupees? For one rupee you can't even buy tea in most shops in Calcutta! But that was our system. In the villages and places where people invited us, we tried to see that people don't sell tickets. If they raised donations for the amount to cover the cost, at least there must not be any distinction between one person and another. First come, first served. Wherever they want to sit; we were strict about that principle though we sometimes got duped.

This term "free" has two meanings: It is free of cost, and the second meaning is wider, not bound, but free. Both apply when the money thing goes and two groups of human beings—the performers and spectators—meet freely as equals not one selling and another buying. I believe that theater is human action. So this free concern is very important to us. Not just the form. We actually feel free, can go anywhere. There are three ways a theater group can raise money: 1) Selling tickets—we don't; selling tickets implies 5–15 rupees! 2) Asking for government grants—we don't even apply for them. 3) Collaborating with business sources like cigarette companies—we can't even think of that, and of course we don't have restrictions, even members don't pay subscriptions. Some small groups work that way, everybody shells out ten rupees a month—but we don't even pay 25 paise a month so far.

And our theater survived. So free theater is possible. Economically we have less problems than other groups.

LINA: That's because you don't have the money.

BS: Yes, but the theater is going on. Many people say theater can't survive without money. In our concept—theater can survive, but their definition of "theater" is different. One is business and the other is not.

LINA: So the audience is the middle class.

BS: I am a middle-class person in Calcutta, I have no starvation problem, my father gave me an education, up to an engineering degree. Then he frankly told me—this is what I can do, nothing else. The rest is up to you. So the plays, the language I write, are about the middle class. They are aimed at the middle class just like me. The protagonist of *Stale News* (*Basi Khabar*) is the Santal revolt but at the same time that is not the purpose of the play. Number one in the chorus is the protagonist. He is reading the stories about the Santals in the newspapers—it's from his point of view. Even in *Bhoma* it is the middle-class person going in search of Bhoma. In *Michil*, again the middle class. "I" is extended to "We"—on the way to getting more and more aware. That kind of journey.

LINA: It's not about maintaining the middle class.

BS: It may be trying to form that nucleus of consciousness and awareness in the middle class. The very small section of the middle class which plays a very important role as a catalytic agent for social change. I do not underestimate that. In the history of revolution or social change—it is done by the energy of the working people. But the conscious middle-class element has always played a great role. Lenin or Mao or the French Revolution! May be our aim in the selection of theater audience is the middle class. Interestingly, I'm saying this in retrospect, as we made our theater free, we could perform in villages. Before we'd have to ask the villagers do you have electricity, motorable roads to take our equipment, money. Now we can just take some bags on our shoulders and carry our own theater. Perform in the open in the daylight. Daylight is not yet taxed. Or even in the evening, put up bamboo poles on four sides and perform in the middle. That freedom we've achieved.

I left the CMPO in1971. As a director of planning, part time, in 1979, I joined the Comprehensive Area Development Corporation. CADC/CMDA was a village project. I got ample opportunity to go to the villages and much of what I put in various plays I got from those experiences. You can read about facts but the facts affect you when you meet people. I can read in the census report about that landless agricultural laborer. Little stories I've heard and things I've seen, that takes one into an emotional plane—not just an intellectual plane. That's when a play comes out. *Bhoma* has radioactivity, dollars, but also underground water. Then we take a play to the village, they find nothing new in it for them. I learned from them in the first place, but they see for the first time that city people are talking about their problems. May be some other people have taken a play about a village to them but that play has been written by a city man who said village people are exploited, that they should revolt. But they have and nothing happens. They have no identification with that kind of false play. But when a play talks about underground water, fertilizer and seed, it is very real to them because they supplied that data to me. The point of identification is there.

LINA: What was the reaction when you showed them *Bhoma*?

BS: In most villages we found wonderful reception. Particularly at Rangabelia—the birthplace of Bhoma, where I got the story of *Bhoma*. There were 6000 people, many children sitting in front, in pin-drop silence. There were inadequate microphones. Then we took a boat and went to another village. Absolutely open, no covering

on top. There 3000 people with at least 500 children. No microphones
and we had pin-drop silence from the children. Clear indication
that we got across.

In Sunderban villages, certain scenes must have gone over their
heads but they didn't mind. And other things they caught on an
emotional plane which is impossible for a city man. Because things
are not in the abstract. *Michil* performed in a village in Burdwan
district, in daytime had 300 people with 250 bare-bodied Santal
peasants and landless laborers. I got nervous. I thought *Michil* has
so many city images, middle-class images and abstract things, how
can we get across to this audience? The second reaction was to
ask: "Why?" *Michil* was as simple as anything. Nothing difficult to
communicate. By intuition, I told the organizers, I want to speak for
five minutes before we start. I didn't know what I'd say but I had the
confidence. All this happened within a few minutes. I started talking
and explained the play. I told them that we are from the city and
can't write about the villages—we don't know them properly. But
we are bringing *Michil* to you, which is about an old man not wanting
to go back to his home, and a young man getting killed —all being
part of your day-to-day experience. City people read of a young man
getting killed in the newspapers. We always think we are out of it.
For them it's a part of life as real as anything. That attitude is real
to them. So *Michil* is absolutely relevant. We all know that . . .

At every place somebody or another joins us. We'll never forget
the experience when an old Sardar from the audience came up and
instead of holding the hand, he embraced the performer and wept.
Later on they asked him, "Why did you weep?" He said, "I don't
know, maybe because you 'called' me (*Aapnara je daklen*)." In
Burdwan district they know Bengali, maybe they are Santals. They
could understand, a clear indication we did get across. In one village,
I remember there was an old Muslim with a long gray beard—he
was sitting right with the children in the front and we were doing
*Laksmichara Panchali*,[1] always a sure success in villages. I've used
*Kabigaan* and *Tarja*[2] forms—village forms in it, and put in what I
found in the villages. A poor peasant owning one *bigha* of land

[1] Tr. Bad Luck Opera.
[2] Pre-modern forms of Bengali performance verse.

becomes a sharecropper, then loses that capacity and becomes a landless laborer. This process is there. One person takes the view of the bosses and the other takes the view of the laborer, and I use Bengali folk tunes. We are always sure of that whenever we go to the villages. I once asked the village people when I had a chance to talk to them—why do you like this play? There's nothing new in it. They were not very articulate but somebody replied in this way: "It's true there is nothing new but we cannot write the way you've written! And placed it! Somebody's done it—and we like it." It happened once that we went to the village and performed that play and another short one, only half an hour. The next year we performed something else and they said you must perform that other play. I said we are not prepared for it—not rehearsed, not the right clothes, we were in trousers—but they insisted and we had to perform it.

Now this old Muslim . . . when we stay overnight we always talk with people. In the morning we went to a village about three kilometers away and there was a small village project. A lady was there—taking me around, inside houses and so on. We walked in and found that we were in the house of the old Muslim, we'd recognized him and got so much feedback from him. I said I don't know if the things I put in it are correct. He said everything you put in is quite correct. I said there may be things difficult to understand and he said why? He started explaining the play to me though he knew I wrote it! All that was so wonderful.

LINA: You think in the rural areas they are more accepting of city people coming to stage plays? Do you also find them trying to have their own theater?

BS: That can happen. The final answer cannot be that city people from the middle classes will prepare plays, go to the villages and perform: up to a point we can do that and it is necessary. The final answer is that village people will make their own plays. I'll tell you my own experience. I ask them if they have any theater? They say that some people perform during the *pujas*. Nothing else. Why not? We can't afford it. Why, what are the costs? They say erecting the stage, hiring draperies, costumes. I say these things are not indispensable in theater, they won't believe me. They have that image, that's why it's necessary for our group to go and perform, then they see that theater does not need all that paraphernalia—does not cost so much. That is one function of the city group. Then when you say—now what do you think? They say we are illiterate—we can't even read a play let alone write one. Then I can't convince them that a play needn't be written. No one has to write or read for the play. For that I do a workshop with them—it's the bread and butter of the process of doing theater. If I do a workshop with them as I have in Rangabelia, they get confidence. What we deprive them of is not just good food, shelter and clothing but self-confidence. That they're worthless—because they're illiterate, they are fools . . . means that we have caused them to think so. The process of the workshop is to give them confidence. It's participation oriented not achievement oriented. Everyone thinks equal in a workshop. After that, at the end of the workshop there is play-making. Each participant has to make a five-minute play in 10 minutes. In a seven-day workshop, I'll probably do it on the sixth day. In Rangabelia, I tried on the second day. I was certain at that time that they'll fall back on *jatra*, all the things they've seen and do a play like that. They surprised me. There was time only for six persons to make plays and all six did plays on their lives, on problems and stories that had happened there. They observed all the rules of the game. Took exactly 10 minutes to prepare a five-minute play.

Later on, at Rangabelia, they continued the workshop process. I didn't dare suggest it to them. When I do it in middle-class workshops they don't follow up but here they decided that twice a week they'll have workshops in the evening. At least half of the people in the workshop were illiterate. The intake was so intense that due to my middle-class upbringing, I thought it was a derivative of education. They have the midday meal working in someone else's field. Instead of going home to eat, which may be 2 km away, they are all very hungry, they come and do the workshop for two hours. Later when I visited the village, I asked casually what are your problems. One of the said: "We are very hungry when we do the workshop." Then I realized what was happening and I raised some donations so that they could get *chola* (roasted chick peas) to eat. Then they made a half-hour play which I saw and later another half-hour play about their problems in their own language, which wouldn't work in Calcutta, but it would work in other villages.

LINA: How is the reaction when you perform for the middle classes in Calcutta? Are plays about the middle class? How would it be if you brought a play prepared in a village to the city? Would they react the same way?

BS: The plays we perform in the city is the same play we take to the village. The reaction in the city is on two different planes. The example of *Michil* I gave you—the concept of Bhoma being killed and the old man not finding his way, city people understand it, but in an abstract level. It's a derivative of our culture and education. It's important and necessary to do that, but the villagers' reaction would not be on an abstract level, but on a much more real plane. Both are very important. *Spartacus* is a better example. It's based on the novel and apparently the structure of *Spartacus* is very sophisticated and middle class. For example, it doesn't tell a story in a narrative fashion. Secondly, space and time jumps the audience backwards. There is more than one scene where two different items and spaces are in the same scene, happening at the same time, and city people take in sophisticated structural things. *Spartacus* was done equally well in cities and villages but in the cities I could see that the appreciation was on an abstract level. In the villages, it's the toil and the suffering, the blood and the sweat, and the revolt of the slaves—that's what they identify with at a real level. In Bengal, the only folk form the villagers are exposed to is the *jatra*. *Jatra* has a lot of dialogue and melodramatic acting. A long heroic speech goes on and up to a crescendo and the performers and the owner of the *jatra* company expect applause at that point. There is a story, real or a joke, that if a performer does not get applause at an exact time, then he doesn't get fish for dinner! In *Spartacus* when the first revolt takes place, the gladiator doesn't speak. Shouting and energetic action—quite unfamiliar to them. Almost invariably we had applause then. It's quite easy to understand because they wanted for a long time for the slaves to revolt, so when they actually revolted, they applauded. I directed *Spartacus* in the Manipuri language—there was a three-week workshop ending with a work-in-progress performance. I said I wanted an arena, they had *mandaps*: mats on the floor, beaten earth, roof, small raised walls. They invited people to come in and sit, but people stood outside, waiting. They didn't dare come in so I told the authorities, can I ask the people to come in? They didn't like it very much but couldn't object. So I went out and asked them to come. The children came in happily but the adults refused. They knew that the Secretary of State, the Big Boss was there—they didn't want to come in and sit on the same mats. They stood there! At the revolt scene, applause came from outside.

LINA: So you do translations from other non-Bengali stories?

BS: We take from any source. Our purpose is certain themes and certain subjects, things we feel about strongly. So an adaptation doesn't matter! For example, when we did Brecht's *Caucasian Chalk Circle*—most of the Brecht productions here were done because the people wanted to "do a Brecht." That wasn't our case. We did it because I thought *Chalk Circle* is very much an Indian play and contemporary play. That's my fundamental understanding of the play. The child should go to the mother who loves the child, the land should go to the tiller who digs the soil. That is very real, very contemporary. We had the greatest appreciation in Rangabelia when we performed. We had 3000 to 4000 people in the audience. I threw away the entire prologue. I edited and adapted it in our language.

   *Woza Albert* was on apartheid. It's a peculiar history, two black South Africans—actors, singers, dancers got together in a theater company and read some books on theater like Grotowski and Peter Brooks and became serious. They gave up smoking and drinking and started exercising and they had a dream of doing a play themselves—the two of them. Ultimately, when they were unemployed they approached a director, presumably white (it is not written in the book), who made a name doing theater with a mixed cast and an all black cast and also working out a play while working with the performers. They approached him so when the book was published the three names are there, the two performers and the director. They had a novel approach—very foreign to our country. When Jesus Christ comes back, the Second coming, and he comes to South Africa—what will happen to him? The Bible image is very foreign here. Maybe some middle-class people know about apartheid. The other day I found in a village a woman, a graduate teacher. I didn't even mention the word "apartheid" but asked if she knew anything about South Africa and what was happening there. She knew that Africa is a continent and that's where we stopped. I liked the play but we couldn't possibly communicate with Bible images and South Africa. They didn't listen to me, and we had two performances in Calcutta which was all right. It is called *Sada-Kalo* ("White and Black"). A member of our group directed it. We don't know about the Bible but the play communicates a lot. It took a long time and the performers made a good job of it. Next Sunday we are going to perform it in a village for the first time.

LINA: It's like the play in which Krishna is born in a prison—that kind of symbolism.

BS: It came to me whether I can transplant the whole thing to an Indian context—but I refrained from it. We are talking about South Africa, so to put a Krishna or mythical image is to destroy the whole thing. So I added some lines and almost indicated the story of the Bible and introduced a new song right in the beginning where I mentioned the principal facts of South Africa—10 percent land owned by 90 percent black people—that kind of thing. The song explains, so there should be no confusion. In this village, next Sunday, I intend to talk for five minutes, about what has happened in South Africa, and then we'll perform the play. It will be our test case.

LINA: Do you feel there is hope for Calcutta? It has changed a lot over the last few years and it keeps deteriorating slowly. Do you feel hopeful about Calcutta now? About theater in Calcutta? Do you feel you can write plays about a dying city? Or you don't think it is dying?

BS: The second question I've already answered. I do not consider myself a writer. Sometimes I write a play in seven days and for three years I don't write anything. If I finish I think this is the last play I've written. When I wrote *Michil* (*Procession*), Calcutta was very much in my mind. In the beginning I had an intention, which was to write a collage on Calcutta. I started from that and somehow it got transformed and became *Michil*. Calcutta is the city of processions. I have little pieces in my notes on Calcutta collages which I did not use in *Michil*. I do not have any intention to write a play on Calcutta now. Calcutta is a city I have always loved and hated. In your sane mind you cannot "like" Calcutta. You either love it or hate it. A colleague of mine asked me if I do like Calcutta? The answer came to me—you can't like it! If I stay away from Calcutta for a long time I miss it. It is my work place and at the same time I try to escape it. Our motive force is not hope.

From 1957–59 when I was in Britain, I missed Calcutta like anything. Even in 1964–67 when I was in Nigeria, I missed Calcutta. I made absurd plans to go back though I couldn't afford it. I don't feel it's my home. It's my work place. Where else can I work? Maybe I can work in other places now, but the language is the question. I don't know if I'm up to learning a new language. I'm not very good at learning languages. There is a lot of action in south India. The workshops in the south always get very good response. But I can't see myself learning Tamil or Kannada or Malayalam now. The way I work: what else could I have done? It's not hoping to achieve something. It's become a way of life. Right from my early days I couldn't conform to just going to office, coming back and occupying myself with the family. In the leisure time I had to do something. So now naturally I have lost all social contact. My relatives and old friends—that kind of life I can't have. My society, my life is with these theater people. Not even belonging to my generation. If we want to go see a film we try to see if some people of our group will go or not. It's about groups now, colleagues, groups.

Many people ask me what I hope to achieve through my theater. Is what I am trying to say through theater being communicated? In some ways I think this is irrelevant to us. We can hope to achieve communication—get across to five people out of 500. And one can never gauge what the depth of the effect is on that person. He himself may not know it. I've made choices, we live by choices— minor and major. And every choice at a certain point in time is a result made in the past. How can we really analyze when we make a choice—that this choice has been influenced by such and such book, or such and such talk. Why try to gauge at all how much effect it's had. But in some ways—like this old Muslim peasant explaining the play *Bhoma*, the people digging the canal in Rangabelia and the headmaster of the village, who was also the project director, trying to provoke him, we said: "You like it, you say you understand it. What is there to like: no costume, no nothing." And he just looked away for some time and said: "There is nothing difficult in it for poor people not to understand it. Maybe rich people won't understand it." That reply is an asset to us, and hope. That, or the old Santal embracing somebody and weeping—this does things—it's positive. Helps us to fight many frustrations. At the same time since we perform during the day there are 300 children and only 30 adults. The children are unruly and the adults don't stop them. So it's extremely frustrating to perform in such a situation. While performing I can still see the impressions on the faces of some of the adults, despite the (children's) noise. They are trying to get it. In our kind of theater we get a direct feedback. The audience is never hiding in the dark. Not really trying to estimate the result of the achievements. We have to go on because we have no other way.

LINA: They say that Calcutta is 63–64 percent non-Bengali, and eventually there will be less and less Bengalis since they'll move out to the suburbs. Non-Bengalis, mostly migrant laborers from Bihar and so on—does that bother you and is that a theme you are interested in?

BS: It's difficult to answer whether it disturbs me or not. Many other things disturb me much more. I think this is bound to happen in a country like ours—a colonial country. The difference between the metro area and the rural areas is bound to happen. The non-Bengalis coming is happening at two levels: laborers come to the city, because of destitution and poverty. That's bound to happen if the total economy doesn't change, and the rural areas do not become self-sufficient. I would much rather deal with that phenomenon on the level of the country as a whole than be bothered by what is happening only in Calcutta or Bombay. It's a part of the whole and the whole is more important to me.

LINA: But as a Bengali and looking at the phenomenon in Bombay with the Shiv Sena—Maharashtra for the Maharashtrians—will this happen in Bengal?

BS: I don't know. For the last one or two years we (like-minded people in theater) are becoming very concerned about this tremendous onslaught of big business in our culture. If you take culture in terms of TV serials—they are making a drastic change in the urban culture. At one time, for the serious theater people, Sunday was the best day to perform. Some theater halls charged more on Sundays than other days. Now Sunday is one of the worst days. Because a Hindi film is scheduled every Sunday, as a theatre group we cannot compete with the TV. In winter we have Third Theater performances at Ahindra Mancha and Muktamancha. In Kanchrapara, we preferred Sundays. Each Sunday different groups would come. Last Sunday our performance had very poor audience. There were 500–600 people but we were expecting many more. Everyone was watching TV. These things are happening. And it's big business—TV serials are big. Sports, for example, are a craze deliberately being created. First a slow process of craze for "stardom." Whether cricket star or film star—it's the same thing. The whole phenomenon of comic strips is a cult of idiocy. An absurdity, and people become addicts. There is no difference between addiction to food, or indifferent TV serials, Hindi films, comic strips and in a way sports also—there isn't any difference from drug addiction—brown sugar or cocaine. It's the same thing. We are very concerned, it's hitting us directly. It is becoming increasingly difficult to pierce through this wall.

Calcutta has always been enthusiastic about certain things like Test matches, or a Ritwik Ghatak film—when he was alive, nobody saw his films but now they'll go. Calcutta people will always flock to see whatever, dancing, singing or the Soviet circus. They'll not only go, they'll wait day after day, night after night to buy tickets. It's a craze, it has a snowball effect. They have spent so much energy and time and money to get a ticket that after they go they have to convince themselves that what they've seen is a lifetime's experience—a psychological thing.

LINA: I thought it was a hunger for culture!

BS: It used to be at one time but not now. Now it's the "craze," the thing I've got to see so that I can tell others I've seen it. That's the greatest enemy of culture. This wasn't there in Calcutta before but it's spreading fast. Even today, there are discerning sections of the middle class but this onslaught is very difficult to withstand. People do write in the newspaper about the idiot box but it's not enough to fight the craze. When TV came I thought it was going to be contained among the upper classes, but now people will starve to get a TV set!

LINA: So you would look at the problem of why people are pushed from the rural areas into the city instead of looking at the problem of the city?

BS: I wouldn't make distinctions like that. Rather take different facets of truth which are relevant to the question of awareness and the necessity of social change.

LINA: Fifteen years ago, Bengalis used to get agitated about the level of awareness and now they seem apathetic.

BS: I have my own reading that the youth have always been on the Left politically—a revolutionary thing has always been there. I believe the political consciousness of the Calcutta students may be compared to any place in the world. In Britain and America it's practically dead. They aren't knowledgeable about what's happening. But Calcutta students have always been quite knowledgeable about what's happening internationally.

LINA: Not today though.

BS: The Naxalite movement came and many students thought that revolution was round the corner. Many brilliant students left their careers, got beaten, suffered, were killed . . . the revolution did not happen and there's bound to be a tremendous frustration. Some people conform, some become inactive and cynical. Only a small minority realize that revolution will not happen tomorrow or in their lifetime—that it is a painstaking process. Those people are searching in their own ways. Going to the villages, doing theater, various movements in small schools, in slums . . . but the apathy is there.

Fascism would never happen in India because it needs efficiency! This huge host of unemployed, this apathy—the youth is easy prey now to drugs, alcoholism. Even today West Bengal is one of the least communal states, least conscious of differences even in villages. All these religious obscurantism, today is amusing to youths, but it's not impossible that they'll sway one way or the other. This is the time strong revolutionary leadership was needed but . . . I don't know which way it will go. But just now I find that this kind of idiotic culture or idiocy culture is taking them over. But there may be some other cult which may be far worse than this—the minority consciousness will face odds which can't be overcome, that's what I'm afraid of.

LINA: Someone defined you as an avant-garde playwright. Do you object to that?

BS: I don't object to anything people say about me. These terms don't mean anything to me. I do not do theater to become avant-garde. It may be a valid reason for an artist to explore new possibilities in that art form. We do explore, but for a completely different reason. We explore a new form to find a form most suited for our theme. As effectively and intensely as possible. Apart from the content, ours is not an experimental theater that way. At the same time we have to do a lot of experiments. *Sada-Kalo* was a challenge. We've never worked on such a play before. In its time *Spartacus* was a challenge, *Bhoma* was a challenge and poetry montage—when we began theater work we didn't even know the meaning of poetry montage. And the play we're working on now is also a challenge. It's a play collage so I do explore but not for the sake of exploring and evolving a new form. It's the theme which is important. Avant-garde is applicable to those people who for many valid artistic reasons want to evolve a new form.

LINA: Calcutta will allow the performance of much varied theater—political, traditional; is there possibility for all of your open theater.

BS: I still think that Calcutta is a place where this can be done more than any other place. But it depends, maybe in another place it hasn't yet been tried . . .

LINA: But at the same time, theater in Calcutta is not just entertainment.

BS: As a matter of fact that is also a part of the history of the theater movement. It's what we call a "group theater movement." It started in the early 50's.

# Utpal Dutt

LINA: Would the anti-fascist period in Bengal have been the right time to stage Brechtian plays?

UTPAL DUTT: On the contrary, it would have derailed like the anti-fascist movement itself: it would have gone over the heads of the people, especially the peasants.

LINA: Most of the plays are not for peasants!

UD: Yes, but in the country, where an overwhelming number of people live—if one wants to create a theater movement one has to link up with the masses. If one wants to be successful financially or make avant-garde theater one will end up in the cities. To have a truly successful theater movement one would have to analyze the needs of the masses: content wise and form wise. Anti-fascism was great content, but not the way it was presented to the masses. During the Emergency we used Brecht and called it *Barricade*.

LINA: To go back to the concept of theater. Is it necessary to have a moral quality in the plays and if so, where does the luxury to choose come from? Is it for a particular elite to decide in a city like Calcutta or for the rural people say in Bankura.

UD: A play need not have a moral point. A play should avoid moral points because theater has nothing to do with morality. But a play should make a political point.

There are two kinds of plays and both are equally important. Agitational and Propaganda. An agitational play takes a stand on a day-to-day issue, day-to-day politics. Then there is the openly propagandist play which makes its points brazenly. During elections, you find street corner plays which abandon subtlety altogether for the sake of their own party. The debate is fought out on the stage. It's a foregone conclusion that the proletariat will win. If the bourgeoisie are to win, we have to go to a street corner play organized by the Congress (I). The more parties involved, the more truthful it becomes.

LINA: So you find that the ideologically based plays are more successful in Calcutta? Yet Calcutta is ideologically divided.

UD: The agitational plays are all over West Bengal. Cooch Behar and Siliguri to Canning.

LINA: Isn't that a new phenomenon since Independence?

UD: It is. In 1961, the entire Communist Party leadership was behind bars so street corner plays were organized to popularize the information. But the other kind of play is called propaganda. Propaganda must be subtle to be successful. It tries to destroy people's confidence in the current social order and the more surreptitiously it works the better the result. For example, Maxim Gorky never wrote a play in which the class struggle is even directly mentioned, but the audience watching his plays had something happen to them unknown to them—they began to lose confidence in the social order. They began to wish for its destruction. Brecht would say the play should make people think.

LINA: What would you say?

UD: I would say the play should rouse emotions. Thinking is good but is only a part of the mental make-up of the audience. They should be emotionally charged. To make revolution you need courage and hatred. A person has to hate so much that he can no longer sit still.

LINA: I can hear one of my uncles talk. What would make Bengalis move? What type of play would change minds in this city? I have been coming here since 1967, since I was an undergraduate, and to me it seems that Bengalis in Calcutta have reached a pinnacle and they've come down, and never went back up to where they should be. As an outsider it appears to me that something is not happening.

UD: I think you mean qualitative change all at once. When change is qualitative, there will be revolution.

LINA: It's almost in the make-up of the Bengali person never to accept what's given! Now I find that they take anything. They are not agitated enough to change anything. And I'm wondering if there is a medium for change.

UD: The Bengali audience is ferociously critical. They don't accept everything that you show just because it's there. They have to ask, criticize. Theater is only a part of the entire cultural web in the hand of the proletariat. We must think about the weapons in the hand of the ruling classes. They are far more powerful. TV, radio, newspapers: it's a miracle that the people can take all that and stay cool and judge for themselves. This can't go on for long. They must either lose or win everything, as Mao Tse Tung put it.

Theater is only a small part of this arsenal. It is significant that the ruling class can't use theater. They have no effective weapon in theater to counter our propaganda. No theater group to take their ideas to the people. After all these years and money they haven't been able to form an effective theater group or theater.

LINA: Are you talking about the national government or the local government?

UD: The central government. They try to buy people off by giving them contracts on TV. But they haven't been able to form an alternative theater movement. What they do is bring outside theater groups from West Germany, New York—people often rejected by their own people. They always make a point of saying that they are touring India but actually they come straight to Calcutta, perform here and go back to Europe. In Calcutta, they try to counter our propaganda this way.

LINA: According to your understanding of theater and propaganda what is the distinction between theater as a basis of a particular ideology and theater as a part of a culture? If one can really distinguish politics and culture.

UD: I can't.

LINA: You are a Bengali and have a distinct political leaning to the Left—do you find an ambivalence in yourself?

UD: I know that only if my country overthrows the ruling class can it protect its own culture. Otherwise this country will be destroyed. The working class has no culture of its own. It has nothing to lose but its chains. Marx meant that literally. They have no culture, no tradition, nothing. They drink in the evening and they are so exhausted and drunk that they have no time for cultural pursuits. So they are given cheap entertainment. In all the industrial areas of India, the people who preserve culture during the feudal period and the bourgeois regime are the peasants who still retain some old elements, traditional forms of the past. Provided they live far away from the city. The more so-called capitalist civilization advances towards the villages, the more local people lose everything. Capitalism mechanizes their lives without giving them anything in return.

LINA: You don't think that a Left ideology would also mechanize their mind?

UD: No. But they should think differently from what they think now. The peasant is not a conscious guardian of culture—just the inheritor. That's why he loses it so easily at the first impact of industrialization. Britain, for example, had beautiful folk dances which they lost. You can still see some in Scotland but not in England. Look at the Soviet Union, a vast country with at least 250 different peoples or nations living in it, and they've saved them all. I wish we could see tonight at Kala Mandir a lot of folk dances . . . The Soviets have also industrialized, but since their industry is not for capitalist profit, they also take care of the people building the industries.

LINA: Someone told me that you are running a TV serial?

UD: We made a four-part serial called Insurgent Theater out of which they showed three parts and banned the fourth.

LINA: Why?

UD: They've given us objections. Ridiculous!

LINA: Were you doing a historical analysis of theater?

UD: Bengali theater was used as an example. We were trying to find out the principal ingredients of theater in general, and to illustrate we used the history of the Bengali theater. The fourth part was about violence in the arts. We were trying to explain why all great drama depends on violence, towering acts of violence. Starting from *Othello* we made our way to Bengali plays and *Arturo Ui*. We were trying to make the point that theater shows violence because life is violent. If theater did not show violence it would be naïve. If it wants to be truthful, theater has to be violent until violence is abolished in society.

LINA: Perhaps they interpreted it as violence perpetrated by a particular government in power.

UD: Also, there was a montage. We took the Odessa steps sequence from Eisenstein's *Battleship Potemkin* to show how various art forms deal with the state's preparation of violence. Their objection was peculiar. It's worded like this: "In the middle there is an old Russian film which is too long"—they didn't know what it was!

LINA: It's almost like turn of the century Bengali theater when they were having problems with bans. They have to go around it like in *Karagar*: symbolism is perhaps where the difficulty lies. Theater here is connected to everything else. I don't see theater in the US playing a revolutionary role. Perhaps theater in Egypt, Latin America.

In your vision of Calcutta of yesterday and today, what are some of the things you feel have gone astray? A lot of people talk of a general apathy of Bengalis to their city: seen in scenes like someone dying and nobody comes to help . . .

UD: This happens in Delhi—not Calcutta.

LINA: It happened in Ballygunge, the Swinhoe Street area, where a bleeding man was lying on the street. The whole day I was obsessed with this. I thought I knew Calcutta. He was there for an hour and a half bleeding—and I was just standing there screaming: finally somebody called the police.

UD: Where were the people sitting around? Had they beaten him up?

LINA: He had been hurt before and fell right there.

UD: And you spoke with Bengalis? It cannot happen!

LINA: I thought it happened only in Delhi and Bombay.

UD: This is one city, where if you're in trouble, people help.

LINA: But nowadays people don't like to get involved. You must admit that there is a new person emerging in the city now.

UD: And he is a very nice person. He's far more disciplined and really interested in life, politics, the state and the country.

LINA: But there is also a person emerging here, who is uncaring, self-centered, and only interested in furthering his own gains. And I really think this goes across classes.

UD: For example the petit-bourgeoisie, the lower middle class, is the most selfish, ignorant, self-centered class ever, because it is dying.

LINA: Yes, but they are the people whose forbears held some values once. Now they are gone.

UD: They are no longer guardians of values because they can't see them themselves. They've been taken over by other classes. It's just taking time. I have heard these condemnations about changes in the city—mostly from the petit-bourgeoisie. They used to love it once, they can't now.

LINA: So you're saying, if it's dying, that's fine.

UD: A dying class should die quickly.

LINA: And the new class will have fewer restrictions?

UD: They've got nothing to lose and so they don't try to acquire anything. They know they can't save money. What's happening, for example, is that a large section of the petit-bourgeoisie used to own land in the villages. They used to take away the surplus from the peasants, and spend the money in Calcutta. This class has been destroyed in Bengal by the *Panchayat* system. It's their constant lamentation that the Left government has robbed them. They are the ones spreading stories of how terrible everything is. I hear them always when I go to shoot outside in big houses in the villages.

LINA: The upper classes don't bother with values. Do you see a parallel between what happened to the elite who made it big during the time of the British and during the twenties and thirties? They lost out to the younger generation not interested in imbibing Britishness but bringing out the best in their own culture. Do you see the same thing happening now? The same class losing out again now?

UD: The British created a class of clerks and that class was supportive of the British.

LINA: What are you working on now?

UD: Doing a Bengali translation of *Mother Courage*.

LINA: Are you still active in the rural areas?

UD: Yes, especially with regard to agitational plays. About 80 to 100 theater groups go out into the countryside.

LINA: Are things better in rural areas in terms of a reaction to plays and the themes presented by you?

UD: I would say that the best audience is in the industrial areas—especially where there are Bengali workers. Hindustani workers find it difficult to understand Bengali plays. But the slightly more politically conscious Bengali worker is the best audience, followed closely by the peasants. But the Calcutta audience is definitely third. Nowhere near.

LINA: But that's a new development for Calcutta over the last six or seven years. A change in thinking. It used to be the place where you could see Left-oriented plays which had a message other than just entertainment. But not today. More and more people see plays they don't have to think about. They can go home, eat their *bhat* and *dal* and forget everything.

UD: Except for a few theater groups like ours many groups play to empty houses. Twenty years back this wasn't the case. Any play would be packed. But you go outside the city limits and the tickets are sold out—25000 to 30000 people at a time. Huge *jatra pandals*.

LINA: This must terrify any political party with a different message—like the Congress (I). Would they impose a ban?

UD: The law for bans has been abolished in West Bengal, but they can attack directly. *Goondas* and so on. It has happened to us but it doesn't stop us. We did a play called *Nightmare City*.

LINA: In Calcutta?

UD: Yes, first here and then all over. In 1975 or so when Siddharth Shankar Ray—the then Chief Minister of West Bengal—used to shoot the Naxals. We were frank. And they attacked with bombs. They started a case: Sedition Law Section 124. As long as the court case is on, the play can't run. They lost the election and we changed the name as we toured West Bengal.

LINA: Who wrote it?

UD: I did. There was an English translation.

LINA: Why did you opt to go into TV?

UD: You use every medium you can. People like my work, especially the old plays. They found the old theater far more dramatic, colorful and full of action than present-day theater.

Are you coming back to Calcutta? We'll be back from the Soviet Union in June.

LINA: How about doing *Nightmare City* Part II?

UD: These agitational plays are very difficult to stage after some time. All the references are so current.

LINA: Does it disturb you that 46 percent of Calcutta is Bengali and the rest are non-Bengali?

UD: This happens in all metropolitan cities. Do they want that only Bengalis should live in this city? And who built this city?

LINA: It's a historical accident that the British built it.

UD: And all the masons who built the houses. Hardly any one of them was Bengali.

LINA: But people are upset because they feel that in a decade or two this city will have no identification with Bengali history, language, values. However they don't realize that they too have changed. They criticize people for imbibing western education, but they're doing it themselves.

UD: You can't put history back and the further it goes ahead the happier we shall be.

# Jochhan Dastidar

LINA: How do the media you use look at the idea of Bengali culture? Is it important to worry about Bengali culture?

JOCHHAN DASTIDAR: I do theater, write plays, and I have a business—interior decoration. I have begun to concentrate on TV serials. I am now working on *Sei Somoy* by Sunil Ganguly. This was a controversial novel. When the British first came, the process, the state in which Bengalis were at the time, the type of people the *babus* were, these are the subject of the novel. The author has facts that people dispute. The controversy has made the novel very popular now. People are very keen on watching the serial on TV and will attack me if I make any mistakes. About 18 percent of West Bengal reads, 25 percent read newspapers. Novels are read by eight percent so the rest who *may have* read the novel is a minute percentage. But three million people watch TV in a single day in Calcutta/West Bengal. Naturally I am worried about my neck.

I have been doing plays for at least 30 years. Non-professional or "group" theater. I belong to Charbak. I have had quite a few experiences over these 30 years. We are social beings and our plays reflect this. In today's newspaper there is an article on the 15 percent increase in the price of petrol. That will mean a rise in the cost of theater production. We take the taxi to work and the cost of props will also rise. It will all come out of the pocket of the public: the price of tickets will go up. Everything is based on the economy. If your financial position goes up by even a little bit it will influence and affect us.

I'll talk about performance and plays, problems and what can be done to solve the problems. When we started doing plays the rate for hiring halls was 500 rupees for four to five hours. That was the highest rate. Usually less. Now the minimum is 1200 rupees. But income hasn't doubled. All the things we needed we used to get cheaper. We can put up fewer shows now than before. We put up more plays nowadays than before because more people invite us to do so. They "hire" us, so to speak. But there have been changes in the economy, industry, politics. Those were the days when people believed in the Communists but they have been in power a long time with not much improvement in peoples' lives. So the belief is fading. People used to come to theater out of ideological belief, now that belief is gone.

The social condition is such that there are no ideological and intellectual conflicts—at least there are less. There was a time when we felt that if we perform a certain play it will be good for the community. Now we see that we can do very little to change society by doing plays. Then we felt we could make a tremendous difference. That is the negative side. Also at that time the economic structure was not unfavorable. Now it is frightening because the majority of youth who come to do plays are unemployed students. As soon as exams come up or they get jobs, they give up theater. Those who are unemployed get insulted at home but they continue. But as the recriminations at home increase, they give up theater. As a result, the questions of motivation, ideological commitment and unemployment are very major.

LINA: Why don't upper-class people do theater? Status? They and the middle class are the audience.

JD: I haven't analyzed it but I think that they are born and brought up in such a way that they feel no responsibility towards society. They are selfish. A friend's son acts with my group. His father didn't really like it. The son loves theater, mixed with theater people but if he were to take up the theater with me day and night, his father would object. But his son has gone to America to study for four years away from his country, a loss for the country. A typical middle-class attitude. The British have left many years ago, then it wasn't such a craze, but now to study English is a craze. As soon as a child is born people try to get that child into an English-medium school. There is a reason for it. If they can get into an English school they can get better jobs. It is the orientation to get a job. That's the important factor. A play of ours, after five shows, experiences a 15 percent change of performers because actors leave. A core remains which keeps it going. You have to understand that the mentality has to go with the economic situation at present. I get home at 11:30 pm, sleep at 12:30, wake at 5:30 am and I am ready by seven. It's not part of my livelihood—but because I've done theater for 30 years I can't stop, it's an addiction. Those who in earlier times had this same passion for the theater were whole-time theater people. Now they are part-timers. If I put all my time and intellect in theater it would benefit, but I can't do it.

LINA: That's the problem with Bengalis. They talk about theater as best they can but they don't support it.

JD: The plays being performed and the groups which do good, committed theater are all Left-oriented. IPTA, Ramaprasanna Banik . . . x, y, z . . . are all Left-oriented. I am Left-oriented. But I am not conservatively Left. I think that whoever is doing good work is my kind of person. That's my personal philosophy.

My dramas should be bought and performed by people of any political persuasion. The political-economic situation in India is so terrible that there can no longer be friendship between members of "opposing" party platforms. Party affiliation is primary. Elimination is the goal: physically, culturally, philosophically. I don't want to convey or let differences stand.

Throughout India things are static. The cultures are static. Theater can't be good and progressive where the politico-economic situation is static. In West Bengal our culture entailed respect for elders; not to hurt our parents; to help and advise our juniors; to stand up for the underdog, the ill, the attacked, the homeless; to tell the truth.

Our festivals deal with this truth—bring up the truth that you must not introduce partisanship into them since they are for the enjoyment and for community spirit. I face a dilemma if four people beat someone up on the street. I will want my son to be involved. But I will not tell him to go and help! Each to his own—we are becoming selfish. Individual houses become an oasis. We talk to each other, but soon even that will go.

This society must be changed! The whole Indian society. I feel that India—*Bharatvarsha*—is slowly disintegrating. It may or may not happen in my lifetime. It will be terrible if India breaks up and I become a West Bengali. I will need a passport to go to Bihar. A tragedy but it will happen because we don't think what harm can befall if India disintegrates. We don't see the danger because we are too self-seeking. We need to be united, to work for others.

Recently there has been a lot of controversy about *sati* in Rajasthan. The evil rituals and practices, religious dogmas keep us back. We have to keep telling everyone how awful it is. We have to educate, to create anew after breaking this system! Caste, all discrimination, everything.

All cultures are breaking up in India. If by culture we mean that I can worship the way I have for 100 years and the ritual is the same, than I'll say it's not culture but blindness. Under-educated conservatism. Culture means progress. I must know whatever is going on in the world that is of value, and I shall use it to build myself as a man.

This is what is static now. We have to reconstruct a sense of our old values in order to have our real culture.

LINA: Who is trying to have the old values?

JD: No one: theater has some duties—writing and media like newspapers and TV.

LINA: Not TV, it is controlled by a single ideology.

JD: It is mostly privately owned. Our new dramas are based on reality. Before there was *Satidaha*; now the name is different, the process the same. That is the theme of our new drama. I had a paper cutting— we have Manasa *Puja*. People from all over wanted new problems solved. Suddenly somebody said that for all the problems and evils three people were responsible and taking a knife he killed them. Then the police came and took him away. People were fleeing in fear, a baby fell and was crushed to death underfoot. Later we heard that there was a land dispute, which is why the incident took place. See how religion can camouflage so much; we must fight against this! But at the same time we want to be in control of the needed social changes. My wife, my son, and I work together and understand each other. But we can't share our prosperity. We don't!

LINA: Whether you are Janata, CPI(M) or Congress and the director of a play, can you get across a Bengali sense of culture and maintain your political views?

JD: I don't belong to a party. I believe in Marxism. I am not a member of CPI(M) or CPI. Supreo is an intimate friend—I see him only occasionally. If I have any problem he'll come. Philosophically he belongs to the Congress side. I believe in human deeds, mankind. He may belong to any party, but he's my friend, my man. And I must do something for him. That is my philosophy.

LINA: Do you consider yourself to be a universal person?

JD: You don't stop at a crossroads and decide. You just go along one road without question, whether right or wrong. We have a narrow point of view.

LINA: In theater, can you distinguish between politics and culture?

JD: No. Politics is part of your life. If the price of petrol goes up, ultimately people pay. In the life of every individual the social problems are manmade: a part of political strategies, processes, and ideologies. From the time you are born you are in a political periphery. In democracy the so-called "Representatives" control government and you have to see what motivates this handful, what propels their actions which lead to the fact that my son can't have milk to drink and go to school. How can I, a man of drama, solve it? I have to think of politics. Those who say "I am neutral" are fools.

LINA: But will your ideology overshadow your values?

JD: No, it won't. In my work I try to convert by exposing the truth: showing who are the enemies of the people, not any party. Things are bad in India—all over the world—but I can speak of India. They are becoming incapable of understanding the present situation.

LINA: They lack leadership. In Sei Somoy, it is not political. Do you only do political plays?

JD: They do but I don't care. In Doordarshan there is a report, "How did J. Dastidar get a time slot. He's a Communist, that's why." I am a license holder though, given by the central government. I am a playwright—I am a citizen of India and no matter what my political predilections are, I have every right to say what I feel. I can put my opinion out. I chose *Sei Somoy* because it criticizes *babu* culture. Bengali people lived so lavishly, but now their position is pitiful. In *Sei Somoy*, Sunil Ganguly addresses what the Bengali culture was in a particular situation. If you are a widow you had to observe certain customs. An 11-year-old girl has to return home, is barely given food to eat. Goes to the theater and asks for water, she's licking the tears, the water, off her cheeks. Any changes? Maybe five percent. But not really.

LINA: So it is a social community and Bengali society? Can you say there is a uniform Calcutta culture today?

JD: What's that? I don't know. It could be an admixture of many cultures. I belong to the *babu* culture—a mixture of so many things.

LINA: How can you attack it then?

JD: Because I know it, because I belong to it. I can criticize it. I am a citizen of a bad area.

LINA: When you say *babu* culture, do you mean a class culture or a traditional culture?

JD: A middle-class culture. In certain villages—the moneyed people ran everything. Even now but there are more people. Now not only the financially well-off, but also the political big wigs. The physically powerful control the strings. But it's still an elite—a fraction of the total population. Calcutta is a mixture of many cultures.

LINA: But 100 years ago they spoke of a typical Calcutta culture.

JD: That is gone now.

LINA: Somebody recently told me that a new Bengali is coming up and he's not a middle-class *babu*, but a lower-class person who will bring new values and culture to society.

JD: I do admit to this.

LINA: But this new person will aspire to *babu* culture too. How can you stop it? You see that in China, Russia, anywhere. The new man has to be a Left politician?

JD: Congress isn't going to survive. There is going to be a regional party breakup. What Utpal-da says about the emergence of the new person is going to be partial, he'll be partly *babu* culturized after a process. But I know that in my own life a new force will emerge, control, and change the entire cultural scene. It'll be good for Bengal.

LINA: Congress won't make a headway in Bengal, but Communists are losing Calcutta because the middle classes feel threatened.

JD: That's not the fact. The Congress work is not much here, but their name is in the blood of Indians because of nationalism. In every history book you see the Congress. Why people believe in CPI(M) is not philosophically but because they feel it works well. Often the CPI(M) works only marginally in places. Traditionally Congress stays on: a blindness. But this is disappearing rapidly. Even in theater my audience is Left-oriented. Now we get a mix. We have TV stars because people want to see them. At our last show we had tickets selling in the black, to see the stars. After seeing the stars, they watch the dramas.

As long as things are in the hands of *babus* there will be obstacles.

LINA: Do you object to the fact that Calcutta is falling into the hands of non-Bengalis?

JD: Definitely. But nothing can be done. Look at the Maharashtrians. They're mad because they don't want Punjabis and Gujaratis in their state. Something will happen now. As long as Communists are in West Bengal there won't be factionalism, regionalism, communalism, but the anger is there.

LINA: Is it because Bengalis lack parochialism?

JD: Yes, and also the party preaches internationalism—a different kind of nationalism. After Mrs Gandhi was killed, there were no reprisals against Sikhs in Calcutta.

# Samik Banerjee

LINA: When did you start the work with Seagull?

SAMIK BANERJEE: I was a university lecturer in English Literature and Theater at Rabindra Bharati University at Jorasanko (Tagore's House). In 1973, I became an editor with Oxford University Press in Calcutta. I was already writing about plays and was basically a drama critic, independently, even while I was teaching. So when I came to Oxford University Press one of the first things I took over was a series of Indian plays in translation—a series called "The New Drama in India." We published about four or five scripts. This was the first series of contemporary Indian plays in translation. But we had a lot of other work. In 1982, I left and Seagull Books came to me.

Basically, there was an organization called Seagull Empire which was doing a lot of things. Seagull Empire has a wide range of impresario sponsorship of shows which included Bengali language theater in Calcutta, music and dance and western plays. There was an important tour; the National Theater of the Deaf from the United States. The entire Indian tour was looked after by Seagull. The tour started in Calcutta, around 1977–78. But I didn't have anything to do with it. What happened in 1982 was a chance thing. In 1982, I had come to have a strong ideological resistance to the English language theater in Calcutta. Plays being done by local actors in English, Shakespeare, and contemporary stuff. Plays which had no bearing. Fashionable exercises for upper-crust society. A sort of gesture. I was ideologically committed to Bengali theater, Indian theater. This is a middle-class city with a whole code of thinking. Ideologically I had nothing to do with Seagull but somehow in 1982, as a kind of a fallout of the tour of the National Theater of the Deaf, there was also an organization for a Deaf Theater called The Action Players in Calcutta, which was already there and had been working in close collaboration with the National Theater of the Deaf. The Action Players were being supported by Seagull. I saw an Action Players' show and at that time I used to write a regular weekly column for one of the English language dailies in Calcutta. I had a lot of good things to say about the Action Players and what I said at one point was why Seagull has to support this kind of stuff—a slant to this piece. After this, the Seagull people came to me and appreciated my criticism and said that they had also started feeling for the first time that there was something grossly irrelevant about the kind of work they were doing. They had enough commercial sponsorships to do other kinds of things. So they asked if I had any ideas they could promote. That was the beginning of my contact with Seagull. The first thing I suggested was that I had been watching something happening in theater in and around Calcutta. For 200 years of Bengali mainstream culture, as far as theater goes, initiatives had started in the metropolis and spread out. Even *jatra*, which claims to have a 400-year-long history, goes back to the Vaishnavas. They claim that Chaitanya had taken part in performances. But if you go into the history of *jatra*—you'll find that it was a kind of portmanteau theme for all things of theater in the open, musical or whatever. So there is no continuous tradition of *jatra* from Chaitanya but there were other things as well. You also have the Midnapur, *Krishnajatra* which has nothing to do with theatrical *jatra* you see here. Plays in the open I've seen in Orissa, Manipur, Assam and different places in Bengal—so (a) *jatra* is not a continuous tradition, (b) the *jatra* we have here in Calcutta at the moment is something which began in the early twentieth century.

The professional *jatra* companies now located around Chitpur all came into being roughly between 1900–1930, at least 75 percent of them, 25 percent evolved later. Throughout the nineteenth century, particularly the second half, professional theater companies from Calcutta traveled to the villages, and even now if you locate an old *zamindari* estate (and quite a few survive in Bangladesh), there will be a *natmandir*—a theater platform with a basic stage.

These are the places to which the Calcutta theater companies would travel and perform. Occasionally, there would be amateur theatricals on the initiative of the *zamindar* himself. This was all the theater there was, even for amateurs the model would be the professional theater company from Calcutta. Around the 1930's, there was a major technical reorientation or improvisation in professional theater. A lot of sophisticated stage gadgets came from the USA because in 1929 Sisir Kumar Bhaduri, who was the major figure in theater at the time, went to the US with a number of plays. The tour was a disaster but he and the company were exposed to theater in America. It was also the period of Eugene O'Neil and the Provincetown Companies but they never came into touch with that. In New York they had glimpses of Broadway and one of their technicians, Satya Sen, stayed on for more than a year. He came back in 1931, and brought in lighting gadgetry, and the revolving disc stage for the first time. These became entrenched as the latest fads in professional commercial theater. This theater could no longer travel. Then came a lot of plays showing rivers and boats getting sunk so the more dramatic elements, the psychological and historic elements, went under and the spectacular elements were emphasized. This gadgetry couldn't travel so theater got stuck. This is the gap into which the Calcutta *jatra* companies stepped in. They were located in Calcutta, so they could take over all the historic parts of theater, apart from gadgetry, in the late 20's and 30's.

LINA: How does that parallel the move of *jatra* theater into the districts?

SB: It remained Calcutta metropolitan theater imposing its models and dominance on the rural areas.

LINA: There was never a sense of theater other than the traditional *jatra*?

SB: There are a few traditional forms. Basically these are skits, not for stage theater as such. These could be like the traditional Italian and British strolling players—*commèdia del arte*—stereotypes, social action. Even attacking local targets.

LINA: I lived in Bishnupur for four years and we saw a lot of *jatras* which had a moral aspect—when the Calcutta *jatra* moved out, did they do the same?

SB: Every *jatra* company, and there are about 50 companies in Chitpur. They exist for a season (9 months) starting immediately after the rainy season (during which they can't function). *Jatra* companies reorganize and reshuffle every year, stars move from one group to another. So a company functions for one year, starting in September and going on till April. May to August is usually taken up in reorganizing, rehearsing, building up a new play. They normally have a repertoire of two or three plays per year at the most. One of these would be straight mythological, with a strong moral core— from the *Ramayana*, the *Mahabharata*, or *Chaitanyalila*. Another play would ostensibly deal with something more modern: a condemnation of modern fashions, modern European or foreign values, including women as vamps, traditional values, suffering wife, stereotypes. The stories are formulaic, the values are very backward, traditional, and superficial. There was one phase around the early 70's when there were plays with political content. You have a repertory of the so-called political play. Maybe the same company would do a play idolizing Ho Chi Minh and as part of the same season's repertory, do a social play in which the greatness of old religious values, "Dharma," "Ishwar" [Faith, God] would be dealt with. If there is an invitation from an industrial town like Durgapur, Asansol or Ranigunj in the industrial belt, with trade unions, they do the Ho Chi Minh. But if they go to a Bankura village they offer the mythological. Depends on the local sponsor's taste. Very commercial.

There may be companies which even idealize some of the old Muslim rulers—Shah Jahan for example with the clear understanding that these plays will do well in a Muslim-dominated area. Normally, a company would have a repertory of three or four plays with a mix. Even when it's mythological, social, or political, it's something worked out in Calcutta.

LINA: Would they create a new culture and impose new values?

SB: Not this theater. But the *jatra* has at one point. The local *jatras* are basically modelled on the Calcutta *jatras* and the scripts are printed at Battala in Calcutta. I spoke to the Battala booksellers at one time and they said that the largest number of texts don't sell in⋅ Calcutta. All semi-professional, amateur or local *jatra* groups use Calcutta scripts and sometimes their director or a lead actor comes to Calcutta to see a performance of a play. They have a model in their mind which they try to follow.

LINA: So Calcutta is still transmitting culture?

SB: What was happening around the early 70's was something different. When Badal Sarkar broke from proscenium theater four or five of his modern psychological plays (which have been taken up by experimental theater companies) were being played on proscenium circuits. He moved to a different theater, intimate, where he could identify his audience directly and communicate with them directly rather than create a distance of rhetoric and histrionics. When he broke off, his theater became very physical, a departure from Bengali urban ethics. Because in Calcutta's middle-class ethos there is a strong pressure inhibiting physical expression, nudity, and so on, so we go in for verbalization. From this, a move to express things physically and ideologically. He has been experimenting and it has been a relentless struggle. The first opposition came not from big commercial theater because they weren't affected, they have their own audience. It came from Left-wing theater because they thought the theater they have created—a verbal derivative ghastly adaptations—they even made a Left adaptation of a non-Left radical play, Arthur Miller's *Death of a Salesman*. You have created in 25 years an audience for that kind of thing. Now you are challenged. You are asked, to whom are you talking, whom are you reaching? They weren't prepared to face this challenge. They revisited Badal Sarkar and carried on working toward a total commitment to the theater.

What happened in the early 80's was that smaller towns around Calcutta, not really interior Bengal, but in a radius of 20–30 km around Calcutta, in five or six small towns (now about 10 or 12) small theater groups emerged, committed to this kind of theater. Committed to what I call a suburban theater and ideologically suburban. The first group that came into prominence was one in Khardah 20 km from Calcutta. It was called the Living Theater, their history is complicated and poses questions. They began with a strong commitment that they were never going to Calcutta to perform. Calcutta was not their focus.

The problems they were raising and trying to explore were typically suburban. For example, one of their first plays, which I found very exciting when I saw it, is a play in terms of its form, around the daily passengers, the daily commuters. Economically, 75 percent of the people of Khardah came to Calcutta to work. It is a supplier of labor. That train journey to Calcutta every day and back and what it does to individual relationships within families, all this is fraught with a suburban mentality and culture. This is a play which couldn't have been written in Calcutta. A play which wouldn't have a ready response in Calcutta unless a sensitive individual is able and willing to relocate him/herself. They were quite happy performing in Khardah and would tell us, if you have any interest in what we think, come. It takes a half hour to go from Sealdah to Khardah. That's how we started going, I and my friends, social scientists, writers, people interested in theater, musicians. It became a travel theme, and we started writing about these groups. There were 3 or 4, now there are 7 or 8 groups. In that sense, I mean it when I say that the culture, the issues, they tried to present are suburban, not Calcuttan.

LINA: Do they also portray a different political point of view?

SB: To a certain extent. More left of the Left.

LINA: So you find, since Independence, the topics of Calcutta plays changing in phases? From '47 period—nationalist plays, then a lax period.

SB: You can break up the plays. In the immediate past, the '47 period, the so-called New Theater movement in Calcutta began under the leadership of the Communists within the IPTA (Indian Peoples' Theater Association) in 1943–44. In 1948 when the Communist party was banned, the IPTA was also banned because it was regarded as the cultural part of the party. When the party went underground—a small core went on working. It was a heroic phase. It's easy to print things underground but it's harder to stage things underground. But it happened. I have childhood memories (I was eight or nine at the time). There was at least one member of my family active in that kind of theater. I saw her act. I know how it was done. My sister-in-law was involved (my eldest brother's wife) and I went to see her play. There would be a kind of protective shield of men standing on guard at street corners. There were occasions, I heard from my sister-in-law, when they'd go for a show and the police had already surrounded the place. So they couldn't perform. Sometimes the site would shift by word of mouth.

LINA: Do you think such passion only happens in Calcutta?

SB: I don't know. I'm trying to get more information but I feel a similar thing happened in Hyderabad in Andhra, and maybe in Kerala in the same period.

LINA: Is there something in Bengali culture which creates this need to express oneself in a literal way, to assert oneself expressively? Today, you can talk to people and they'll tell you about Tagore. Even the common man identifies literally with him. Whereas if you ask about nationalism, they stand aloof. I find a difference in the way in which people address problems in Calcutta today. Did people become lax? Do you see it happening in theater?

SB: During the Emergency, at the urban middle-class level in Calcutta, there was no strong resistance. It was taken lying down. There were 10 or 20 very dramatic gestures by some writers and journalists, but I personally don't give much importance to that. If you are not that strong and influential, take a stand. You know you are going to be arrested for a month. You become a national hero, and you're sure to get released. You won't be beaten up. Everybody will know about it. These gestures don't mean much in the long run. Beyond these gestures, nothing really happened in Calcutta. But right at this time, Utpal Dutt staged a play called *Barricade*. This was set, significantly, in Germany between 1933 and '37, immediately after the rise of Hitler and the period of elections/ non elections, and the SS going around. It became a roaring success. A big production. So, at one level, people would buy tickets about the Emergency. And the government, being intelligent, knows that if they intervened, it would mean that they were identifying themselves, which they couldn't do. Utpal knew it was safe, so did the audience. So I don't know what kind of attitude you are talking about: At one level, it was a time of protest. That's why you went to see that play, registering your feelings about the Emergency. At the same time it was a cowardly and sheepish mode of protest. If that's all you can do, buy your tickets and clap in a theater! This is typical for all the Left-wing radical experimental theater in Calcutta operating at the urban middle-class level. And also, the upper crust of the urban middle class—the people who can afford to go to the theater were helped to work it out of their system. Whatever anger is generated within you on a social or political issue is expressed characteristically at that level. It's quite natural that whenever certain issues become important there are plays to match them.

LINA: You still think that theater is a powerful medium?

SB: It has started dying out in the last three or five years. It's in bad shape.

LINA: They don't have support? Not because people can't afford it?

SB: Many reasons. Four years ago, in sheer terms of crowds, people were doing the same kinds of plays. It's the same people. An excuse is put forward by my theater friends. They say its TV, but I am not entirely convinced. The other thing that has happened during the 40's, 50's, 60's till the 70's, there was a greater emphasis on themes, and the problems and the kinds of play that were being done.

# Pratap Chandra Chunder

PRATAP CHUNDER: Job Charnock was the founder of the British town of Calcutta and it is reported that he saved a Hindu widow from the funeral pyre as she was about to perform *sati* and married her. I have written a play *Job Charnocker Bibi* which has become very popular. It has been translated into Hindi, Marathi and English.

LINA: Were you talking more about the *bibi* than about Job?

PC: About the life of Job Charnock in India, from documents, correspondence.

LINA: I wanted to ask you about your connection with Calcutta. Do you identify with the past or with modern Bengali culture?

PC: I am very interested in the present but we cannot enjoy the present unless we know the past. The present is the product of the past.

LINA: There seems to be a lack of interest in language, values . . .

PC: We have become very oriented to politics nowadays but the substructure of culture is there alright. It's going on its own course. Today there is something imposed from the top like modern media. TV or even the Press. Even in villages, people are aware of the existence of the outside world. A large number of people are illiterate, therefore they depend more on radio and TV. Through these they come in contact with the outside world, so culture is not lost but modified.

LINA: What gets lost?

PC: They have their own culture—the village folk have their traditional festivals and discourses, *jatra*, puppet shows—that culture is continuing but also changing. Popular dramas on Lenin, Mao Tse-Tung, struggles between landlords and peasants also find a place as themes of dramas. There is a lot of contact with the urban areas, not only Calcutta but smaller urban areas like Kharagpur, Burdwan, Asansol. People have lost some degree of isolation. Whenever there are two cultures coming in contact there is mutual influence.

LINA: Do you think Calcutta "feeds" rural areas with values?

PC: Calcutta is the only major city in West Bengal whereas in the other states there are many other cities. Bengali culture, the modern variety, is Calcutta centered. Calcutta sets the trend in music, dress, education. Particularly the influence of Calcutta writers like Tagore, Sarat Chandra Chatterjee. Though their themes were village events, they saw life from a Calcutta perspective. I have written novels about village life. I have a country house at Falta, 30 miles from Calcutta on the river. One novel is based on the life of a shaman who exorcised ghosts. I got the original charts which he'd written in some exercise book. I made use of that. Another was about the daughter of a prostitute who was married to a villager. But when her identity was disclosed, she was thrown out of the house. And she reverted back to her old profession. All these are based on truths. I know because I am a lawyer by profession and I come in contact with such clients.

LINA: What made you a lawyer and a writer of novels?

PC: I write, I paint, I am connected with politics.

LINA: Is that a remnant of the nineteenth century renaissance?

PC: Just for the pleasure of it.

LINA: But there are people like that. Take Badal Sarkar who is an engineer involved in theater. I met another person who is an engineer and publishes books for children. I don't think this is accidental in Bengal. There is something within the Bengali person that makes this possible and I'm trying to get a handle on it.

PC: I don't think it is peculiarly Bengali. This is the Indian tradition.

If you read Vatsyayana's *Kamasutra*, apart from the sexual aspect, there is advice on taking life as a whole. A citizen had to earn his living and devote some time to culture: painting, music.

LINA: But I don't find people like that in Bihar, Punjab or Orissa. You come across more people like you in Bengal and Calcutta in a day than in a year in Punjab. There must be something about the Bengali person.

PC: Thank you for the compliment. Speaking for myself, I have too many interests. I have been a teacher of law for 37 years, one of my students is the Chief Justice of the Bombay High Court, another a Governor, more than a dozen judges of the High Court, the Finance Minister—about 20000 students throughout India. I have been a practicing attorney. My son is so busy he had to discontinue his fortnightly paper—*Jana Sangbad*.

LINA: You must admit that your generation was special.

PC: Even now among the younger people there is this vitality. I mix with them. I am connected with dozens of organizations in Calcutta: cultural, musical, artistic, and religious, because now I've almost retired from politics. I was president of the West Bengal State Congress from 1967 to '69. It was a troubled period. My house was attacked by the Communists five times, they even wanted to set fire to the house, then we became friends in 1977 when we fought Mrs Gandhi after the Emergency. Strange bedfellows. Then I was elected to the Parliament in 1977. In the Janata Government I became Union Minister for Education, Social Welfare and Culture.

LINA: As a Congress person: which of the two parties, Congress and the CPI(M) is really concerned with Bengali society and culture? Do you think they differ?

PC: Well, the difference is only outward basically, they come from the same stance.

LINA: Congress seems to go more for a universal rather than a regional identity.

PC: Within the Congress there are people interested in regional culture. Regionalism is still a big platform though we all tried to make it into a party. Similarly, the Communists may be influenced by Marxism and Leninism but they all go to *Durga Puja* ceremonies, Ramakrishna Mission and try to help local festivals.

LINA: A localized Communist Party? Maybe this coexistence is possible only in Calcutta. Ideologically they may have differences but deep down they share the same roots. Nobody's interested in destroying the roots of Bengali society.

PC: The Communists are encouraging old dramas, *jatras*, music, folk songs and dances. As Minister of Culture I had called a meeting of all the state cultural ministers so that we could evolve a single cultural policy. We had the blueprint, but then the government fell and I couldn't carry it out during the Janata period. I left Congress when there was a division in the Party in 1969. That's when I parted with Mrs. Gandhi and remained with the old Congress, 10 years before Emergency. For 10 years we were in the wilderness.

LINA: Why was it important to have a universal sense of culture? For all India?

PC: You can't understand modern India without understanding the old.

LINA: How far would you go back?

PC: 7000 years! A book published by Cambridge University Press *The Rise of Civilization in India and Pakistan* by the Allchins is excellent on this point.

LINA: I personally think that it is difficult to come up with a blueprint for an all-India culture today.

PC: The Allchins have tried to prove that the Indus Valley Civilization which continued for about 2000 years had unity as well as local variations or diversity. That tradition has continued in India.

LINA: What connects a Bengali, a Bihari and a south Indian is perhaps the basic tenets of Hinduism. The *Ramayana* and *Mahabharata*. Linguistically they are different, cultural traditions may differ, kinship relations differ, but when you try to turn a model and into everyday activities—there is trouble. People will look at it as an imposition.

PC: That happens with the small nuclear family. After the introduction of modern thought there is too much individualism. Many
marriages are breaking down, even in village areas. Formerly there
was some understanding but now there is no give and take. Then the
joint family is also breaking down—partly because of individual
changes.

LINA: Having studied rural culture in Bankura, I have a sense of
what is of value for a household. When I come and do a historical
study of culture in Calcutta, I am faced with problems. The
development of culture out of contact between the British and
the three early villages was one of animosity and curiosity. These
changes and the emergence of an elite, the rise of the Brahmo
Samaj constitute an imbibing of Britishness and then comes a break.
People today talk of "Calcutta culture." Is there a difference between
the culture of today and that of the 1800's?

PC: There has to be a difference because no culture can remain the
same. If it does it dies. Whenever there are outside influences there
are changes in the culture. Before the British came to India, among
the Bengali elite, apart from the traditional village culture which
was indigenous, there was the imposition of the brahmanical system
with Aryan gods. Some of the local gods which had dominated local
cultures were made a part of the all-India brahmanical system. Then
came the Muslims and the influence of the Muslims on Bengali
culture was intensive. Persian influences and the Sufis contributed
to the integration of Muslim ideas into Bengali culture: the Vaishnava
movement, and at the local level, the worship of Satyanarayan. Then
came the British and western culture. It started around Calcutta
and spread to other nuclear areas like Uttar Para, Srirampur, but
Calcutta was the kingpin. A composite culture was created. Music,
dance—the Tagore family also contributed. Bankim Chandra
Chatterjee developed the novel form in literature from English
literature. Before that there were no novels. The first great novel
was *Durgesnandini*, said to be modeled on Walter Scott's *Ivanhoe*.
Take the drama. The Russian Lebedev moved to Calcutta in the
1790's and translated some English dramas into Bengali. He learned
Bengali from Pulaknath Das and set up an English stage behind the
present Writers' Building. He produced Bengali drama with Bengali

actors and actresses. In 1796 or so. About 80 years later, the public stage was created. But drama is very popular, it is really an offshoot of European culture. The Brahmo Samaj was a limited movement. It tried to take liberal ideas from the West but it was also based on old ideas. It served its purpose for a while but the movement's work was nipped in the bud by the activities of Ramakrishna and Vivekananda.

LINA: They were more dynamic because they didn't take their ideas from outside?

PC: Their faith was based on traditional religion, the worship of Kali.

LINA: In the 30's there was almost a collapse. The children of the so-called *babus* came in contact with a movement that seemed more real, forming a society capable of fighting the British. What kind of culture were they creating at that time?

PC: Politics became very important from the last part of the nineteenth century. Some of the policies of the British in Bengal actually highlighted Bengali aspirations, like the partition of Bengal in 1905. It relieved a sort of emotional upsurge among the Bengalis. Later on politics dominated everything and culture was linked to politics.

LINA: You see that in plays, novels, nationalist plays . . .

PC: The religious element was also present, mixed with politics. Bankim Chandra's *Anandamath*, a play called *Karagar* written by Sachin Sen Gupta about the life of Sri Krishna's parents. Kangsha represented the British in India and the play was banned. Then Bankim connected the worship of another goddess to the worship of the motherland. *"Bande Mataram"* became a slogan for Bengali revolutionaries. The British also contributed ladies like Sister Nivedita, Annie Besant. They wanted to modify the past with the present.

LINA: You have that group in the 30's and 40's. An exciting time. Today, I don't get a sense of that national fervor—call it Bengali or Indian, whatever. Upper-class Bengalis criticized the elite group and the Bengali renaissance, and they formed a parallel identity for India. Today the remnants of the same group are looking to the West and Bengali politicians refer to Calcutta culture as a bastardized video culture. It's repeating a cycle.

PC: That's only at the top level. It hasn't really affected the masses. Video is too costly for ordinary households. TV has some influence, but it is a compendium of cultures. State and national production. The latter seeks to integrate India and shows the cultures of different parts. A good thing I should say. As for the problem of integration and disintegration, that happens to every society. Modern history is replete with that sort of conflict—centrifugal forces which keep people apart and forces which keep people together.

LINA: So you are not pessimistic about what is happening in Calcutta?

PC: No. I'm in the thick of the cultural movement. I head the Rabindra Bharati Society which seeks to spread Tagore culture. His literature sells well so many years after his death! Songs, exhibitions draw crowds. His collected works are good. Sarat Chandra as well, but the collected works are fairly expensive.

LINA: The CPI(M) politicians I have interviewed were disillusioned and very down on Calcutta.

PC: There are a number of professional groups regularly performing theater in the city which you won't find in Delhi and Bombay as much. There are large numbers of amateur groups producing plays. When I was in University I started . . .

LINA: I like your optimism. Academics say there is no such thing as Calcutta culture. They are very pessimistic.

PC: They have become mentally old.

LINA: Then you talk to a generation that was active in the nationalist movement and you get a completely different picture. You get a sense that things are still happening and everything is not dead.

PC: I am also President of the Indo-American Society in Calcutta of which I am a founder member. Last Sunday we organized a "sit and draw" competition for children, nearly 1500 children participated. Now in almost every locality you'll find some art school for children.

In sports, they may not thrive in competitive sports, but football and cricket have become a way of life in many localities. What is culture? It's not always success in competition. It is how you conduct your life overall and whether you enjoy life.

LINA: Talking to you, I get a sense of something positive coming out of the British encounter, and the nationalist movement. It wasn't totally a waste. Many people say they can't live outside Calcutta. I know they are serious. When you ask, "What is it about Calcutta that you don't want to leave behind? They say, "My culture. My language, I can take with me." Maybe it's the ambience of the city.

PC: From the beginning of Calcutta's history it has created a composite feeling, a universal feeling. The British in and around the Dalhousie Square area, Park Street, and the Black Town in the north. In my two historical novels, *Job Charnocker Bibi* and *Lebedever Ranjini* I tried to stress this interaction.

LINA: Do you think that today class is an issue? In colonial times there were distinctions between Whites and Indians based on language, culture and race. People did distinguish rich and poor but not to the extent that it would further separate them as classes. Today class is a very important issue in Calcutta, there is a kind of antagonism among Bengalis themselves which does not look at shared features but at differences.

PC: That deals with a very small group of the people in institutions like the Calcutta Club or Saturday Club, those who drink and take drugs or spend too much on clothes. Only at the top level. But beyond that, the Bengali middle class hasn't got that kind of inhibition. In many localities a large number of clubs have been set up which integrate people culturally—people who come from different states. You have the very rich and the lower middle class.

LINA: So that still happens? But as you build these high-rise buildings that will die!

PC: But high-rise buildings don't represent India.

LINA: But they represent something that is happening to Calcutta and it is very disturbing.

PC: The question is, how far can its impact reach?

LINA: There used to be a sense of *para* and if you have a *boro bari* and other houses around there were communal *pujas*. But in a high rise . . .

PC: I agree with you but what percentage of people live in high-rise buildings? Considering the total population of the country?

LINA: Just look at Calcutta alone. Go to Southern Avenue: I am shocked about the fate of all these old buildings. In the last few years I have been diligently taking pictures of old mansions but now they are not there any more.

PC: Take our house. We have been in this area from 1781. The nuclear house was extended and this large house was constructed. We have the Durga *Puja*, Kali, Kartik and Saraswati *pujas*. Hundreds of people come here. Your Consul General and his wife attended, the British Deputy High Commissioner came. Ordinary people unknown to us come: the door is open wide. I'll show you a big room next to this one. It's meant for public meetings, cultural meetings, musicals, examinations for the local music school.

LINA: What was your family doing here in 1781?

PC: They started as Banias for the British. They acted as links between the traders and the country people. Then they amassed some money. My great grandfather took to the legal profession, Ganesh Chunder. He became a big man in his time. A member of the Lieutenant Governor's Legislative Council, a member of the Senate of the University, and amassed a fortune. Our street is named after him: Ganesh Chunder Avenue. By primogeniture all the eldest sons joined the legal profession: great grandfather, grandfather, father, myself, my son. Other branches are in other professions.

LINA: That is a long connection with the city! Did anybody write a history of your family.

PC: No—this is sad! There are very few families apart from the Tagores which are still active. We have not only *pujas* but activities outside the home. I am involved in politics, law, teaching, cultural movements. I guide the puppetry movement in this region. I have taken to law for a living because I don't like full-time jobs. This gives me a sort of independence. Although I belong to parties, I have always had an independent stance. I was one of the first important members of Congress who had protested against Mrs. Gandhi when she first brought about a split in the Congress Party. Apart from the cultural ministry, I was in charge of the law ministry for a few months under Prime Minister Morarji Desai, and I was the head of the Council for Scientific and Industrial Research Laboratories—that is, the forty national laboratories. I introduced the first national adult education program. We wanted to train 100 million people in five years' time to acquire the fundamentals of literacy.

LINA: I hope somebody like you will carry on this work.

PC: I am also a painter and had four solo exhibitions in Calcutta and Delhi. Last year I painted 50 paintings on American life and it was shown this year in Calcutta.

LINA: What you're saying is that you can be an Indian, a Bengali, and also take the best of another society different from your own, west or east.

PC: That is quite possible. I have visited China and Russia and most of the east European countries. I have been to America twice.

# Sisir Bose

LINA: How do you see the role of the Netaji Institute?

SISIR BOSE: We don't have to be chronological?

Well, it started like this. Rather oddly. We were a group of medical students and doctors who had come together and formed a group to do relief work during the 1946 riots in Calcutta, which were followed by floods too. That group used to operate from the house where the Institute is today. And eventually, my father decided that the house should be turned into a public institution and it was named Netaji Bhavan after my uncle. It ceased to be a private house. Soon thereafter (the house actually belonged to four older brothers including Netaji), all the house shares were converted to the Institute. My father said, it can only be Subhas' memorial, a living memorial. Not a statue but an institution. Of course there is a museum, one part of the house, where he lived and worked, but apart from that it's a working place. There is a research library, relating to the freedom struggle, and an auditorium. As we proceeded, this social service group used the house as rehabilitation camp for INA men returning from Asia. They lived there. We still have somebody—the resident caretaker—who belonged to the INA. Our social service group came into contact with the INA, and I don't know whether this played a role or if my presence had an influence. We all thought that if we did not take steps for the study and research of Subhas's life and work, nobody else would do it. That was our impression even at that time. That's how it has turned out to be. He would have been forgotten.

LINA: Why?

SB: Because there was a time in India in the early 50's when even his name wasn't mentioned on All India Radio. R.C. Majumdar, our great historian, said how thrilled he was on the night of Independence as he listened to the radio all night and heard all kinds of names but Subhas's name was not mentioned even once. So we thought . . . this was because he never came back. If you do not put in an appearance in politics this always happens. An absentee politician is always pushed out.

LINA: But that seems unlike Bengalis.

SB: There was emotional support from common people because of the impact of the INA soon after the end of the Second World War, which is why Independence came. In spite of official Indifference, his birthday was celebrated spontaneously on the streets! Most people participated on Bose's birthday rather than on Gandhi's. That was the ceremonial part, but that doesn't keep a person alive. We thought there should be some solid foundation.

LINA: How about Calcutta as a city? When did it begin to recognize Netaji?

SB: The emotional response has always been there, particularly that of the younger generation. Today, there is another wave. There was one generation, the Naxalites of the 60's, before that young people were interested, and following that there is a new awareness among the younger generation. Even now, as a pediatrician treating patients, children seven to eight years old, even when they come as patients, when I ask about their health, they ask me about Subhas Bose. Even they are interested about who the leaders are but it's all artificial. It is an artificial interest. I sound cruel, I shouldn't blame anyone, but people are foisted on them. You have to call somebody your "grandfather" or your "uncle." It is part of the socialization process, it sounds more spontaneous. I don't know how and I don't know how long this will last. The middle generations are lost. Those who had seen him and remember the nationalist struggle naturally see differently. Calcutta has always been responsive. It was the first city to name a street after Subhas Chandra Bose. Now there are two or three roads named after him. Before, Netaji Subhas Chandra Bose Road was Clive Street! Just after Independence.

ANOTHER VOICE: They also removed the Black Hole Monument of Holwell's. It was part of Subhas Bose's programme to move this monument.

LINA: So, he became a feature of Calcutta.

SB: He was inexplicably linked with Calcutta. When Subhas Chandra Bose left and used to broadcast from abroad he made moving references to Calcutta. I remember once he said, "When I think that war will come and Calcutta may be bombed, I feel terrible because the lanes and by-lanes of Calcutta are familiar to me." He grew up here, except for schooling in Cuttack, Orissa. That was a part of the Bengal Presidency. He came back from Cambridge and became Chief Executive Officer of the Calcutta Corporation. He was Mayor of Calcutta. It was in this capacity as Mayor that he was beaten up and badly wounded near the Ocheterlony monument, now called Shahid Minar. He led a procession against the British ban during the civil disobedience movement. Even when he was immersed in all-India politics, he had to look after so many things, tour around the country, he still took active interest (not just dabbling) in a local problem! He'd be interested in the development of clubs and associations. It wasn't only a political issue, Calcutta was a part of his life.

LINA: As a member of his family, do you feel that Calcutta has honored him enough? Is there a difference between the way in which Calcuttans honor literary people, the artists, and politicians?

SB: He was more of a politician, but I do not think that Calcutta has done enough or that Calcutta has been able to take enough from him. It's not just true of Calcuttans but of all Bengalis—we are very fond of "crazes," "fads," and hullabaloo about something. When we launched the Netaji Research Bureau, back in 1957 (I had been quietly collecting material even before that), the response I got from nearer home was the least! I sent out letters requesting people to give us materials for our archives and museum but the response was poor. People were not interested. Actually our archives were based principally on two sources: first, fortunately, my mother saved a lot; also, our European friends sent us a lot. They are very conscientious. Even though they had gone through the ravages of war, they had preserved so much material. I made links after the war—my father supplied contacts; I got Calcutta newspapers like *Amrita Bazar Patrika* from Europe. Nobody in Calcutta would give us these. People will not part with their possessions. They'd throw one out. The response of such work—of building up a man's life—was not there. Even now it's not enough. I don't think that one lifetime is enough to complete such work: I'm not complaining I'm just stating a fact.

LINA: I was walking on Park Street and I saw an *Amar Chitra Katha* on Netaji and bought it. The popular media seems to spread his memory as much as they can.

SB: They deify, and make him a semi *avatar*, like many other people. Because many people love to make of him a mystery man—which I think is very unfortunate. He was one of the most straightforward, forthright people.

LINA: Is the commission discussing Netaji's disappearance still going on?

SB: They've finished and submitted a report to the government.

LINA: I remember as recently as the 1970's there was still some controversy.

SB: There was one commission in the 50's when Nehru was there. Then there was the Khosla Commission in the 60's. When he escaped and we created a myth, we told people that he renounced the world . . . and in so doing we mystified everything. We laid a tiger skin in the room yet he never did that sort of thing. He was a deeply religious person but his religion was his own, he never made a show of it, of meditation. He was never in that room in seclusion. It was only declared that he'd go into seclusion, but he escaped the same night. There was nobody there, only the light was burning. It looked as if somebody was there. We deliberately created a mystery and now we are paying the price. He disappears from Germany, no one knows where he's gone, he travels in a submarine for 90 days, comes to East

Asia. Even to the British Intelligence Service it was a mystery. I have heard that even while he was travelling to the East, there were some rumors that Bose may be going east through Siberia, but some thought he'd go by submarine and take a risk. So many people thought he had supernatural powers when something happened perhaps a crash, people said this is nothing. He must have disappeared again. Life is such that people want to mystify. Also there is a mass psychological phenomenon. Masses of people in India want him to be alive because he was a leader of hope. His being alive gives people hope that good days will some day come to us. He will come and deliver us of our problems!

LINA: Let us go back to the point you raised about Netaji as a symbol connected to nationalism and the literary world of Calcutta. Why is it that the present generation is reviving Netaji . . .

SB: I only talked of children because they're not professionals and they are not parasites.

LINA: It seems that a sense of nationalism had died. So does Netaji's worship have anything to do with politics or nationalism? Is this the age for such worship? If so, it suggests commitment and activism. Look at Tagore, you can be indifferent to the man and his work, you don't have to act one way or the other. What is happening to Calcutta today?

SB: We are bereft today of all ideology. We are living in the age of power and patronage. For instance, this literary world you are talking about—they are just parasites. Let us look at the journalistic world— you take a batch of newspapers and read one then another. You get the impression that Rajiv Gandhi is an angel. Same date, but the other says this fellow is a scoundrel. If you try to go deep you see the whole thing is motivated. Nobody is balancing the situation. Everybody has a motivation. Subhas Chandra Bose is a difficult problem. You are right there . . . Tagore had an ideology and he had very definite social, economic and traditional ideas but those things are difficult and people avoid them. They go for his songs, his poetry, dance dramas. Subhas Chandra Bose is neither a writer nor a poet. If you want to accept him, you have to accept so much ideology. You have to accept real Indian nationalism which is tough.

LINA: It demands action.

SB: A lot of sacrifice which people are not prepared to make.

LINA: The perception and treatment of national leaders in society is changing.

SB: The same fate has overtaken Mahatma Gandhi and to some extent, Jawaharlal Nehru—all these people are in the refrigerator, I think.

LINA: You still see them on the walls.

ANOTHER VOICE: Others take whatever advantage they can of these people.

SB: Yes.

LINA: How do you see what's happening to Calcutta in terms of demographic change, residential change, and changes in values? What is this new Calcutta culture one hears about?

SB: We proudly declare that Calcutta is a city of culture—most of this is rubbish.

KRISHNA BOSE (Sisir's wife): You have to stay in Calcutta to understand.

SB: I said it to provoke her [referring to his wife], but most of it is rubbish though there are some remnants of substance—some culture is Calcutta's way of life. There is some content. But most Calcuttans are not involved in culture anymore. They have no time for it.

KRISHNA BOSE: Recently there's been a change because Calcutta no longer belongs to the Bengalis.

SB: I'm not taking that view yet. They could be absorbed, Gujaratis, Marwaris . . .

ANOTHER VOICE: But they don't become "Bengalified."

KRISHNA BOSE: Rather they change us . . .

LINA: You have a universal culture but not a Bengali culture.

SB: Why do you compare so much?

LINA: Because of language.

SB: There are so many Sikhs, Gujaratis, who speak Bengali like Bengalis. So it's possible to have a common culture. Our pattern of life has become so fast. We spend all our time rushing from one thing to another, no one has time for anything else.

LINA: That changes values . . .

ANOTHER VOICE: Economic changes . . .

SB: The economics of life affect our values . . .

LINA: So there is a new culture now?

SB: The music I want to hear, my son doesn't want to hear. I'm not blaming him, with the generations it's not the same culture.

KRISHNA BOSE: Dress has changed.

SB: I was always extremely angry when girls cut their hair. Now even I think they are looking nice!

LINA: Coming to this city off and on I see major changes . . . Maybe these have to do with the influx of people.

SB: Calcutta is losing its character.

LINA: It could become Bombay in another decade.

SB: An attempt could be made to preserve.

LINA: But it would be crushed because few are ready to take up the challenge. That's why it is easier to read Tagore than to practice what he and other national leaders have begun.

SB: Tagore's socio-economic views are very well thought of.

ANOTHER VOICE: I always say he was the greatest "women's libber" in some of his stories . . .

SB: Almost a crusader.

LINA: He had powerful sisters-in-law, strong women . . .

# Amal K. Dutta

AMAL DUTTA: I'm in charge of the most populous district of West Bengal—namely 24-Parganas. It has the longest border with East Bengal (Bangladesh). The influx of populations has adversely affected the economy of the district but it has also helped to nourish the economy. The East Bengalis who have come from there are fishermen. They have found their occupation in the South 24-Parganas—in the Diamond Harbor Subdivision, Basirhat Subdivision, etc., which has rivers. Formerly, the West Bengal people were concentrating only on inland fishery, now part of the Salt Lake area. The fish supply of Calcutta and its adjoining areas used to come from there. For growing wheat, rice, jute, the East Bengalis have brought with them the know-how. They are industrious. Therefore, they gave a boost to the economy of the district as such. But the population pressure is continuously rising. After every disturbance (including the changeover to Bangladesh) a fresh influx occurs. In the last three to four years because of bad politics in Bangladesh, we are facing again an influx, Hindus as well as Muslims. You will be surprised that in many of the houses in Calcutta, Muslim girls are working. They often take a Hindu name. This has come to our notice. They brought their food habits from East Bengal too. That follows the cultural changes.

LINA: What was the effect of the influx on Calcutta? Was it positive like in the 24-Parganas?

AD: Lots of them have come over to Calcutta in search of employment. Calcutta city was initially conceived for a population of one million or so, but today there are more than 10 million and a lot of people are coming in. The electric trains bring in at least another 50 lakhs of people—commuters, every day.

LINA: Is there a way to stop the influx?

AD: Very difficult, unless Bangladesh also develops equally.

LINA: But obviously they wouldn't be interested in stopping the influx of Bangladeshis into India.

AD: They want the Hindus out.

LINA: But also the Muslims—they wouldn't make an effort. So, in Calcutta—the presence of migrants is mixed? There is the majority—lower class—they took over a lot of lands around the city, but the professionals really benefited the city of Calcutta. If you look at every profession you find that seven out of nine are from Bangladesh, holding prominent positions.

AD: I think Supreo Bonnerjee would be able to enlighten you. Even before the 1947 partition, East Bengal used to send out a lot of educated people to West Bengal, or educated people used to come in search of employment to this town.

LINA: From the 1800's?

AD: The elite. They used to work here and go back to Dhaka for the pujas. With the partitioning of the country, the people who could afford it—the educated class—the professionals, the physicians, teachers, etc., all came to Calcutta. There was a complete drying up of intellectual sources in Bangladesh. That problem took 5 to 10 years to stabilize after partition.

LINA: But still, if you look at most of the early literary people, they were mostly from West Bengal. Major leaders like Rammohun Roy, Bankim Chandra. Most of the big names in literature and the social reforms are from West Bengal.

SUPREO BONNERJEE: I am from Calcutta, West Bengal but the people on whom they depended are East Bengalis. The majority of the educated class are from East Bengal.

LINA: Today, the majority of people in literature, theater, are people who came after partition. What has happened to the West Bengalis? I don't know if you can comment on this switch.

AD: Supreo keeps track of this development—but, I'll say that East Bengalis are very insular. Chittagong people like to live in their own area. Only the Dhaka people were energetic and dynamic and used to come in search of employment in Calcutta. In Chittagong the standard of living was low but people were happy with that. Though we have a few poets, Nabin Chandra Sen for example, they were insular.

SUPREO: Lina's empirical observation is that WBCS officers, IAS officers, senior members of the medical services, people writing short stories—they are mostly people from East Bengal. This was never so apparent before.

AD: In East Bengal, before partition—the Hindus dominated the administrative scene. They were also clerks. The ICS officers and IPS were mostly Englishmen, but below them—the *munsifs* [magistrates], the *baro babu* [head clerk] were mostly Bengali Hindus.

LINA: So they were basically transferred and because they were uprooted they were more aggressive about getting on to the top. Is this correct?

SUPREO: You must understand the very great attraction that people of our generation have for their own district. Now there is a new generation of Calcuttans who take this as their home and who are more Calcuttans—or as much Calcutta-*wallahs*—as the original people.

LINA: If I was to ask you where is your home—you would say Chittagong, this is my experience with people coming from Bangladesh. The parents were from there, but even if they came a long time ago, they say they are from East Bengal. Now, in looking at Calcutta, to me, it seems there are three crises that could happen here: 1) The kind dealing with work—work related. Typical of migrants, laborers. 2) The ones dealing with Bangladesh immigrants. 3) General. Would this be your three areas of concern too?

AD: No *Bangal* and *Ghoti* problem exists today as such. There are quite a few pockets here and there with that feeling. East Bengalis are called "Germans" (because Germany was divided!). From 1947 to 1987—two generations have elapsed, so these things don't affect my son. Doesn't affect the new generation coming up in the colonies. This word "colony" is a very significant term. We Bengalis use this word with a sense of contempt. Living in segregation. A sense of temporariness. A colony in Delhi means something else.

SUPREO: You know Bagha Jatin, Bijoygarh, Ramgarh—all had "colonies" attached to them. Now the word "colony" has been dropped. No longer Ramgarh "colony." They have become *paras* of Calcutta.

AD: They are named for martyrs of East Bengal.

LINA: But . . .

AD: But that kind of diversity between East and West Bengalis has diminished, the feeling that East Bengalis are encroaching into our areas—employment . . .

LINA: So even children born in the colonies don't have these East-West distinctions.

AD: But East Bengal and Mohan Bagan [popular soccer clubs] supporters behave fanatically. This is a bad sign. This fundamentalism is bad—especially with Mohammedan Sporting [another soccer club]. In my early days when I was living in East Bengal I was a supporter of Mohan Bagan.

In the colonies, they have started *pheriwallah* [vendors with handcarts] business, and selling, vending, pulling rickshaws. May not be adequate but that is something. The pressure on the land is too much in West Bengal. The high rate of fertility doesn't help, the population problem is staggering. The land distribution has progressed but it wasn't taken into consideration if a family could actually live off a particular piece of land. As a result, the family cannot fend for itself. Additional income has to be created by cottage industry. No family in Nadia is unemployed! You should go to Phulia.[1]

---

[1]A semi-urban village, now town, near Ranaghat Railway Junction. Apart from being the birthplace of Krittibas, the poet of the Bengali *Ramayana*, it was unknown. Now it is a thriving center of handloom, designs brought from East Bengal. Also connected with poultry development.

Those people who had nothing in Bangladesh now constitute part of the prosperous families because of handlooms.

SUPREO: What you are saying is that the new Calcuttans who came from Bangladesh and settled here are much more industrious and they give more dignity to their labor, so long as they earn money for themselves, for their livelihood. As a result, their competition was not with the old Calcuttans who never had this tradition but they were competing with migrant labor from other states—like Bihar.

LINA: But more lower-class refugees?

SUPREO: Lower class is a difficult term. The point is, there is a middle class—those who are not Brahman, Kayastha, Baidya—they come here, take advantage of the upheaval and move higher up the caste hierarchy. They may claim to be Kayasthas or Brahmans. There is nobody to detect. They have used this to become part of the so-called *bhadralok* class.

AD: That's correct. Except for one or two big estates in East Bengal, the *zamindars* consisted of the *bhadralok* class. This class degraded slowly.

LINA: One question you have dealt with—the problem between East and West seems to have fizzled out. What about problems of the neighbors—say Biharis versus Bengalis, are these on the increase. I lived in Bankura for four years and the problem cases there were different, mostly about thefts, land problems, bazaar thefts, occasionally a murder. In the city after Independence—obviously, there was an increase of one type of crime. In Delhi there seems to be a rise in crimes related to women. Victimization of women. In Calcutta, still it's the same as 20 years ago. So, are there any patterns which might indicate changing types of crime in Calcutta. Changes that might alert us to urban problems?

AD: From the crime point of view, conventional crime is on the way out. House burglary or dacoity is not found to be very rewarding nowadays. Other types of crimes are important. Wagon breaking was big 10–20 years back. Now, crime is highly sophisticated, similar to other states.

SUPREO: A lot of violence—political violence, etc.

LINA: I was here at the height of the Naxalite era.

SUPREO: Naxalite crimes were different. They were a group of people who were at war with society. Today's problems are different. The control today is with the *mastaans*, a problem for law and order people. If left to themselves, the law and order people would deal with them like the mafia.

LINA: Why does *para* need a *mastaan*?

SUPREO: A *para* never needed a *mastaan*. They are adopted because of political reasons. A completely different type of problem.

LINA: How is pressure alleviated from the city and Calcuttans by building suburbs?

AD: You were asking about the influx of people from outside the state. That is noticeably high. Though Bihar and Orissa are developing quite fast—the number of persons from there is high because a Bihari would like to encourage another Bihari to come to the metropolitan area, especially from north Bihar they tend to send out a lot of people. They work as cart pullers, construction workers, factory workers—and I don't know whether I'm competent to say this—it has come to my notice when I am in the districts— that earlier, the labor welfare officers in all the factories used to be "sons of the soil," i.e. Bengalis. Now this officer class is being supplanted by people from outside. What they do is bring in their own people. They feel safer. Biharis, Rajasthanis. Bengalis are left out.

LINA: Is that a concern for you? Does this lead to law and order type of problems?

AD: Ours sons won't get jobs. In Bihar there is provision for recruitment only from the "sons of the soil" (Biharis). When I went to Jamshedpur I was told 90 percent of the workers including the number two officer after the M.D. were from the state [Bihar]. You can't enforce this rule here in Bengal.

SUPREO: Does this problem have any communal overtones?

AD: Yes. Religious—sectarian.

SUPREO: This is also a commentary on Bihar's development.

AD: Earlier we could take them in now we can't. Another feature about modern Calcutta—most of the multistoried flats are inhabited by non-Bengalis. Today, Bihari graduate engineers will get preference over our local Bengali boys.

LINA: I talked to many educated elite Bengalis in Calcutta and I usually ask them if they are disturbed by the fact that in Calcutta they have 60 percent non-Bengalis. Their answer is always "No"—that it is the cosmopolitan nature of the Bengalis that allows many non-Bengalis to settle in Bengal. It's our heritage, we are not parochial. But only now I realized that all of those people were employed. I'll get a totally different reaction from Bengalis who are unemployed, and who have to compete with Biharis and Rajasthanis.

AD: Some Bengalis try to project an image of being non-parochial. But there was a time when we Bengalis went to Bihar, Orissa, Assam and we dominated them; we felt we were culturally superior—intellectually superior. So the oppressed turned them out from their states. Today we are all in Bengal, we are insular and resent leaving the state, even Calcutta. I was recently chairman of a board for bank recruitment. I asked an employee if he would be transferred to Jalpaiguri (north Bengal). Many did not want to entertain the idea of leaving Calcutta; nor to the suburbs because they would have to commute. Bengalis in their mind do feel neglected. You see it every day: the style of living—in Park Street and elsewhere is flagrantly clear. The contrast is the Punjabis.

LINA: I'm glad to hear somebody in Calcutta say that. But that is because you're looking at it from another angle. You have more information than a number of these people. You are looking at actual crime, frustrations, that affects Bengal. I don't think there is a solution because even Bengal won't come up with a "sons of the soil" policy—like the Shiv Sena. You can't buy land in Madras unless you are a Tamilian.

SUPREO: Today none of the Bengalis are in big companies—top positions are gone. Except for some of the development consultants—Bengalis don't control any big enterprise.

LINA: Can you, as a Commissioner of Police, suggest some changes and who would you suggest them to? Can you say that in the next seven years, these are the kinds of problems Calcutta will face and we can't control them?

AD: This kind of parochial feeling must go. We are part of the Indian Republic—but some legislation may be necessary keeping in view the disastrous consequence for the state. Today, big solicitor firms, the big companies of Calcutta—which the Marwaris have taken over, they will never employ Bengalis, there is no trust. Now they employ Bengali professionals—but a very small group. Then there are the physicians. They tend to select their own. So they are creating a problem.

LINA: Of quality.

SUPREO: Our best doctors are Bengalis. There are a few—like Dr. Chhetri—that some Bengalis go to. Marwaris—like our women who will not consult a male doctor but go to a woman, so Marwaris go to their own doctors. Marwari women never go to male gynaecologists.

LINA: So, because there is a lack of Bengali parochialism they—the outsiders coming into Bengal—can use their own parochialism to manipulate the situation.

AD: Unless I come to a political platform I can't do anything about that.

SUPREO: Do you think a Shiv Sena type of movement is possible? Bombay is one of the most prosperous cities in the country. We are in the same situation except Calcutta doesn't have the same fame as Bombay for business and money.

AD: Even today, the Bengalis are romanticists. But the course of history forces changes in their attitudes.

LINA: Creates the conditions . . . There are two groups competing with each other and they're not working on the same principles. They work against each other. I don't think your generation will have the leadership. The younger generation—and the service class that's hurt the most will come up with alternatives.

SUPREO: The use of a new middle class who have lesser values—who are more practical. And the older middle class as represented by Mr. Dutta and myself—will be opposed to that.

LINA: Just like the way that the earlier *bhadralok* found themselves lost in the 1930's when the new generation decried westernization.

SUPREO: There is no accountability in any sphere . . . a lot of things have to be done . . .

# Sakya Sen

LINA: How did you begin to conceptualize the idea of your party?

SAKYA SEN: How I came to get acquainted with *Amra Bangali*, well at first, it was a cultural organization. It approached me as an organization. You may know that there are a group of islands here in the Sunderbans known as Marichjhapi. A few hundred thousand refugees from Bangladesh came and settled there, all Hindus, perhaps driven out of Bangladesh. As you know there is always some political conflict between Hindus and Muslims. At heart it may be nothing. But it's so politicized that people always think that Hindus are against Muslims and Muslims are against Hindus. When Bangladesh came into existence (1971) and after that, as long as Mujibur Rehman was alive it was all right. Then, things started turning. There was a tendency to drive out Hindus and there was an influx of Hindus here. It's still continuing. Sometime in 1979–80, a few hundreds of thousands of people came over from Bangladesh and were accommodated in Marichjhapi. Perhaps our government was indirectly involved because of their consent to let them settle there. After they settled—the refugees had to earn their livelihood and there were reserve forests there. So the government said that the refugees were cutting trees and trading in wood, while the refugees said they were not timber thieves. They were trying to set up trades like bakeries or handlooms. Then there was fishing—they had set up fish breeding structures and so on. Contention apart, the government one day appeared and said: "You can't continue to stay here. Evacuate this place." They were told to go to Dandakaranya. These people said that they were unwilling to set up a new settlement again in Dandakaranya—they resisted.

The government then tried pressure tactics. They created barricades. Since they had to sell their cloth or bread, the government tried to prevent them from selling. Injunctions and so on. At that point in time they came to me for an injunction against the government. The refugees were represented by certain leaders. There were quite a few people—more than 100 persons signed the petition. In 1980, in the application to the High Court, *Amra Bangali* came into the picture independently, as an organization. There were basically two parties in the petition. One was a group of persons representing the people of Marichjhapi and one was *Amra Bangali* who said that they were supporting the cause of Bengalis, in the support of Bengalis. We shouldn't treat them as outsiders. Why should they have to go to Dandakaranya.

LINA: Did the refugees accept the connection with *Amra Bangali?*

SS: Very much so. *Amra Bangali* tried to help them out. After this there was a turmoil in the court. We came into the court—and we got an injunction and there was a commission with a direction on the lawyers of the government as well as the petitioners to go personally to Marichjhapi and find out the state of affairs. After this the government resorted to some "diplomatic" tactics. Overnight, they sent military forces to demolish the structures on the island (of Marichjhapi) The government made boats ready and said those who wanted to go to Dandakaranya could go and the others would be thrown out. Almost the entire island was depopulated in about 48 hours. We came up with a contempt application against the court but that came to nothing because the mischief was already done. You can say we lost the case diplomatically. We got no relief for the refugees. They scattered. Today I do not know where the people who signed the petition are. But this is how *Amra Bangali* came into contact with me. After this they petitioned about quite a few things (through me—I am a lawyer). The government had often claimed that there were bad sorts in the organization *Amra Bangali*—so they made applications in court subsequently. This was my link with them. One day, they said: "We want to contest the elections. Are you agreeable?" I said, "Yes."

LINA: How old is the group *Amra Bangali?*

SS: Age wise, it had its existence back in the 1970's. The stronghold was in Tripura. Even now they have a parliamentary seat.

LINA: The members would be in their late 20's, 30's.

SS: Yes, also the people in the forefront have changed a lot. So there has been trouble maintaining unity and integrity of the group.

Anyway, they asked me to stand and I agreed. Whatever little reputation it fetched in the election I got—people knew Sakya Sen as a part of *Amra Bangali* and *Amra Bangali* as a part of Sakya Sen, I was in the limelight. Perhaps because I was a public man— a lawyer. The political relationship with them gradually broke up. They approached me again but I said I was no longer interested in standing in the elections. It brings up problems in my profession. They still come over once in a while for legal advice, for a seminar, etc.—that's the background of the party.

LINA: Why do you think that the movement did not pick up well?

SS: One of their slogans was to wipe out English and Hindi. We always had an antagonistic relationship with Hindi. We do not want Hindi to be imposed on us and the government is always saying that we have to read and write in Hindi. But simultaneously *Amra Bangali* says that we must get rid of English. You will see that the signs by the roadside or at stations are written in Hindi, English (often left out), Bengali—you find that they have scratched out Hindi and English. I had told them that they shouldn't try to get rid of English like this. Those among the Bengalis who belong to the elite—the intellectuals—they will never support you. Another thing I'd said was that English is an international language. Even in India—there are so many states (linguistically defined). If I want to communicate with anyone I will have to speak in English. I could hardly talk to a Madrasi in Bengali. I have often had to face allegations like, "Mr. Sen, we had a sign board with English on it and they have scratched it out. Why?" To tell you the truth, I couldn't really answer them properly.

*Amra Bangalis* say that they don't want English because people among Bengalis have a tendency to privilege anglicization. That is a fact. Today, if I go to a high-level Bengali family, in the drawing room I will find English books. Alfred Hitchcock, etc. If I want to hear a song, I will get English pop songs!

If you want *Rabindra Sangeet* or *Nazrul Geeti*, those Bengalis who have gone up to that status will not appreciate such songs. I know people who are successful in business, and some of them have asked me who Sarat Chandra Chatterjee was; and when I recited a poem by Rabindranath they called it "trash." I felt it. I thought, "You are a Bengali and you are saying that Rabindranath is 'trash,' you are asking 'Who is Sarat *babu*?' You will see that the average Bengali youth of today does not know the works of Bankim Chandra Chatterjee, they haven't read classics like *Gyanjoga, Bhaktijoga, Karmajoga*.[1] They haven't read Rabindranth's classics like *Gora*. We weren't able to explain this to such people. I had told them about *Amra Bangali*—that they should have a programme of finding out Bengali families of high status in Calcutta. Go to them and ask them why they refuse to read Rabindranath, refuse to recognize Sarat Chandra and Bankim Chandra. Why do they feel that they can come into the social limelight by naming a few English authors? They did not accept my suggestion.

LINA: When they say they are *Amra Bangali*—what do they mean by that? Do they primarily refer to the cultural and social aspects? Do they mean something more? I heard discussions about the high percentage of Calcutta's population, 46 percent, being non-Bengali, and I am just wondering how a political movement like this *Amra Bangali* will tackle the problem?

SS: I would say that we haven't been able to explain to the masses about this. The definition of Bengali—for *Amra Bangali*—is not someone who has been born "there" and even speaks Bengali according to them. They will treat as a Bengali anyone who, irrespective of caste, creed, religion, will not/does not act against the interests of Bengal. For example, if I am a Marwari businessman who is carrying on a business in Calcutta and if I channel the proceeds of my business into Bengal for the betterment of her

---

[1]These were written by Aswini Kumar Datta, a very well-reputed Congress leader, freedom fighter from Barishal.

economy—that is, I reinvest, then I am a Bengali. But if, say, I am a Bengali who has a business in Bihar—and invest some of that profit in Bihar then I am not a true Bengali. Therefore, to have a house in Bengal or to have been born here, are not the criteria. Someone who works for the welfare of Bengal, who does not seek the economic disadvantage of Bengal, is a true Bengali. We haven't been able to interpret this concept well at all. People have got the impression that if they are non-Bengali ethnically, we will kick them out of Bengal! That is not a fact, we don't want any violence. It is possible that during the elections, our speeches were a little aggressive—so people got the impression that we would beat them up if they were non-Bengali. We were unable to explain what we meant by "Bengali." The least we wanted to say was "Please don't ruin the economy of Bengal. If you ruin the economy of Bengal you are not a Bengali. We can see that today, people from different states come and do business, and work in Bengal and profit, but the profit goes out of the state—it is drained out."

LINA: Every month you can see that effect at the post office, people lining up to send money out.

SS: That's right. Money orders go out!

LINA: Then *Amra Bangali* was not a movement targeted against the upper class? A *rickshawwallah* sends money home out at the end of the month. So it's not a class-based movement?

SS: No, it's not a class-based movement, it is a cultural and a political movement. Cultural because those of higher status are being requested not to forget Bengali/Bangla. They can read English but shouldn't forget Bengali. And because of this, the movement may be a bit aggressive—they are striking out English words from posters, in stations and so on and to me, it is not the way to make a man understand. You can make a man understand but not by "multicoating" their signboards.

LINA: They are coming with an aggressive tactic from the top down and obviously any group of people would react strongly to that whether you are CPI(M) or Congress (I). Talking to people I found everybody had something negative to say about *Amra Bangali*. Even though there is some attraction to the idea of a "Bengal Renaissance" but they don't know how to cope with the political aspect and there is a tendency to fear what might turn out to be like the Naxalite movement.

SS: I'd say that our failure lies in our deficiency in explaining and in our communication in trying to influence our "boys" (party workers) not to become aggressive or sentimental. When they say that the Bengali elite and the business people who forget Bengali should be wiped out—it is a sentimental statement—a casual statement in a public "lecture." Shouldn't be said in that way and because many Bengalis have been scared away. A negative wave has been created.

LINA: What is the difference between the *Amra Bangali* sense of culture and the CPI(M)'s sense of culture? I understand that they are also coming around to take up the issue of "Bengaliness."

SS: Interestingly, the proposals that we had put forward were 100 percent employment for Bengalis (or at least 80–90 percent), a reserved employment quota is usually kept for "sons of the soil." If you go to south India, or anywhere in Bihar or UP you will find the "sons of the soil" policy. But you won't find any reservations for Bengalis here.

LINA: Because of the politics?

SS: Yes, and because of the votes. Our government is more interested in getting votes—so there are no reservations here.

We wanted 100 percent employment of Bengalis but were agreeable to negotiation (you don't find 100 percent employment anywhere). But we wanted at least a certain reserved quota. At the primary education level, we wanted Bengali language as a must (compulsory). You will see that the present government has started to push these demands and these were all our proposals. I can foresee that one of our proposals that Bengalis need a position, a place for themselves will be taken up.

LINA: What is this "Bangalisthan" issue?

SS: By "Bangalisthan" what we have meant is that where there are more Bengalis that is, a greater population of Bengalis, the states should be reorganized. Look at the Bengal-Bihar border, or the Bengal-Orissa border. Where there are more Bengalis, taking land from Orissa or Bihar, they could include it in the boundary of Bengal.

LINA: So, what you are saying is that there is no real difference between the *Amra Bangali* sense of culture and the CPI(M) sense of culture. It is only a matter of politics. At base they both agree that there is a problem in Calcutta or Bengal about the percentages of Bengalis and non-Bengalis.

SS: CPI(M) doesn't say that directly, they are more role oriented. Maybe in their heart of hearts they are thinking in a like manner but not as openly as *Amra Bangali*. Because they have another interest which we don't, we are not fighting for political power.

LINA: And you're not fighting for a Marxist ideology either.

SS: As a matter of fact there is no logic in a Marxist argument.

LINA: Doesn't have a role to play in Bengal [i.e. Marxism]?

SS: We have instead even said that the ideology left behind by Vivekananda should be followed. That might be equal if not better than Marxist ideology. You may know a story about Vivekananda—he went to a shoemaker's (*muchi's*) house and said, "Give me water to drink," and wanted a smoke. The shoemaker was amazed that person of a high family would want to do this, but Vivekananda was obviously not concerned with such things. You can't find a greater Marxist ideology. They say we are Marxist, Leninist . . . why draw in the culture of a foreign nation when among Bengalis you can find a better culture?

LINA: Do you think that *Amra Bangali* is going back to a renaissance of Bengal? Rabindranth's sense of culture? The nineteenth century sense of the Brahmo movement, the reformation?

SS: That is it! At that time there was a rush of Bengali culture—there were many Bengali people in the limelight, in literature and every sphere—you can say that this phenomenon was a gift of god. You don't find that now—so Bengalis are forgetting Bengali culture, you can say brainwashing, television-video culture.

LINA: Video culture is what someone told me.

SS: If you compare a classic by Rabindranath with a present day Hindi film . . . terrible. Today Bengali youth is better acquainted with Hindi films and film stars than with the Bengali literary classics which have been filmed. We wanted to bring *Amra Bangali* into the social limelight—not into politics as such. But we wanted to make a social base out of a political status.

LINA: Social base out of a political status?

SS: Come close to people through politics—not a politics meant for catching votes—just an awareness that there is an organization called *Amra Bangali*, that we think about Bengalis and are concerned with social issues, a renaissance. That was the purpose of our getting involved in politics.

LINA: What is your opinion about the *Desh* culture or magazines like *Ultarath* and popular novels written in Bengali? After all, their medium is the Bengali language—what is the position of *Amra Bangali* vis-à-vis such "popular" Bengali culture?

SS: There are some undesirable elements in that genre. Jatin Chakraborty, one of the ministers of the present government, tried to harass a Hindi pop singer, probably Usha Uthup, by saying that she sang vulgar songs and was a bad influence on people. Tried to stop her from singing so she went to the high court and said that her fundamental rights—her freedom of expression was being curtailed and won the case. I personally feel that there is nothing really wrong with her cultural stuff as such. Jatin Chakraborty was being over zealous trying to prove that the CPI(M) is doing so much for the Bengali people/culture, that's not the real way of doing it. It was our proposal that loud, vulgar, disruptive elements which are not really "Bengali" culture are a problem. Our culture is decent— we don't easily indulge in excess, we are opposed to such articles, we should be guarded against. So, we are opposed to articles in the journal like *Desh* which may have a bad influence on people.

LINA: Are we talking about a puritanical society? Nineteenth century values?

SS: We feel things as they stand now are rather out of bounds and if we don't fix our foundations in the nineteenth century, we won't be able to do anything to right matters.

LINA: What is the place of western education in the scheme of culture?

SS: There will be western education, but the excessive elements in it will have to be weeded out. Compare Japan. They are very westernized but if you go to Japan you will find the family is Japanese to the highest sense.

LINA: They pick aspects of culture and drop others—sometimes picking aspects which have no foundations, values, history.

SS: I am not saying European culture is bad, but we have to have some symmetry between Indian and European cultures, turning 100 percent European will not help matters.

ANOTHER VOICE: This nineteenth century renaissance may be seen as a largely urban phenomenon but the culture of *bhatiali* songs, the stories of the Bengal weavers, of north Bengal—where do these aspects fit? Are they amalgamated into your notion of a Bengali culture. I mean these rural elements. Or is that notion of culture mainly urban?

SS: What do you mean by "Bangla culture?" Specifically we mean Bengal but we don't want to see India separately. India is an integral part of Bengal as Bengal is an integral part of India. States adjacent to Bengal cannot be said to have Bengali culture—but whatever is of value we must definitely take from them.

ANOTHER VOICE: I am asking about parts of West Bengal. If you go to Cooch Behar, the culture there is not the same as in Calcutta.

SS: We need to push these cultures, bring them into the limelight.

LINA: What you want to do is carry on the work of Tagore? To bring Purulia, Bankura into the limelight? What he did for the tribals? The difficulty is how do these people in the districts understand/ accept a sense of *bhadralok* culture? I don't mean a sense of class but say nineteenth century families who decided to look into their own values instead of foreign culture. Right now you have a Calcutta sense of culture and the "*akulin*" or the *other* sense of culture, which though they may speak the same language but the perception of symbols and images is different. You find that Amra Bangali may go back into the roots of what is Bengali whereas people in the districts will opt for a more bastardized version of that culture. The city has seen it—what it means to take the elements of western society— and now they are coming back into tradition. But in the districts, how to stop that?

SS: It is a very difficult question. What is happening in the city is a kind of deformation and in the rural areas, there is another kind of deformation. In any city—in Calcutta, this video culture is being thrust inside the family. Let us assume there is an intellectual family—parents, children. If children are watching videos from a young age, their minds are immature before they know what is good or bad for them. A mark is being left. We can compare this with the rural areas. There the adults are in the same position as children in the city. When they see the video culture—adults and children— their brains are not so mature (they do a particular type of work: farming, weaving . . .), they are not intellectuals, mentally they are not well founded. When they see video culture, their own (better) culture disappears gradually. Videos are a craze and whenever something is a craze, alcohol or video, culture begins to break down.

LINA: Can you say that in Calcutta we see the social development of culture while in the districts we see a political culture? If you take the different parties—Congress (I) gives you a universal sense of Indian-ness, CPI(M) gives you Marxist, not nationalist sense— if you see Amra Bangali, they'll talk about culture.

Would you say that in the districts, it would be difficult to exercise control to bring the rural people into the limelight of Bengali culture because they are really immersed in the political aspects?

SS: It is much easier in the city to get the masses in control so far as imbibing Bengali culture is concerned. It is much harder in the districts. I suppose the basic education should be molded in a way so that instead of thrusting Marxism down their throats for votes . . . this is an incentive for votes. They take advantage of the fact that their brains are not mature enough to understand what is good or bad for them. Doesn't mean that getting bread every day makes a government very good. But that is what they are doing in the districts. Because it's easier. If they give bread each day to an intellectual class nobody would be convinced.

LINA: You see Calcutta as the repository of Bengaliness more so than the districts?

SS: Yes.

LINA: How do you feel about the fact that only 46 percent of Calcutta is Bengali and the rest is non-Bengali?

SS: This is our misfortune. We cannot say that non-Bengalis must leave. We won't say it. There would be a civil war and that would be the last thing we want. If we said it, *Amra Bangali* would immediately lose its ground. Perhaps during the elections, people misunderstood us on that score. For us a true Bengali is one who has the good of Bengal at heart. But we can't explain that to people.

LINA:    What is the symbol of the *Amra Bangali* movement?

SS: Everything we want is freedom. Some of this is from the point of view of the group, but personally I have also met many Bengalis who have forgotten Bengal.

LINA: But many feel that *Amra Bangali* is fascist?

SS: We haven't been able to explain ourselves. We have been too sentimental which is why people are wary of us. When I have spoken in public I have found that I was crying when I spoke about Bengal. I couldn't control myself. So people think that if we find a non-Bengali before us, we'll dismember him!

LINA: It is a pity that they interpret sentimentality with the fear of how it would affect them.

SS: I remember a young member of our party who went to a party meeting and said: "We have come here to be established as a Bengali power and we will succeed. And we will kick all non-Bengalis into the Ganges." That was a very childish and embarrassing statement.

LINA: That's what will go to the press.

SS: This is what went to the press. People got scared and were asking me what it meant? They shouldn't make such loose statements.

LINA: I think that there is also a fear of the unknown.

SS: People who don't understand what we want or what we are doing, are trying to do some guess work and frightening themselves. Specially when we enter the elections and say we are not fighting for political power, we are fighting for Bengali culture through a political plane, they cannot accept it. The least we are trying to do is by some means make Bengalis aware of one thing: "Don't forget Bengali culture," a Bengali sense of identity and values which made Bengal what it once was and may again.

LINA: How can people listen to Rabindra *Sangeet* and not be moved?

SS: If you do a percentage survey, you'll find they are more attracted to and acquainted with Hindi songs, or "trash."

If I can bring the analogy of the knowledge of English to Bengalis—we brag about our knowledge of English, I am someone higher than my neighbors if I know English. You'll find the person who says he/she knows English doesn't know anything about English culture. He picks up the "trash" of English culture. The "loose" side of culture. If you say to him—start from Shakespeare or Oscar Wilde—they won't. But they'll pick up cheap detective novels, Hitchcock. I'm not saying don't read [sic] Alfred Hitchcock—but don't forget the better side of English culture.

LINA: Are any of the parties more sympathetic to *Amra Bangali?*

SS: No. They are afraid we'll come into power. Don't have an organization as such which can take up the administration of the country. We aren't harried that way. Citizens have asked me after the election campaign that if we get maximum votes, what will we do? I say, I'll do the inevitable. I'll ask my party to take up the administrative side of the job. They ask if our party is equipped with the capacity to do that?" There was no answer. The real answer is "No." We are not going in for power, but this much is true—if we ever get power in the normal course of things, we'll have to take up the administration and reorganize Bengal. But that is out of the question.

LINA: How do you say "Bengali culture" in Bengali?

SS: *Bangali aitijhya, Bangali kristi.*

# Parimal Ray

LINA: In this city anybody can say something about Calcutta. In the last 20–30 years of post-Independence Calcutta, I notice that things have deteriorated. Somebody like you, who collects artifacts from Bengal, and you preserve them, you have a respect for the collected art.

PARIMAL RAY: It's our heritage and culture.

LINA: But a lot of people want to leave heritage and move on to something else.

PR: It's my personal feeling that our basic education from childhood doesn't emphasize our culture nor an awareness about preserving it. Second point is, that art objects are so expensive and people's basic economic capacity is so low that their daily needs come first. Third point is that, if they can sell old things and can meet their daily needs then that is their priority. You have to eat first, live first. So they don't learn to love old things. They see old things as objects for sale.

LINA: Do you think that collecting art objects is a luxury?

PR: No, that's not so. From birth there should be an eye for something, love for something. There is a group for whom pride of possession is major. Something may be worth one lakh rupees— you could take it to him and say it costs 500 rupees. He won't buy it. He requires something that has to be priced at a lakh or two lakhs. Another group buys and keeps things out of love.

LINA: People go to museums?

PR: If we could we should take children to museums from kindergarten age. Teach them to love our heritage, that would be useful; after that you can learn about the rest of the world. There are many people who have never been to a museum. It's a concept. For many going to a museum is a negative concept. Such people would probably fix all their money in a bank and enjoy the interest. If I buy something for 2000 or 3000 rupees and tell my wife (although it's not coming from any surplus income), she'll tell me I am mad, that I should sell it. Now I'll tell her I've bought it for 200 rupees! Sometimes I also wonder if I'm depriving my family or not.

LINA: When did you start thinking of preserving culture by collecting artifacts?

PR: This started from my younger days. When I was in school, I liked collecting things, papers, cuttings of sports, matchboxes, cigarette boxes. When I wasn't studying I would roam about where the army camps were and collect what I found there. One day I found a small purse in my father's house. There were about 30–40 foreign coins. I wondered about collecting coins. So from 30 coins, my collection reached 7000! I gave up foreign coins and now specialized in Indian coins, primarily from ancient to contemporary times, Mughal coins, and from the Sultanate period. I am engrossed in this. Sometimes I feel that this may be a selfish pleasure. I have sculptures, paintings, bronze; whatever I could, I collected. But no longer. Because a kind of madness has set in all over India—buying artifacts. In affluent society, the craze for artifacts is major. Lots of people have destroyed ancient coins by melting them. There is no law against it. This happens because there is no awareness.

LINA: I also wanted to ask you about value and tradition in Calcutta. Some people say there is something called Calcutta culture. *Babu* culture, political culture, class culture. What do you think of when you hear this?

PR: I have traveled a lot, but even now there is a sense of culture in Calcutta. *Babu* culture still exists in a modified form, people don't have the capacity for it. Also, people would ridicule this. The western influence is too pervasive. The kinds of clothes and things my son likes is about being part of English/American culture. At one time, Japanese women wore kimonos. Then it went out of fashion because it took a long time to wear and because it restricted movement. They took to European dress. But now they have opened kimono schools to teach women how to use them. *Babu* culture had become too expensive and time consuming. People have no time or ability for it. But, there is a tendency to keep bits of it alive for the sake of tradition.

LINA: But the middle class of Calcutta don't have the economic means, otherwise there would be full-scale *babu* culture in Calcutta. The idea is there but the economic ability is not there. Those who have the economic capacity are not interested, they are westernized. But what about the lower class?

PR: There is nothing they can do. The affluent are not interested in *babu* culture but are going for antiques. There is a boom for show, not love. I had found a bronze figure from the Pala period, very expensive, I told the seller, "Brother, I can't pay this price for it." He told me, "Parimal, keep that figure next to your bedside for 15 days, see it every day, than you'll develop a tie with it. You'll talk to it, keep it." I'll tell you—I talk to all the statues I have in my room. Small children must be taught. If five boys learn, that's enough! The problem is that of poverty. Even if you want to, you can't afford to collect. If my daughter is getting married, I know I can sell something for 5000 rupees. You'll see the *bikriwala*, the rag collector, go from house to house collecting old shawls, saris, spectacles, watches, old things and exchange sometimes old gramophones, hairpins, photographs. All valuable stuff. It's terrible that I don't object to things going out of the country, that is bad, but it's better than destruction. If somebody, anywhere in the world, preserves something, there is no sin in that. If I break something and destroy it in my own home, breaking coal on a tenth century statue, then it's better for it to leave India and be preserved. It's because of ignorance, then somebody comes along and says I'll pay you 50 rupees for it! Sheer lack of basic education regarding our heritage makes us do crazy things.

LINA: Do you think it's the responsibility of the educational system, the political leadership to preserve the heritage.

PR: The educational system and the leaders.

LINA: In Calcutta, the CPI(M).

PR: Certainly. But there is no one. There are a few organizations trying. INTACH, I am a member of it. It's organized from Delhi. They're trying; they try to preserve old buildings etc. But it has to become more organized and on larger, wider scale.

LINA: In Calcutta, there are channels that preserve something of Bengal's past. Theater does that, literature and perhaps the media, like cinema or TV. What else? The family? But the family is changing too. If the theater wasn't there, Calcutta would be in the same situation as Delhi and Bombay. What is your opinion?

PR: I'll tell you my feeling—I don't really know. *Jatra* has become so filled with techniques and gadgets. Before, boys played the role of women. There was fun in it. Now it's different. Before people would sit in a circle around the players, now one row is closed on a side and open on three (like a stage), with lights, etc. Before they used hassock[1] lamps! A tea chest was used for a throne, now everything is authentic. Dress has changed. I had once seen a *jatra* in Midnapur. At six o'clock in the evening the field was empty. My brother-in-law was in the police; he said there would be a *jatra* that night, at 9:00. From 6:30 on things began to arrive on carts. A round shelter (*pandal*) was erected. Shops were set up with kerosene lamps. People were frying snacks—puffed rice, people were coming from far away villages. Bringing small children, about 20000 people! Those were the night *jatras*.

LINA: Have things changed because of TV?

PR: That and the use of small transistors which can be carried in the pocket. Why carry the big one?

LINA: Has the content of *jatra* changed?

[1]Pumped petroleum lamps, Petromax, etc.

PR: An element of sophistication has entered *jatra*. The language of *jatra* has changed. The realistic language of theater has penetrated the ornamental language of *jatra*, nowadays theater people work with *jatra*.

LINA: Which of the two, *jatra* or theater, uses and promotes Bengali values?

PR: I think theater, now. Because even villagers get to see theater. Calcutta theater people go regularly to the villages to perform.

LINA: Why?

PR: Money!

LINA: I think it's for ideology.

PR: I can talk big and you can tape it—that's not the way I work! Ideology is all right but the hard fact is that people need money. They can see *jatra* people earning a lot. Rupees 50000 just for booking charges. Before it was 1000! They have their own buses, food, costumes. Nowadays, cinema is at low ebb. The cinema artists have taken to *jatra* and theater.

LINA: What happened to Bengali cinema?

PR: There is so much western influence in the cinema, the next generation doesn't go for it. It's like a circle. Perhaps the wheel will turn. Hindi films do well because of sex and violence. Bengalis are trying but their films flop. There's no one to invest in Bengali films. Saytajit Ray, Mrinal Sen, Gautam Ghosh, Utpalendu Chakraborty are making some good films for international prizes. Not for commercial purposes because they don't succeed so well. *Debshishu* hardly played for seven days. But it's a beautiful film—it's not for the masses.

LINA: Do people see more theater than film in the villages?

PR: Villagers go to theaters and *jatras*.

LINA: In Bishnupur, there weren't many theaters.

PR: I'm talking of theater groups going from the city to the rural areas.

LINA: Now I heard there are theaters for the suburbs.

PR: Before, people wanted a theater hall to perform, now that's immaterial. Simplifies things. Badal Sarkar is someone special for open-air theatre.

LINA: In this respect his plays are very symbolic.

PR: His plays are not for common viewers. Not for a village girl. She will prefer Ram and Sita.

LINA: Then for whom do they do it?

PR: I can't tell you. But this I know, that until education penetrates to the lowest stratum this will happen. Cultural education is important; practical information, not just books. They must see old coins, the plays, etc.

LINA: Which has more influence on rural Bengal from Calcutta? Theater, *jatra*, cinema or TV?

PR: TV is widespread. You can't get rid of it, like the radio.

LINA: How many people can afford a TV?

PR: In a village, the local government has probably bought them four sets.

LINA: CPI(M)?

PR: Not just them, all over India. There are TVs in the *bustees* (slums.) This is one way to communicate. We still have two channels. Slowly developing sports, educational programs, etc.

LINA: Isn't it propaganda?

PR: Could be, but if people hear/listen, something goes in! Even that is all right. Afterwards we'll see.

LINA: So you'd say TV is the most powerful media coming from Calcutta to rural Bengal.

PR: At the initial stage you can let it be. First the awareness must come. You speak of TV, but the people in my village can't buy TVs whether color or black-and-white. When it's one to one, you can think about segregation and quality. My eighty-five-year-old mother will watch TV, that's OK!

LINA: I talked to Jochhan Dastidar and he said there'll be a TV program called *Sei Somoy* by Sunil Gangopadhyay. I saw one or two episodes, very powerful. I was thinking: everybody in Bengal watches TV and will understand some of what Sunil Gangapodhyay is telling them. They will understand it visually as Jochhan is trying to show them, everyone will have an idea of the past.

PR: True, in a remote village, a woman frying rice with a baby at her side, if she watches TV it is OK, let it reach her at least. Later she can decide which she likes and which program she dislikes.

LINA: If there is a play about *sati* or bride burning I want everybody to know. They are social observations. If that's on TV it's OK, but if the Congress (I) or CPI(M) or the Janata government tells me how to think I worry, that's politics, not social . . .

PR: That's the truth. I am saying you must build the foundation first. From childhood a boy must be taught to cross streets on the marked walk. But when I am a man of 52 and you tell me to cross streets differently, I will not listen. What you are talking about is the question of education from the middle. Also, what is politics and what is not is too difficult to distinguish. The bank advertises, they'll give me money, but they'll shave off my head first. You [in the West] all have a system, you can get all kinds of help. I have seen a Pala age Vishnu, eight feet basalt stone, for which the price is eight lakhs. I know it's nothing, but I can't afford it. If I had the opportunity to turn to a group which loaned me the money, I'd buy it! That's the problem. Nonetheless, Bengal is still alive. I'll say this, Bengal has been neglected by Bengalis and non-Bengalis.

LINA: Both?

PR: The non-Bengalis have contributed to building Bengal. Birlas have given museums, etc. They do cultural programs. We owe them; if there were only Bengalis we'd never have managed on our own. After Independence, compared with Punjab, Delhi and Orissa, West Bengal has stagnated.

LINA: Is it because of the Bengalis?

PR: I don't know the politics. All I know is that nothing gets done. There is unemployment everywhere. How will I get my son a job? It's a headache. What can you expect from such a place where all this goes on. Yet there's still something. If a good exhibition comes, you should see the crowds! You could barely get in.

# Aniruddha Ray

LINA: I would like to approach Calcutta through locality and history. Is Calcutta different? How would you deal with history, locality, and culture in Calcutta?

ANIRUDDHA RAY: I really don't know how one compares Bombay and Calcutta for example, but surely one major difference that immediately springs to mind is the fact that the intensity of the colonial impact was different. Private investment in Bombay dates to 1322, showing difference between the eastern and western India. Actually Bombay, western India as a whole, felt the colonial impact more after 1818 when the Maratha plunder and the first phase of British colonialism was over. Whereas Calcutta not only feels the impact, but in a sense shapes the impact. Important factor following from this is that in Bombay the business community was and is strongly entrenched. They are not overthrown by British capital. In Calcutta two things happen: in the nineteenth century Bengali entrepreneurship is curtailed and then again beginning with the 1930's through the 40's and the 50's, it becomes increasingly slower. English capital itself is losing control to the growing Marwari capital, a very important phenomenon for contemporary Calcutta.

So there is a two-fold displacement in Calcutta from the late 1800's through the 1950's and 60's.

LINA: Can one talk about a city as early as that?

AR: Why not? In early nineteenth century you could talk in terms of Calcutta.

LINA: Which Calcutta?

AR: I would say to a very large extent, except for the area south of Box Street, the city as it stands today physically was already very much there by the late nineteenth century or even the mid nineteenth century.

LINA: We can talk about Calcutta as a colonial city?

AR: That's one phenomenon which comes to mind immediately.

LINA: The colonial and the local need not be homogeneous.

AR: But the colonial capital loses out to another kind of Hindu capital which is not Bengali, which is not native to the city

LINA: Is that already a dominant feature at the end of the nineteenth century?

AR: No, that's not it. I would say that the process starts from the 1930's and very prominently from 1947 on. In the 50's very definitely so. In a sense, Calcutta was a very strong Bengali city in its early formative state but, through the twentieth century, this Bengali characteristic has been eroded because the Bengalis have been squeezed out or they are being squeezed specifically from the top by the pressure of Marwari capital, and from the bottom by the working population. I think very strongly that this is connected to the nature of colonial policy as such, the way colonial education is a credit to the Calcutta middle classes. You know they were groomed for clerkdom.

LINA: For the mid ranks in the services but not higher up.

AR: They could not become entrepreneurs but in the nineteenth century they were dominated by the English completely. They hated any kind of labor.

LINA: Now one sees a trickle of Bengalis performing some lowly jobs. Do you think this affects the ratio of non-Bengalis?

AR: Another thing that has happened, since you raised the question of trade. After Partition, the people who came over here from East Bengal and settled in Calcutta increasingly from the late 50's and

early 60's, have taken to small businesses; because they couldn't get
into the services, so they had to look for other avenues to generate
income.

LINA: They are an equivalent to the middle class but coming from
Bangladesh?

AR: Yes, the hawkers and their stores up and down Rashbehari and
Gariahat avenues have become a shanty town. These are hundred
percent refugees. What I don't know is where does the capital come
from? I have a suspicion that their capital also comes from Marwaris.

LINA: Through some kind of middle men?

AR: Not middle men, just retail outlets for a Marwari tailor or a
Marwari *mahajan* who has the money to carry on the business and
charges exorbitant rates of interest. I say this because on Gariahat
Road there used to be a very big hawker's market just opposite the
Gariahat market which got burned down in 1982. It was 10 or 15
days before the *Puja* and the rich men's markets as well as the hawkers
were stocked for the festivals. It got burned early in the morning,
and I went to see what happened. All these big hawkers were saying
that they had taken loans of vast amounts and now they have to
repay. This is what brought the idea to my head that they were
indebted and their businesses were not really their own and they
did not generate their own capital at this point.

LINA: What makes East Bengalis in debt themselves and go into
this so called "enterprise" while a West Bengali would not take
that route?

AR: A person from East Bengal didn't have any connections which
would get him a job in the city, whereas a *coolie* or somebody, from
say Bihar, who had that kind of opportunity was already entrenched
in the city. This is probably a very simple explanation I am giving
you.

LINA: Due to the attitude to physical work and trade that was and
still is to some extent stigmatized by Bengalis?

AR: Yes, but a person pushed to the wall would do away with the
stigma and I think this is what happened to the East Bengali. Not

that he liked going into trade, he still thinks that is inferior, but he does not have any alternative.

LINA: Bengalis in Calcutta went through a period of losing out to the British then to the Marwaris, and now small brokers and traders are still losing out to an influx of people at an even lower level.

AR: The last one I will put as hypothesis. It is to be investigated whether they are losing out or not.

LINA: I was talking to somebody today, who said that jobs at the lower level have increased something like 16 percent recently and are occupied by Bengalis. I told this man: "That's good because finally Bengalis are beginning to realize there are jobs." But he said, "No. I have to correct you, these are descendants of East Bengali families who came and settled here so that there is still that perception of lowering of one's status by doing menial jobs . . ."

AR: And also, always the Calcuttan, the *Ghoti*, has always considered the *Bangal* (the East Bengali) an inferior creature. Saying that he cannot even talk properly.

LINA: Let's go back to the people and the culture. Is there a "national culture" in Calcutta?

AR: My first response is that I would reorganise a division between an ordinary and a refined "high" culture.

LINA: Are we talking about high culture or middle-class culture? Calcutta as a city versus people in the country?

AR: I think you can't talk of a composite Bengali culture in Calcutta, there is nothing like that. I don't accept it.

LINA: Perhaps it is only in the 1930's that a break occurs and refinement cannot maintain a separate existence.

AR: In the 1930's, outside the world of Tagore, right? The major intellectual group you get is the political group. A more sophisti-cated and more refined group than that you can't think of, right? And they are trying to analyze or even at times reject received knowledge from the West, so at an intellectual level I would say that the 1930's is a continuation of that refinement.

LINA: And 1947?

AR: No, I would say, but from the 30's on there is a growing movement which is different or is consciously setting itself up to be a different culture, to be a bridge between the high and popular culture domains. And the major achievement I think is an attempt to use the poems of popular culture.

LINA: What are you talking about?

AR: I am talking about the play called Nabanna in 1943. Produced, written and performed at the peak of the Famine. I am talking about songs written by Hemanga Biswas at that time.

LINA: How should we look at this? Is it purely in terms of a political movement using symbols, images of high and and popular culture, or bringing about a new culture?

AR: That cultural strength will just not come from one or the other. It will have to come from the people because they have a sustained culture of their own which will have to be used, or as you say, recreated in a different way.

LINA: After Independence, there was the euphoria of belonging to a Nation. Then came the disillusionment of the late 50's and 60's, the questioning of national movements, and the idea of belonging itself. Then we have the 70's and 80's, very turbulent times when people are saying: "Well, where do we go on from here?"

AR: It is difficult for me to answer this question because I am part of the confusion.

LINA: I have been coming here from '67 on and my sense is that it is a very dangerous confusion mixed with ambivalence and anger. Ambivalence as to what people should be doing; the anger comes with the recognition that you are forced to sell your property, partition the household, and the family which is very important for Bengalis is split up. That anger is not yet expressed but can be seen in small frustrations.

AR: I think the ambivalence part of it is right. I see it in myself in the sense that I am angry at the Marwaris since their value system is not mine. But I know this is the irrational part. The intellectual part of me knows that we must resist this reaction. I do not let this racist reaction dominate my feelings and actions because this can lead to a very fascist kind of response. I am sure that the Germans once felt this way about the Jews in Germany in the 20's. So there is this anger, and I think you are very right in the . . .

LINA: You know every year I come it gets a bit worse. The old middle class is dwindling without doing any thinking and then you have a lower class that is indifferent. It is a drain on the city.

AR: But why do you think the upper class has decided to collaborate?

LINA: Well, they have the upper hand, they do not have the kind of economic or political pressures of middle-class families. The latter have to ask, "Can I afford to send my kid to Jadavpur or Xavier?" There is still the old sense of value education. For the upper class this is not an issue. It is accepted that everybody is going to get education if they can pay for it.

AR: For them I use the term "beautiful people."

LINA: These people are not bogged down in issues of regionalism, cultural differences, and values.

AR: Irrelevant, but still they have a strong hold.

LINA: They are still making decisions which affect the middle classes in terms of setting goals which are difficult to attain. What do you do when you cannot meet your goals? You become embittered and revert to something you still hold and use it as a way to differentiate between "us" and "them." The middle class is on its own, whether they are lawyers, doctors, or in government service. They perform a viable function in the community.

AR: Not only a viable but a very important function which can be shown in that most of the lawyers who are advising the Marwaris cannot afford to buy property or even evade taxes; because they are Bengali, they cannot be in that game. I have seen the beautiful people and I have a strong feeling that if Bengalis were to be among the beautiful people of Calcutta or Delhi, they would be out of place. They have different styles and they don't have the proximity to power.

LINA: Where is Calcutta going?

AR: I do not know where it is going now.

LINA: Are we going to see a city like Delhi here? Even more people will be accommodated from all over India?

AR: I don't think that something like that is possible in Calcutta. Delhi has no character in that sense. Some areas have a character, Nizamudin has a character, may be the great avenues also have character. But all of this put together doesn't have any character at all.

LINA: But Calcutta's character has changed.

AR: It has changed, but it still has a character.

LINA: I can still go to Ballygunge and feel that I am in Calcutta.

AR: Which part of Ballygunge?

LINA: Around Gariahat, not beyond . . .

AR: But half of the houses are gone. Still "Third" Boro Bazar is a code name for it. The first Boro Bazar is the original one. Ali Boro Bazar [i.e. Alipur] is the second and that is the third. And you know, I have it on very good information, but this is completely alleged, that there are orders from the Birla house that in one mile radius from the temple, (you have seen that hideous temple!) any property, even if it be just a room, they are willing to pay 20 percent above the market price.

LINA: What has happened to Bengalis? Irrespective of class, education and politics; they were a "prime mover" who started the nationalist movement, and handled the British! Why are they so apathetic? People are not stupid, they see what is happening, they analyze and talk about it, and from a vegetable seller to upper class politicians, they tell you straight out "what is happening to us," yet you get a sense of withdrawal.

AR: No, I would go back to my original argument: being the first victims of colonialism, and not just colonialism as an economic system but also as a cultural system. I think that we are still trapped in the curse of Macaulay. Just to give an example; somebody who has a son who is plain—he has no academic French but maybe he is good with his hands. The family would pressurize that son to go through the motions of becoming a graduate because that is very important. It earns him respectability. Whereas the son, if he went to a technical school, would learn to utilize the skill he has with his hands. Would be better off and would not waste his time. Now he becomes a good-for-nothing, he can be nothing other than a very bad clerk in some bank. He is completely bored and does no work. He arrives at 11 o'clock in the morning, asks for a cup of tea, then reads the newspaper and discusses yesterday's football match, and then has his lunch and tea again, and then he is finished. It is our fault that we accepted this stupid system and have not been able to get rid of it. I think the roots go back as far as that. An education system made for the specific purpose of creating a class of people who would perform these tasks.

LINA: There are few technical schools here.

AR: I know of just one. I am sure that there are others, but . . .

LINA: There is a college where I did research that teaches everything, history, economics, science but a young graduate is not guaranteed a job. Training youths in technical skills, carpentry, or metal work may be more beneficial.

AR: I think, increasingly, for more than one reason, Bengalis are getting marginalized here in Calcutta.

LINA: They will move out to the districts?

AR: Not to the districts, to the suburbs.

LINA: This is what I asked you! Will there be a Bombay here soon? The smaller suburbs will spread out and turn into satellite towns. Salt Lake will be the new middle-class city of Bengalis. But I understand that even there more and more land is sold to non-Bengalis.

AR: Look I am absolutely certain that in 20 years I will not be living in the area I live in now!

LINA: Well I am glad I saw Calcutta in the 1960's. You refer to a colonial system of education for a particular purpose but that is not the case today.

AR: Historians working on cultural history will work this out. The books that my father read in school, like *England's Work in India*, were straight about the civilizing mission. Apart from that if you look at the syllabus in the nineteenth century, you have a rebel in 1857 somewhere in north India saying: "I don't believe that the Bengalis decided they are only fit to teach rhymes and Shakespeare."

LINA: I wonder what good is that today? I was once on a train heading to Calcutta, I met a group of Bengalis who were returning. They were starved of conversation. They work outside Bengal but they have to go home for a bit of history and literature, or just plain old intelligent conversation. I find that in rural areas the level of intelligent discussion, whether it is about plowing, *puja*, or symbolism in religion, is just astounding. I do not find this level of intellectual curiosity and commitment in other areas of India.

# Epilogue: A Conversation with Tarun Mitra

*On a visit to Calcutta in 2001, we sat down with Tarun Mitra, an old friend, to discuss the 1986 conversations which form the bulk of this volume. We first met Tarun-da ("elder brother," as we call him) in 1967 on our first research trip to India and we have been close friends ever since. We talked about Calcutta since Partition and Independence, the 1960's, the people represented in this volume, and especially the changes since the 1980's, in an effort to give the addas a wider perspective. This final adda is reproduced below.*

LINA: People tell us that culture is dead in Calcutta. How do people think about this? What's in this city that makes it Bengali in culture, or something else?

TARUN MITRA: From the mid-eighties, it is difficult to say how much of Calcutta is exclusively Bengali. But the city is definitely Bengali in its orientation and moorings. Bengalis with the help of English people built this city. Englishmen came here to trade and eventually they ruled from here but it is the Bengalis who made the city. If there is anything called Calcutta outside "white town" it was because of the cultural activities of the Bengalis. These people were either "middle class" or rich; middle class meaning those who came to Calcutta from outside to make money, but came in contact with western education and western notions like rationalism and the like: whatever was deemed good in European culture at that time, in the context of Indian culture. What we call today Bengali culture was created by those people, so Calcutta is still a Bengali city even though now a substantial fraction of its population are non-Bengalis in origin . . . Control by non-Bengalis extends to the economy only. Very few of them contribute to Calcutta culture as such. May be the various groups like Gujaratis, Maharashtrians, have their own cultural institutions. Punjabis have gurudwaras. Then there are the Kerala, Andhra and other associations, but they have not contributed anything to Calcutta culture. Don't forget that nearly a hundred thousand people commute to Calcutta every day, they also contribute in one way or the other. With the electrification of the trains, and the modern communications systems, the suburbs are not culturally away from the city.

LINA: Are you saying that the idea of class is central to the city?

TM: You can divide classes money-wise and economy-wise. But, the moneyed upper class contributes very little to culture. Lower classes, economically speaking, are so hard pressed for a living that they also do not contribute much to culture. But they also have their own cultural entertainments. It is the middle class that really produces cultural artifacts.

ÁKOS: So, what should we mean by Calcutta culture?

TM: It is difficult to say unless we refer back to the nineteenth century. It is very difficult to talk of Bengali culture even in the late twentieth century. In the nineteenth century English education, western ideas, the educated and professional classes, the Brahmo Samaj and other movements created a new consciousness, and established a very close relationship with western ideas and institutions. Till the other day for instance, in the Foreign Publishers Bookshop, right under the Grand Hotel, I could buy any book published in London. If I saw a review in *Times Literary Supplement*, I could have the book within a month. And let's take a nineteenth century figure like Vidyasagar, whenever a new ship came to the port he would look at the new books, buy a few, tear off the covers, saying, "These are my books. Send them to such a binder and he will bind them for me." Some of these books are now at the Sahitya Parishad. Even in my student days you could buy books in the Pelican series like the *Managerial Revolution* for a few *annas*, later a shilling. We were more or less up-to-date all the time! Our literary movements, our schools were very closely connected with the West. This held true for the last 200 years, except for the period in the earlier part of the century when nationalism, patriotism, sought to find the roots of the old, traditional India which was reflected in neo-oriental school of paintings of Abanindranath Tagore, Nandalal Bose, and their students. Also, in literature, until Bankim Chandra, our entire Bengali prose literature didn't have any tradition of novel or short stories; even in Sanskrit, there are no novels.

Our writers flourished, made international reputations and were translated into many languages. Calcutta always was a different kind of city, yet so much a part of Bengal. All this time, influences went both ways between the rural taste and urban taste. Let me give you a funny example: A friend of mine once told me that you can understand how closely a village is related to the city by listening to the songs girls practice on the harmonium in the evening. So that was it! Calcutta influenced the country that way. On the other hand, look at the great stalwarts of the twentieth century Bengali novel like Tarasankar Banerjee, Bibhutibhushan Banerjee and Manik Banerjee and a little later, Satinath Bhaduri; they all drew their inspiration from rural Bengal. They hardly ever wrote about the city except Tarasankar in his later period. But right now most Bengali authors write about the city and urban people.

LINA: A new and different kind of Calcutta emerged since the 60's. Are these the changes you are referring to?

TM: Calcutta changed physically but when you talk about the culture, good, bad or indifferent, it is not something you can quantify, you cannot pinpoint, you have to talk about it. At best through your personal relationships, you get a sense of personal values, what people consider good or bad, permanent or transient. There is also the western, mainly American impact.

LINA: Not English any more?

TM: Not English: first of all, English universities don't give grants to that extent, they cannot afford to, secondly England is not doing much by way of literature, and painting. America is not doing much either but still, through media and other contacts we are coming closer to the Americans. Also through the Peace Corps, John Hopkins cholera research, the Ford Foundation, hoards of people came: academic and non-academic. TV was practically unheard of in

Calcutta in the 60's. It's a later phenomenon, but still the impact was there. American movies had a great role to play. British and a few other foreign movies used to be shown at the Metro, Hollywood movies mostly. The Metro deteriorated however. Bengalis started changing superficially. Young Bengali girls go to college or university in *salwaar kameez* or jeans and shirts. It is not aping a fashion. It is out of necessity also, meaning that Calcutta trams and buses are so crowded that a sari is very difficult to wear, you may come out of a crowded bus with the sari left inside! Then food habits started changing. Not western but Chinese and south Indian food. In our student days there were one or two south Indian food shops in south Indian areas. Now, you can get *idli, dosa, sambar*, Madrasi food almost in anywhere in Calcutta. The changes were superficial at first but became inward later, meaning in the 70's and 80's.

LINA: These changes are so fast and so drastic that there is no connection to the past?

TM: May be fast but the continuity is also there. There is no society which can keep stagnating. Every society is changing, right now due to consumerism. In our time consumerism was shunned. I had rich people's sons studying with me in college. They did not dress differently. I was poor, I worked so that I could study. The rich or upper-middle class could afford a lot but their lifestyle was not very different. For instance, if we were in a tea shop-*adda* they all said the same thing, "I have just this much money." Probably, their father, elder brothers and uncles had cars but they themselves hardly used the cars. Their level of consumption was not different, so that the outward gap was very little.

LINA: Consumerism is something we notice: all of a sudden the choice is where you shop and what brand you buy. Who are the people who enjoy this and what do they spend their money on?

TM: From the 1950's up to the mid-60's, what was there to buy? What did we produce? Naturally, because of our foreign exchange difficulties we had to restrict the import of many things, so what did we buy? A transistor radio (which revolutionized the rural areas), and a long-playing record player costing 350 rupees! You could also go to a Chinese restaurant or any Park Street restaurant. As students, on rare occasions we used to go and get a full meal for five or six rupees. There was nothing much to spend on, even clothing was cheap. But now sitting in Calcutta, you can buy an airplane, so out went the Nehru style import restrictions. Lots of people go for brand names but many brand products are franchised here and we can get them. The younger generation eats out a lot. Because of devaluation, books have become so expensive that we cannot even dream of buying a hardcover book. We wait for a long time to get paperback novels but B-grade "trash" literature flourishes in the market. Another aspect is the mushroom growth of English medium schools from the 1960's onwards. In our time the best school was our locality school, where the parents didn't have to worry: "Oh, you can come and go with your friends." Now, because of the economy, you have to compete with people and proficiency in the English language is one of the criteria to prove your ability. There is a very good reason: businesses are owned by non-Bengalis so if you want to speak to them you have to speak in English and being employed by those people you may be put in Delhi, or Madras or Bombay.

LINA: Do you find this in Delhi too?

TM: Everywhere it is a class phenomenon, but it is imperative to go to this kind of school. Schools like South Point, St. Xavier's, St. Lawrence, and Don Bosco, just for hundred and fifty seats there are five or six thousand applicants. So you stand in line from the evening to collect the form for the next day at 11 o'clock, then the poor child (who must be six years old), has to sit for written test; if he clears that, he has to appear for an interview. Parents are also interviewed, because if the child does not get feedback from the family he will always remain backward even if he is very intelligent. I studied in a village school, in a Bengali-medium school; that I would ever speak the English language never entered my head. But now people have to do this from the beginning so this is another aspect of change. After all they are not scholarly people or people with deep understanding but you see people change and those who study in Bengali-medium schools slowly begin to change.

LINA: Some say that Bengalis are bad business people but good politicians.

TM: First of all, for Bengalis, business means trade. Bengalis first came in contact with British traders, Banias, Mutsuddi agents, people who paid advance money—*dadon*, from which they made money and they tried to invest in business. There was stiff opposition from British traders. There were lots of restrictions imposed on them. On the top of this came the failure of The Bengal Bank where lots of Bengali money was deposited. Due to the fall of this bank, Bengalis lost faith in business because they said these people had all the facilities, yet we lost whatever we had. So they tried to invest money in land. The return was not anything less. There was a long tradition of Bengali business from the sixteenth century. From the west bank of the Hooghly (River Ganga) came all the Subarnaboniks and Gandhaboniks, Duttas, Sadhus, who are now resident in north Calcutta. They were traders in gold, pearls, spices, textiles and active in foreign trade. Before, the Arabs and Portuguese held sway over the Bay of Bengal. During the British period, these businessmen started to invest in land which not only gave them an adequate return, but also a social prestige. They were chiefs of the village, and did a little voluntary work, mostly at the cost of the blood of the peasants and *ryots* who labored hard on the land. Later on, with the return of the *jamidari*, income from land dwindled. There are different kinds of inheritance law one of which is the *daibhag* system. So, one big *jamidari* is divided into *dashani-chhawani* [i.e. ten-sixteenth and six-sixteenth portions of an imagined whole rupee]. *Dashani* again is divided and subdivided, and eventually these people became small landholders and their income was not sufficient to maintain them in style and status. They formed the middle class which flocked to the professions in country towns and to Calcutta. Yet middle-class people could maintain their families in Calcutta because they were directly or indirectly subsidized by whatever little income they received from their land. The extended family could live in the village and the men who worked in Calcutta could send a little bit of cash back home. These are mainly the people who created cultural artifacts and patronized cultural institutions. They formed the bulk of the professional middle class and elite people.

LINA: What about Bengalis being good politicians. Do they know something that other people don't?

TM: The answer is, yes and no. For instance, how many all-India figures do you find in politics except Netaji Subhas Chandra Bose? Sarat Bose made some contribution in the State Assembly but his name is never mentioned. They do not make good politicians. As a matter of fact Bengalis have a sense of resistance to authority throughout history. The Mughals never had as many problems in other provinces as they had in Bengal. The small territory chiefs like the *Baro Bhuia* (i.e. the Twelve Landlords who revolted against the Mughals, the number is figurative). Even before that, in the ancient period, Bengalis revolted against a centralized state of any kind, imposition of any kind.

LINA: In Calcutta, or in Bengal?

TM: In Bengal

LINA: In Calcutta?

TM: About Calcutta let me be hyperbolic: Around the time when India achieved Independence, we saw gods walking on the streets. These patriots who suffered innumerable, unaccountable miseries for the sake of the freedom struggle, naturally became big shots in the Congress regime but corruption settled in after they assumed power. Corruption was there even earlier in government institutions like Calcutta Corporation, district boards, local boards, municipalities and union boards. So with power came corruption. These leaders were trained in agitation but they didn't know how to run an administration. Not that they were all corrupt, but corruption flourished through their agencies. The Congress people were neither intellectually nor economically equipped to handle the economy and the immense burden of the refugee influx. They were thinking in terms of day-to-day domestic care of the people but there was no plan. The refugees came on their own and cleared jungles and ponds, and built shanty-towns. But the first thing they built was a school. Among the refugees there were school teachers who began teaching. So this way, all the suburbs were populated.

LINA: What of the refugee problem?

TM: They were obliged to leave their homes in East Bengal because in the first flush of Muslim domination injustices were done to them. They were deprived of their rights so they came here. But the administration could not give them enough of a minimum, so there was a lot of frustration, a lot of anger; that was fertile ground for Marxist agitation. Among the intellectuals there was quite a number of Marxists. Many of them met Marxism when they were in England, big landlords: for instance Jyoti Basu [ex-Chief Minister of West Bengal] went to sit for ICS examinations and failed, cleared the barrister-ship somehow and joined the Marxist movement. When they returned they found a very congenial ground for themselves because the Communist Party at that time, instead of confronting colonialism, because of the German attack on the Soviet Union, all of a sudden turned the war into a people's war. Contradicting the Congress's freedom struggle, they joined the British. Samaresh Bose has written a novel about it. They organized trade unions in the refugee belt. So they became the mouthpiece of that anger and frustration and Congress didn't do anything to counter it.

If you talk about the cultural contribution of Marxists in Bengal or Calcutta, then you see the Indian Peoples' Theater Association, Anti-Fascist Writers' League and such things. Apart from drama, they had not produced a single worthwhile piece of literature. Some poets like Samar Sen or Bishnu Dey were a kind of Marxist, and they were patronized by the Party. They were thought to do things for the Party but they did not. They were theoretical Marxists. In drama, we must admit for the sake of truth, that they started the theater which eventually influenced subsequent groups who were not even Leftists, some were even anti-Marxists. Their contribution to painting is nothing. Marxists who really shouldn't, or didn't, believe in parliamentary politics entered parliamentary politics, and within a few elections came to dominate the state legislative assembly. For a short while during Emergency they were thrown out but after the Emergency was over, they again fought the elections. They came back with overwhelming majority in the state legislature. They had a very disciplined party organization from the Calcutta Central Committee to the district committees, village committees and this way they spread their tentacles. So nothing can get done these days unless you have a patron in the Party.

LINA: So, politics is not helping the city but retarding it.

TM: Yes, since you are elected by the majority of the voters, a first rate *literati* has one vote and a first rate criminal who was three times in jail has one vote too. So people vote in a group. Look at the shanty shops all over the place; nobody can do anything because they have votes. Congress won't do anything because they are also hoping against hope that these people will some day vote for them. CPI(M) controls their votes. But they have done some good things in rural areas.

LINA: At the expense of Calcutta?

TM: Not at the expense of Calcutta. The effect on Calcutta, as I explained, was that the middle class had some kind of subsidy from rural property. The village people benefited, however marginally, because of other government services. When I was in the villages, there were few government officers: Thana (police) Officer, the Post Master and others like the Jute Regulation Officer. Then there was District Board Officer (my father was one), and village health officers, on the preventive not curative side. Occasionally, the District Board would have a charitable dispensary which had doctors and compounders. They had very little funds but distributed drugs like quinine. My father's job was supervising inoculations, vaccinating people against smallpox, cholera, cleaning the ponds with bleaching powder, organizing students, clearing the water hyacinths which were the breeding ground for mosquitoes. Now, every government department has an officer at the village level and they are coordinated by the Block Development Officer. Imagine the number of people going to the villages! Even if they do one-tenth of what they are expected to do, it's bound to be a lot!

LINA: And Calcutta.

TM: Calcutta is a city Kipling described as "chance directed, chance erected." It was never imagined that one day Calcutta will have more than one million people. Right now, we have close to 10 million people and they have little to do with the villages. They are deprived of landed property, there are no village industries and villagers all flocked to town. Calcutta's problem was that it was the only city in the eastern region of India. Dhaka was also a big city but the Calcutta port's hinterland was entire Bengal, Assam, Bihar and eastern Utter Pradesh. From the Orissa and Midnapur border villages people came to get a cook's job. From Bihar where even today the situation is terrible, people came as laborers in factories, if unlucky then rickshaw-pullers or porters; from eastern Uttar Pradesh and Bihar, to set up *paan* shops or cobblers you see at the street corner, mending shoes. From Orissa, we get most of our plumbers, but Calcutta, unfortunately, despite Dr. B.C. Roy's great efforts to develop Durgapur and Kalyani, Calcutta is still the only city. The neighboring states are developing but not in keeping with the needs of the people so there is always a surplus who come to the city. At the street corners you must have seen quite a number of beggars. A beggar knows that during the entire day, about 10000 people walk by. If people give just five paise, at the end of the day, he will earn 20 rupees. Even doing nothing, just by shouting and sitting he can make 20 rupees a day. So people come but the amenities are not there, the jobs are not there and on top of that government doesn't have the kind of money needed.

ÁKOS: What has happened to politics in Calcutta since the 80's?

TM: I think from the 80's on Calcutta didn't vote for the majority party. They voted Congress not out of love but because Congress is the only Opposition party in the state. Even if the government wants to do something for the city it cannot do very much. For a perceptible change, the kind of money or the kind of machinery they need they just don't have.

Whatever little money comes from Planning Commission, World Bank loans and other funding agencies is put to use but some is eaten up by ghosts. Let's say if there are 10 million rupees, you will never know who has taken one million. We have a chain system: such and such people supply stone chips, such and such supply asphalt and our PWD—Public Works Department—supervises. But unless you pay something, the PWD clerk may not approve. Again the accountant who will pass the bill may have to be paid. Some funding agencies make stipulations now, so some benefits you can see.

ÁKOS: Today, many of our friends tell us that there is no culture here, everything is finished, no painting, literature, music, and everyone is running after money. Whatever we had in the 60's and 70's is all gone by now.

TM: My reaction will be a very conditional yes and no; because you see for every creative cultural artifact, you need consumers. How can you say that we have not done anything in the creative field, that's not true! Let's take literature: even during Tagore's time a bunch of very good poets and prose writers, Sudhin Datta, Buddhadeb Bose, Bishnu Dey, Jibanananda Das, tried to go outside the direct influence of Tagore and were trying to introduce new phenomena, deriving their inspiration from the West. We see the same kind of thing in the West also: Eliot, Hopkins, Spender . . . In the 30's, here we had Tarasankar Bandopadhyaya, Bibhuti Bandopadhyay, Manik Bandopadhyay, later Satinath Bhaduri also wrote good literature. Every country, every society suffers from a dry period, you cannot maintain stalwarts all the time. The poets who followed in the 40's, Arun Sarkar, Naresh Guha, were not bad poets, but after their generation, Alok Sarkar, Alokranjan Dasgupta, Sunil Ganguly, Sakti Chattopadhyay were quite good. Not only that, we were the first people who, with the help of Signet Press, held a poetry conference. Nowadays poetry conferences are held weekly not only in Calcutta and suburbs but in the districts as well. In literature, a new generation of prose writers like Samaresh Bose and Sunil Ganguly. Look, everybody cannot be great, but Sunil Ganguly is not a bad writer. He has a sense of history, he knows the situation of Calcutta, competition and the like, so he writes short stories and plenty of novels. Probably he writes too much for his own good, but in those days people didn't earn much money. In literature we have not run out of talent. But may be we do not have great names now.

In music for instance, Calcutta never had many great classical musicians; Girija Chakraborty, was one. But north Indians, from the *guru-sishya* relationship, came here. *Gurus* keep their best for their sons or sons-in-law; that is the tradition. In this century, we had Karim Khan Saheb, Alladiya Khan Saheb, Rajab Ali Khan, Allauddin Khan Saheb, Enayat Khan Saheb, Vilayat Hossain Khan Saheb, Omkarnath Thakur. In no other 50-year period, even a century, will you find such great stalwarts. People who paid them money and honor were Calcutta people. We did not create great musicians but good ones like Tarapada Chakraborty, and we always had a great number of connoisseurs; many people, sometime out of fashion, or curiosity, but also genuinely, love this music. Since the 1970's, people like Ravi Shankar, Ali Akbar, Vilayat Khan in instrumental music, Amir Khan, Bhimsen Joshi, in vocal, are there, but our music conferences these days cannot afford them unless sponsored by Indian Tobacco Company or other industrial houses. These days there are very few music conferences. Bengal's creativity found another outlet. After Satyajit Ray, look at the brilliant filmmakers. Ray is the great stalwart of modern film but his contemporaries are Ritwik Ghatak and Mrinal Sen. And no mean ones. Then Goutam Ghosh, Utpalendu Chakraborty, Buddhadeb Dasgupta, Aparna Sen were turning out very good movies. May be there would be a barren period of ten, twenty, thirty years but then, you know, culture goes in waves. We have a strong and thriving drama movement which can sometimes be compared to the best anywhere in the world.

LINA: Who are some people in painting today?

TM: Jamini Ray started as western academic painter but eventually moved to *pat* painting, and impregnated it with a new meaning. In the neo-oriental school there were Abanindranath, Nandalal, Asitranjan Haldar. During the War years the Calcutta group was formed and held several exhibitions after Independence. They were influenced by modern movements in European art. This group had great impact on painting in Calcutta. Many other people took to modern painting and after that no one painted in Neo-Oriental style except Ramanada Bandyopadhyay. Right there in Santiniketan were two people who were the opposite of that tradition— Rabindranath Tagore and Ramkinkar Beij, the sculptor. The younger generation searched for a modern Indian identity and looking West for inspiration discovered nineteenth century French painting and twentieth century German painters. That is very strange. They were called the Calcutta Group: Nirod Majumdar, Paritosh Sen, Gopal Ghosh, Prankrishna Pal.

ÁKOS: And into the late twentieth century?

TM: The only painter I immediately recommend is Ganesh Pyne. If you look at one of his paintings, it is Indian and also modern: telling tales stylistically not exactly Indian but they remind you very strongly of something Indian. Some of the watercolor painters also paint mostly Indian scenes. An Indian subject does not necessarily mean an Indian painting, still they are trying. A moderately successful painter can make a living. Previously the picture was of a painter dying of tuberculosis. Nowadays you see a change. There is a new cooperative housing for artists near my house. Many of them are my friends, and half of them came in chauffeur-driven cars for the laying of the foundation of the building! Earlier even well-known artists didn't have chauffeur-driven cars.

LINA: Who do you recommend today?

TM: Look, this is very difficult, in any branch of art, to recommend who is one's favorite. In poetry I may bring it down to three. If you ask me who are my favorite novelists? Again I may bring it down to three. In painting, objectively I will say—Bikash Bhattacharya. He is academically so correct that you enjoy his painting. Now, this is the kind of painting that sells, so he has abandoned his previous surrealistic ideas. If you go for watercolor, I would say Shayamal Datta Ray. If you ask me who is the painter I like? I would say the most significant is Ganesh Pyne, and Ganesh Haloi is in the same front rank. Maybe for the peculiar angularity of my psychology, I feel that if I see five paintings of Ganesh Pyne, I've seen them all! Then if you go for graphic arts, I would say that, Amitabha Banerjee, Paresh Maity, Krisnendu Porel, and several others are also quite good. Good thing is that they are selling.

ÁKOS: Who buys them?

TM: That is another thing. Not out of love. This is a kind of investment, status. The gallery owners have their own list of buyers. Often, before the official inauguration, half the paintings are sold. Depending on how influential you are, how you can push your artists, how well organized you are, how many businessmen you have on your list. For instance, Shyamal Datta Ray is my close friend since the 1950's but I don't have any of his paintings. When he was selling at 3000 rupees, I could not afford that; now he is selling at 60000

rupees and I still can't afford that! I own one Jamini Ray which
I bought for 75 rupees, but it would cost 25000 rupees now.

LINA: I want to ask you a question about civic sense: I think there
is so much love and concern for Calcutta, yet there is a disjunction
between what you do for the city and how you feel about it.

TM: I understand your question perfectly. You see, I have tried in my
mind to explain such things. I will give you a very short anecdote.
You know Shatul-da [the nickname of the late Radha Prasad Gupta,
a contributor to this volume], his tram was held up once. A student
procession organized by the Congress Party was passing by. The
reason was that textbooks published by the Left Front Government
had some unkind words about Lala Lajpat Rai, the Congress leader.
So Shatul-da wondered: how with all this garbage, lack of electricity,
no job opportunities, such human degradation, these people are
taking out a procession about a book! How to intellectualize hunger?
How to appeal to these people? That is not exactly the answer but
it is there somewhere. There is also a reverse process: urbanization
and many restless people. Women, who took their bath in a secluded
tank before, now have to take a bath in the open. Gradually the
sense of decency, privacy, sobriety goes: if you have to share a
community latrine with hundreds of men and women, how do
things go?

People who live on the streets say, "We are from Sundarbans,
our area is flooded." Sometimes it is true, sometimes it is not; but
if there is no cultivation for two years, they come here and do
everything right on the street. Opposite the AIIS office, there is a
paan shop. Right under the shop, there is a small hole where people
keep their things. During monsoon, they go to the garibaranda,
balconies extending over the footpath, and take shelter wherever
they can. They try to educate their children and if they get a little
extra money, they buy a transistor radio. From the AIIS office veranda
I see that the maid from the next flat has bought a new wristwatch.
Not necessary, but this kind of consumption is there. On the other
hand, we city people are learning from this kind of thing. Calcutta
Municipality provides urinals but you have to walk miles, and they
are not properly maintained. Nowadays people don't care. Ladies

squat right there, so a vulgarization is entering. And all the shanty shopkeepers—where will they go? The municipality should provide the civic amenities but our taxes are so low we cannot even pay the salaries of the officials. There is very little surplus. So rather than Sanskritization, you see vulgarization and you see callousness, because a group of like-minded people cannot do anything, you need political power, muscle power, and money power.

**East Bengal/East Pakistan/Bangladesh**   the eastern part of undivided Bengal with Muslim majority which after 1947 became East Pakistan; revolted against the central rule of West Pakistan and in 1971 became the independent sovereign state of Bangladesh.

**Emergency**   Indira Gandhi, Prime Minister of India from the late sixties to the eighties with a break of a few years in the seventies, found herself assailed on all sides with allegations for mis- and mal-governance and also for nepotism, corruption and tendency to dynastic rule. The judiciary declared her very election void. In order to counter the loss of power she promulgated Emergency Rule (1975–77), suspending most of the democratic rights of the Constitution of India.

**Emily Eden**   sister of Lord Auckland, Governor of Bengal who visited India and left records of contemporary life and times of Bengal.

**Great Calcutta Killing**   the Muslim League called for a Direct Action Day on August 16, 1946 to work out a final division between Hindus and Muslims hostile to each other, to strengthen Jinnah's demand for Pakistan. Muslims in Calcutta came out in great numbers and started indiscriminate killing and destruction of life and property of the Hindu community while receiving protection from the Muslim League Government in Bengal. After about three days of this one-sided killing spree, Hindus started retaliating and, being the majority, killed Muslims in much greater numbers. It is sometimes claimed that nearly 30000 people of both communities died in that riot which lasted for close to seven days and sporadically long after. The actual number of people dead is probably much less. But the damage it did to the psyche of the people is irreparable and still perceived today.

*goondas*   hoodlums, criminals who coerce by physical force.

*guru–sishya*   master–disciple relationship

**IAS**   Indian Administrative Service, the all-India higher category of civil service.

*idli, dosa, sambar*   south Indian snacks, the first two items made mainly from rice, the last a kind of lentil soup, popular in all parts of India.

**INTACH**   Indian National Trust for Art and Cultural Heritage; a non-governmental organization rather like the National Trust dedicated to preserving the culture and environment of India.

**INA**   Indian National Army. During the Second World War, Indian prisoners of war from the British Indian Army in Singapore and a few volunteers of Indian origin from South East Asian states formed the Indian National Army; effectively led by Netaji Subhas Chandra Bose they fought against the Allied Army for India's freedom.

*Ingraj Tattva–Babu Tattva* the dichotomy of behavior among the leisured class of Bengali gentlemen engaged in dissipation and aping the British habits.

IPS Indian Police Service

IPTA Indian Peoples' Theatre Association. A front organization started by the Communist Party of India attracting unsuspecting talents from the fields of theater, music, movies, etc., many of whom left the group later for ideological reasons.

*jamidar, zamindar* feudal landlord class, who in exchange for a fixed annual rate of rent to the state held the ownership of large tracts of land, and collected taxes in their turn from the tenants on various pretexts. The margin of profit after paying the state taxes was immense, and enabled the feudal families to live in leisure and great luxury.

Janata Party once a moderately strong political party, now with dwindling support base on account of internal splits.

*jatra* traditional theater, still extremely popular in the rural areas. The performance is held in the center, surrounded by the audience on all sides. The general subjects are mythological, religious, and historical and the style melodramatic. Social problems and issues have been added in recent times, with other technical innovations.

Jibanananda Das eminent Bengali poet who greatly succeeded in his efforts to come out of the influence of Rabindranath Tagore. He has a large following among Bengali poets even today.

Kalighat Painting traditional folk painting of Bengal which was sold in the pilgrimage place of Kalighat in Calcutta where the painters also lived. The subject of the paintings were religious and mythological as well as social satires.

*Kamasutra* a Sanskrit text on erotica written by Vatsyayana. It has 36 chapters, supposed to have been composed between second century BC and second century AD.

Lal Behari De, Rev. (1824–1894) came from a rural background and received education in Calcutta, became proficient in English, embraced Christianity. An educationist of repute but better known for his *Gobinda Samant* or *The History of a Bengal Raiyat* and also *The Folk Tales of Bengal*.

Left Front    several Left parties of different shades of Marxists led by the Communist Party of India-Marxist [referred to as CPI(M)] has ruled West Bengal for the last 24 years. They are democratically elected.

Lord Curzon, George Nathaniel Curzon, Marquis of Kedleston (1859–1925)    Governor General of India from 1899 to 1904, reappointed and resigned in 1905. An expansionist-imperialist yet introduced quite a number of reforms, greatly remembered for his Ancient Monuments Preservation Act which actually started   archaeological studies and excavations in India. He remained until his death a powerful politician in his country.

Macaulay, Lord Thomas Babington (1800–1859)    English scholar, essayist, historian and politician. Law member of the Governor General's Executive Council in India in 1834; remained involved in Indian affairs all his life.

Mahatma Gandhi    Mohandas Karamchand Gandhi, great political leader and ideologue of India, called Mahatma (Great Soul) for his saintliness. An unswerving adherent of non-violence, he skillfully honed it as a weapon of struggle against imperialism. Not only one of the greatest Indians but also considered one of the greatest original thinkers of the twentieth century.

Manasa    female presiding deity of snakes. Many medieval Bengali literary works recount her power, indicating her popularity.

Marwari    trading community from Marwar in Rajasthan.

*mastaans*    originated from an Arabic word, has the same meaning as *goonda*, the local strong-arm criminal.

M.G. Ramachandran    noted actor of Tamil films, a charismatic personality, was elected Chief Minister of Tamil Nadu.

Michael Madhusudan Dutta (1824–1873)    great poet, scholar and linguist of Bengal. He introduced blank verse and European classical traditions in Bengali poetry. Drew heavily from the epics and histories for his poetry and drama. Adopted the name "Michael" at baptism.

Mir Jafar    the treacherous commander-in-chief of the army of Bengal under Siraj-ud-Daulah who willfully lost the battle of Plassey (1757), thereby ending Bengal's national sovereignty. As a reward he was appointed *Nawab* of Bengal from 1757 to 1760 and again from 1763 to 1765 by the British East India Company.

Morarji Desai    a strict follower of Gandhiji, considered to be on the conservative and obscurantist side. Was the Finance Minister of India, also became the Prime Minister of India from 1977–79.

Mughals mainly Central Asian people of Turkish strain, invaded and conquered Delhi and adjacent areas under their leader Babur. Their territory eventually grew into a large empire through military expeditions by successive emperors. Completely erased from the Indian scene after 1857. Their reign ushered in a new era of understanding, absorption and acculturation creating great changes in architecture, dress, food, music, and many other aspects of Indian society.

Mujibar Rahman patriotic leader of East Pakistan, fought against dominance by West Pakistan. Freed the country with help from India; turned the country into the independent state of Bangladesh and became its first Prime Minister. Assassinated in 1975.

Naba Kumar the hero of *Kapal Kundala*, a novel by Bankim Chandra Chattopadhyay, the first and one of the greatest novelists of Bengal.

*natmandir* a spacious building typically situated in front of a temple where people could sing and dance for the deity in the temple or gather to hear religious discourses.

*nautch*-girl culture the *zamindars* and big merchants amassed immense wealth. To please the English imperial bosses, they held parties on various occasions and pretexts where wine and liquor were served liberally and dancing girls performed. Calcutta had many such families with social influence.

Naxalite pro-China Communist splinter group who accepted Mao's *Red Book* as the gospel and brought in an iconoclastic movement of minor killing and destruction, ruining the career of many intelligent students. It first started in a north Bengal village called Naxalbari, hence the name.

Nazrul *Geeti* songs written by poet Nazrul Islam and also set to music by him.

Netaji Institute a museum commemorating Netaji (Subhas Chandra Bose), whose records, documents and memorabilia are preserved. It also encourages research on the national liberation movement and publishes Netaji's books and speeches.

Netaji Subhas Chandra Bose (1897–1945?) a great national political leader of India with considerable organizing ability. Despite his great respect for Gandhiji, he differed from him on the agenda of the freedom struggle. Elected President of the Indian National Congress. His inclination towards the left of the Congress policies forced him to resign from Congress and found his own political party: the Forward Bloc. He was jailed and exiled and eventually left India and went to Germany, later to Japan. His tactical principle being "My enemy's enemy is my friend," he raised an army from among the prisoners of war of Indian origin held by Japan and with them invaded British India on the north-eastern border areas. Even though he was defeated in his efforts he holds one of the highest positions as a leader of the freedom struggle. People endowed him with a demi-God status out of love and reverence. His death and its date is highly controversial. Netaji, in Hindi, means "the leader," and he is better known by this appellation.

*Nidhu Babur Tappa* a genre of Bengali songs composed and set to tune by Ram Nidhi Gupta (1741–1839), well known by his middle name.

paisa originally, one sixty-fourth of a rupee before decimal coinage; still the meanest coin of the demesne, one-hundredth part of a rupee.

*Panchayat* literally means council of five elders but is in fact a council of people to settle social and community problems; now it refers to the village self-government.

P.C. Joshi the powerful Secretary of the Communist Party of India during and shortly after the British period. He helped to create many front organizations of the Communist Party and rendered help to the Imperialist Power during the Second World War and effectively opposed the freedom struggle then.

*pheriwallah* itinerant hawkers who loudly shout their wares.

*puja* Hindu form of worship

Rabindranath Tagore (1861–1941) India's only Nobel Laureate in literature. A poet, novelist, dramatist, composer of nearly 3000 songs set to his own music, essayist and a pioneering modern painter. He was also a great educationist. The greatest Indian who lived and worked in the late nineteenth and the first half of the twentieth centuries, and kept the country enthralled by his creations.

Rabindra *Sangeet* songs written and set to music by Rabindranath Tagore.

Rai Bahadur/Khan Bahadur civil honors of the British colonial government awarded to Indians for service to the Empire. *Rai Bahadur* for Hindus, *Khan Bahadur* for Muslims.

Ramakrishna Mission an organization founded by the followers of the Hindu saint Ramakrishna Paramhansa in 1897. Swami Vivekananda, the most famous disciple of Ramakrishna, was the chief instrument in its foundation. Since its inception the Mission has devoted its energy and resources for relief work in natural catastrophes, expansion of education, medical facilities, and publications throughout India and abroad. Their belief can be summed up as "Service to Man is Worship of God." It is a widely spread organization managed by devoted monks of the Ramakrishna order.

Rammohun Roy (1772?–1833) a pioneering figure of the Bengal Renaissance of nineteenth century, social and religious reformer, founder of the enlightened religious sect: the Brahmasamaj (also spelled Brahmo Samaj).

Ravana king of the *rakshashas* (demons ) of Lanka, became the adversary of Rama after he abducted Rama's wife Sita in the great Indian epic *Ramayana.*

*saheb* a Persian word for a gentleman, largely used in Bengal to describe Europeans.

Santoshi Ma a new folk goddess recently become very popular among women who observe the simple propitiatory rites.

Sarat Chandra Chatterjee great Bengali novelist who influenced novel writing in most other Indian languages through the translation of his books. Still enjoys great all-India popularity.

*sati* in some areas in India, Hindu widows immolated themselves on their husband's funeral pyre. It was practiced more in north India. Many such immolations were forced on the widows by the men of the husbands' family and many others considered the practice as accumulating religious merit. There were some genuine cases no doubt but the whole institution was barbaric. Lord Bentinck, at the urging of Rammohun Roy and a few others, abolished the practice by force of law in 1829.

*Satyanarayan/Satyapir* a syncretic form of worship of Narayan (Vishnu) and a Muslim saint or *pir.*

Shiv Sena a political party headed by Bal Thackeray championing "Maharastra for Maharashtrians" only.

Siraj-ud-Daulah the last independent Nawab (ruler) of Bengal prior to British rule (from April 1756 to June 1759).

*Siyar-ul-Mutakharin* an authoritative account of the reigns of the last seven Mughal Emperors; traces the progress of the English in Bengal up to 1780, written by Syed Ghulam Hussain Khan Tabatabai.

Supreo Bonnerjee immensely helpful and knowledgeable friend who glided from one cultured or educated gathering to the other with effortless ease. He used to write precise, witty and sparkling prose which gave his readers an insight into his very kind, sympathetic and loveable personality. He had a great sense of humor.

*The Metropolitan Explosion*　book by Sunil Munshi.

*Vaishnavas*　the worshipers of Vishnu (Narayana, Krishna); a religious cult revived and popularized by Sri Chaitanya and his followers in the sixteenth century.

Vidyasagar, Iswar Chandra Bandyopadhyay (1820–1891)　great scholar, educationist, philanthropist and rationalist; pioneering prose writer of Bengali. People at that time and even now know him only by his academic honorific "Vidayasagar" (Ocean of Knowledge) rather than his name. His charities are proverbial.

Warren Hastings (1732–1818)　first Governor General of Bengal under the East India Company from 1773 to 1785.

WBCS　West Bengal Civil Service, upper category of the state civil service.

William Carey (1761–1834); Joshua Marshman (1760–1837)　Baptist missionaries who all learnt Bengali. Carey along with Ram Ram Bose translated the Bible into Bengali to facilitate the spreading of Christianity. Founded the Srirampur Press for printing Bengali texts and to publish Bengali periodicals. As educationists and reformers they are remembered very fondly by Bengalis even today.

*Under the Shadow of the Metropolis*　book by Sudhendu Mukherjee.

# Biographical Notes

Radha Prasad Gupta (1921–2000). Professionally the Public Relations Officer of a famous industrial group. "RP" or "Shatul Babu" was an antiquarian, scholar and intellectual of considerable reputation. His detailed knowledge of Calcutta history, Bengali printing, and cultural history of Bengal since mid-eighteenth century was phenomenal. Scholars, poets, artists, musicians and intellectuals were among his closest friends, and frequently were glad to acknowledge that an hour of conversation with him imparted more knowledge and insight than twenty scholarly lectures. He wrote very little and mostly on the cultural history of Bengal and Calcutta. He was a consummate conversationalist, holding forth on subjects which interested him, from the learned to the ribald. His hobbies of collecting specimens of early Bengali printing and popular painting, and diverse unexpected cultural artifacts indicated the liveliness of his mind.

M.J. Akbar is an eminent journalist, presently the editor of *The Asian Age*, a daily published from several cities. He became famous as the editor of *Sunday*, a weekly magazine published by the *Ananda Bazar Patrika* group. Later he became the founding editor of the Calcutta based English daily *The Telegraph*, published by the same house. As an editor he made innovations which made the daily popular with wide circulation, and a major journalistic voice. He once contested a seat for election to the Lok Sabha (Lower House of the Parliament). As a serious journalist he writes about many urgent and pressing national political problems.

He has written several thought-provoking books, which received wide attention including *Nehru: The Making of India, Kashmir: Behind the Vale*, and *The Shade of Swords: Jihad and the Conflict between Islam and Christianity.*

After completing his Masters at Calcutta University, Professor **Satindranath Chakrabarty** (1916–2003) taught Philosophy at City College, Calcutta continuously for 43 years. But he was even better known outside the classroom for his devastating polemic. A Gandhian in early life, he later focused on Marxism, and though he had discarded Soviet Bolshevism he retained a strong interest in Marx. He contributed over 200 articles in Bengali and English to the popular press, professional journals and political/cultural periodicals. Two volumes collecting fifty of his articles have been published. He was Member of the Calcutta University Senate and Academic Council for a crucial decade. He was best known for his devotion to the cause of education and teachers, having been General Secretary of the West Bengal College and University Teachers' Association (WBCUTA) from 1957 to 1964, with and without the support of the major political parties. Member of the Communist Party of India from 1948 to 1960, he was also a Member of the West Bengal Provincial Executive of the Congress (I) from 1972 to 1976. He was thus one of the few individuals who knew the inner workings of the two major Calcutta political alignments. He served Calcutta best with his penetrating socio-political analyses and leadership as an independent, anti-establishment intellectual, most recently for example when the ruling party abolished teaching English at the primary school level. He believed that his membership of several famous *addas* of Calcutta and Santiniketan, and his work combined to give him *"brahmasvad."* Professor Chakrabarty passed away on June 6, 2003 but he was carrying on with his polemics and *addas* almost till the end.

Professor **Satyesh Chakraborty** studied Geography at Calcutta and London Universities and has had wide-ranging exposure in the related fields of Economics, Anthropology, Sociology and Archaeology. He has taught at Presidency College, Calcutta and was Head of the Department of Geography, Burdwan University, and Professor at the Indian Institute of Management, Calcutta. Member of the State Planning Board of West Bengal for five years, he was Adviser to the Calcutta Metropolitan Planning Authority (CMPO) and the Calcutta Municipal Corporation. He has served as visiting faculty at many universities and institutions in India, the USA and Canada. He has published extensively in *The Geographical Review of India*, *The Journal of the Institute of Geography*, *Nagarlok: Journal of the Institute of Public Administration* and other publications. His penetrating analyses have influenced the national discussion in the wider area of Urban Development and Planning in all aspects, including Ports, Railways, Transportation, etc. For the last two decades he has been an important voice pleading for Environmental Impact assessment in Development and Planning studies.

He is also a connoisseur of north Indian classical music.

Professor **Sunil Munshi** is an eminent geographer. After completing his Masters in Calcutta, he has taught there at the University, at the Center for Studies in Social Sciences and at Burdwan University. He is a fine scholar with a Marxist orientation, an inspiring teacher and his research breaks fresh ground. He has been Adviser to the West Bengal District Gazetteer Committee, a member of the University Grants Commission and the ICSSR. He has served on the Indian National Land Commission, the West Bengal State Land-use Board and as President of the Geographical Society of India.

His publications include *Geography of Transportation in Eastern India Under the British Raj, Resources and Regional Disparities, Thikana Kolkata* among others. He has been politically close to the Communist Party of India.

**Gour Kishore Ghosh** (1923–2000) was a prominent Bengali writer. He wrote novels and short stories as well as literary criticism. A serious journalist of the Bengali Press, he began his career at *Satyayuga*. After a short stint as the editor of *Aajkaal*, he wrote for the *Ananda Bazar Patrika* till the end. His spirit of independence brought him a Magsaysay Award, but this also caused him to be sent to jail for a lengthy period during the Emergency imposed by Indira Gandhi.

While his early political inspiration came from MN Roy's *Radical Humanism*, in his later years he veered towards the ideals of Gandhi. He always wrote for the underdog. His weekly satirical column was famous as also a series of humorous stories whose hero became a proverbial character. One of his short stories was made into a movie (*Sagina Mahato*). His mature work chose the rather neglected field of interaction between Hindu and Muslim societies.

For a vital decade **Samar Bose** (1925–94) was the human interface between the Calcutta Metropolitan Development Authority (CMDA) and the people of Calcutta. He did his graduation in Economics from Presidency College, Calcutta and his masters in the same subject from Calcutta University. After working in various positions in the Cell of Central Information Services, Simla, All India Radio (AIR) and in the Press Information Bureau, he was assigned to the Dandakaranya Project as head of its Public Relations office. He later became senior correspondent with AIR. As the chief PR officer of the Border Security Force, he was instrumental in helping members of the Awami League (of Bangladesh) establish contact with political leaders in West Bengal and New Delhi. He was later honored by the Awami League government. In 1974, he joined the CMDA as the Director of Public Relations and played a crucial role in giving the organization a people-friendly image. He retired in 1983 and served briefly in the West Bengal State Electricity

Board as an honorary advisor. As an executive editor of the Bengali daily *Bartaman* from 1984–94, he contributed a regular column on current affairs.

**Sunil Ganguly** is a well-known poet, novelist, critic and short story writer and an established part of the *Ananda Bazar Patrika* publishing group in Calcutta. Early in his literary career, jointly with friends, he edited and published a Bengali poetry quarterly, *Krittibas*, which became the mouthpiece of a group of young Bengali poets.

As a young writer he participated in a year long Writers' Workshop program at Iowa University, USA. On his return he gradually moved towards prose and began to publish novels and short stories. Around this time he joined the *Ananda Bazar Patrika* group and its cultural journal *Desh*. His novels are based on nineteenth and twentieth century historical, socio-cultural and political circumstances. He has traveled widely and his writings have been translated into many Indian and foreign languages. Satyajit Ray based the film *Days and Nights of the Forest* (*Aranyer Din Ratri*) and *The Adversary* (*Pratidwandi*) on his novels. He was appointed Sheriff of Calcutta for a term.

**Samaresh Bose** (1924–1988) was a very powerful novelist and short story writer dominating Bengali prose in the era succeeding Bibhuti Bhusan, Tarasankar, Manik and Satinath. Under the influence of Marxist ideology, he participated in labor struggles and lived among the poor working class people in the industrial suburbs of Calcutta. A refugee from East Pakistan (Bangladesh) he experienced the hardships of life from close quarters. His earlier short stories and novels like *B.T. Roader Dhare* and *Bokultala Camp* dealt with life and struggles in this social milieu.

He became disenchanted with the Left ideology and politics of Bengal and turned to other writing. Two novels of that period *Prajapati* and *Bibar* brought him immediate fame and some amount of notoriety and opposition. Nonetheless he did not fail to depict the raw experiences of poverty, the exploitation of labor and the machinations of politicians. His last serialized novel, *Dekhi Nai Phire*, based on the life of the famous sculptor and painter Ramkinkar Baij remained unfinished at his untimely death, but the published portions proved that he had extended himself beyond his earlier work. An "eternal wanderer," under the pen name "Kalkut" he wrote of his travels and also novels that re-interpreted themes from Hindu mythology.

By training an engineer, **Surajeet Ghose** gave up a successful corporate career in order to devote more time to literature, and his work, especially poetry, has been widely published in Bengal. He found his real metier in editing and publishing, and being a good organizer, he established his own periodical and publishing house, which are at the forefront of Bengali publishing. His publishing house never catered to intellectually shallow or vulgar interests, yet the fastidious and highbrow editorial policy has left an enduring impression well-received by the discerning public.

**Badal Sarkar** is a revolutionary Bengali theater personality with over 50 plays to his credit. He performs nowadays mostly in rural Bengal. He was initially trained as an architect, engineer and town planner. An anti-establishment free spirit, he led a revolt against the proscenium theater in Calcutta, started his own group, and writes, directs and acts in his own plays. Some of the best known are *Evam Indrajit*, *Pagla Ghoda*, *Bhoma*, *Balu*, *Baki Itihas*, *Basi Khabar*, and *Juloos*. His themes are related to the economic, political and social problems and constraints and aspirations in the life of common people.

**Utpal Dutt** (1929–93) was a dramatist, a theater director and actor, and a household name in Bengal and also well known all over India for his successes in theater and movies in Bengali and Hindi. He was a Marxist as evidenced by his artistic manisfesto *Toward a Revolutionary Theatre*. His themes for the stage and also for *jatra* (traditional theater), dealt with revolt, anti-colonialism, patriotism, anti-exploitation. In order to achieve his goals, he formed a group, "People's Little Theatre," trained the actors, wrote his own plays and directed and acted in them. He adapted Gorky's *Lower Depths*, revived satires written in the nineteenth century, wrote successful plays about cultural figures and momentous political events. He was a fine serious as well as a comic actor. His political activism matched his solid scholarship, and his books on Shakespeare and Girish Chandra Ghose, (a great Bengali actor-dramatist of the nineteenth century), point to new and interesting interpretations. He directed and acted in both Bengali and Hindi movies, mostly as villain and comedian. His famous theatre productions were *Angaar*, *Tiner Tarwal*, *Dilli Chalo*. He successfully adapted the famous Bengali novel *Teetas Ekti Nadir Nam* for the stage. His well-known plays for the traditional *jatra* are *Jhar*, *Sanyasir Tarabari*, *Joy Bangla*. He played the protagonist in Mrinal Sen's *Bhuvan Shome* and Satyajit Ray's *Agantuk*.

**Jochhan Dastidar** (1931–1998) studied at the Government College of Art in Calcutta. After his initial struggle as an artist he took to interior decoration as a profession. His artistic instinct could not remain confined within the bounds imposed by this, and he found fulfillment in his involvement with "little theater groups." Eventually he founded his own group Charkbak, named after a notorious materialist philosopher of ancient India. A Marxist, he was jailed on the assumption of being a Naxalite (an extreme revolutionary group owing allegiance to the Chinese model of Mao). His whole family is devoted to the theater and has played various roles in different plays. He later directed documentary films and TV serials and his *Sei Somoy*, was a great success of Bengali TV.

**Samik Banerjee** is a widely read critic of literature, theater and cinema, and is best described as an "instigator" of cultural events in Calcutta. After reading for his degree in English literature, he became a highly regarded manuscript editor and publisher, as well as a critically acclaimed translator. He was the in-house editor of the Oxford University Press in Calcutta, and was closely connected to such avant-garde Calcutta publishing ventures as Proma Prakashani and Seagull Books. He has made an intensive study of all aspects of the theater and conducted numerous seminars in this field. He has been intimately connected with major dramatic productions and critical publications on drama. His knowledge of modern cinema is equally profound and he has frequently done commentaries and interviews on television. He has been a member of the Indian Film Censor Board.

**Dr. Pratap Chandra Chunder** is widely known for his academic, political and cultural achievements. Trained in law and history, for a long time he taught at the University Law College, Calcutta. Born into a prominent nationalist family, he also joined the freedom movement, and politics occupied an important part of his life. He held many important offices and was briefly the Cabinet Minister for Education and Culture in the Government of India. He is now connected with several educational, social and cultural organizations, Rabindra Bharati Society being one. His fiction is mostly on historical themes, set, most prominently, in the earliest decades of Calcutta history. For a politician to have earned such universal respect is quite uncommon.

**Dr. Sisir Bose** (1920–2000) was a pediatrician by profession. He trained in Calcutta, London, Vienna, Boston, and Cambridge, and was the Director of the Institute of Child Health, Calcutta for twenty years, and also the first Editor of the *National Pediatric Journal*.

His father, the late Sarat Chandra Bose, was a great national patriotic leader, a most successful barrister of the Calcutta High Court and an outstanding parliamentarian. His uncle Subhas Chandra Bose, better known as Netaji, was elected President of the Indian National Congress (1938), and remains one of the iconic figures of the Indian Freedom movement. In January 1941 Subhas eluded British surveillance on his

Calcutta residence and fled to Germany, eventually reaching Japan and South-East Asia where he helped to reorganize the Indian National Army from among the Indian prisoners of war and others of Indian origin. This army was the first (in March 1944) to reconquer Indian soil in (north-east) India. His disappearance in August 1945, after a reported air crash in Taiwan, remains the greatest unsolved mystery of modern Indian history.

Sisir Bose was instrumental in spiriting Netaji away from India, and was later the trusted coordinator of Netaji's underground organization in India. All members of the Bose family fought the British. Sisir was severely wounded by the police and repeatedly jailed between 1942 and the end of the Second World War. Dr. Bose became a legislator in independent India from 1982 to 1987. He wrote or edited over 40 books, many connected to the life and politics of his father and uncle, including the collected edition of Netaji's writings. His great labour of love was to build up the Netaji Research Bureau from 1957 on, as a major institution with a fine library, museum and active research program in History, Politics and International Relations.

Born in pre-Partition eastern Bengal, **Amal K. Dutta** has strong memories of his adolescence there and in Calcutta where he completed his education. He joined the Indian Police Service and served until 1988, retiring as Inspector General of West Bengal Police. During the troubled Naxalite period of the 70's, he sought to reform and rehabilitate the young offenders through patience and genuine affection.

A lawyer by training, **Sakya Sen** has practiced in the Calcutta Courts from the 1970's, and is one of our youngest contributors. He has studied German language and culture in Munich on Goethe Institute scholarships. His poetry has been published in international anthologies, and he has recently received the Editor's Choice Award from the International Library of Poetry. He campaigned for the Indian Parliament in the 1980's for the *Amra Bangali* Party.

**Parimal Ray** has been an avid antiquarian and collector all his life. Working for a multi-national corporation for three decades, he spent his spare time and spare resources in collecting the material artifacts of his urban environment—Calcutta Old Prints, oleographs, unique film posters and lobby cards, cigarette packets and match-box labels from brands long gone, postage stamps, enamel signboards that record the city's manufacturing and consumer history. All of this brings his "real" material Calcutta alive, that is missing from history books. More classically, he has collected stone and bronze sculpture, unique autographed letters and manuscripts and coins of east and north-east India, on the last of which he has contributed learned numismatic articles.

**Aniruddha Ray** is one of the most outstanding economic and political historians speicalizing in late medieval India, especially Bengal. Educated at the University of Calcutta and the Sorbonne, Paris, he was Professor of Medieval History at Calcutta University till his retirement. In his numerous publications he has researched archival sources in India and abroad. Author of over a dozen books, his work includes the study of port cities like Masulipatnam and Cambay, translations of memoirs like that of Francois Martin. He has made a special study of the center-periphery relationships in the period of Mughal rule over Awadh and Bengal in his books *The Rebel Nawab: the Revolt of Vizir Ali of Oudh* and *Adventurers, Landowners and Rebels: Bengal c.1575–c.1715*.

**Tarun Mitra** was born and grew up outside Calcutta, in a "Bengal" that was still undivided, and came to Calcutta for his college education. He was in the earliest MA class in Comparative Literature from Jadavpur University. Very active with the Forward Bloc as a student, "Tarun-da," as he seems to be universally called, later became a Gandhian, joining the Gandhi Smarak Nidhi, the Gandhi Vichar Parishad and the Harijan Sevak Sangha. He has worked in the American Institute of Indian Studies for a quarter century and is now their Regional Director Emeritus. He has had an enduring commitment to social service for development. He continues to write extensively on the contemporary art and culture scene of Calcutta and has been a life-long student of north Indian classical music.

**Supreo Bonnerjee** (1933–93) worked for the USIS (American Center) Calcutta, and in later years became its Program Director. He obtained a Master's Degree from the University of Calcutta in Political Science. He had extensive contacts with the liberal world, working in various genres, as well as with musicians, artists, academics, journalists and public figures, many of whom counted him as a friend. This was possible because he took a keen interest in many of the creative expressions of the Bengali intellect and involved himself in matters of public interest. Above all, he was a gentle soul before whom people felt at ease. In him they found a generous, helpful and understanding friend. He was keenly alert to the social changes and movements that affected the life and mind of the people. He would have disdained to be called an intellectual but undoubtedly he was one and of good standing. Eastern India was well known to him. He wrote little but in impeccably polished Bengali prose.